Susan Rose O'Sewall.

# LIFE IN AN IRISH COUNTRY HOUSE

By the same author

# LIFE IN AN IRISH COUNTRY HOUSE

Mark Bence-Jones

Constable • London

First published in Great Britain 1996
by Constable and Company Ltd
3 The Lanchesters, 162 Fulham Palace Road
London W6 9ER
Copyright © 1996 Mark Bence-Jones
ISBN 0 09 474 680X
Set in Monophoto Poliphilus 12pt by
Servis Filmsetting Ltd, Manchester
Printed in Great Britain by
BAS Printers Ltd, Over Wallop

A CIP catalogue record for this book
is available from the British Library

TO BILL AND DAPHNE MONTGOMERY

# Contents

# Illustrations

# Preface

This book gives a picture of life in twenty-three Irish country houses at various periods. It tells of the families, their servants and their guests; of domestic matters, comforts and discomforts, improvements and dilapidations, parties and disasters, joys and sorrows. It also shows some of the houses as they appear in fiction, having been used as models by writers who knew them. The houses are portrayed as they were when they belonged to the families who owned the lands on which they stood for many generations. Only eight out of the twenty-three houses still belong to such families. Of the rest, two belong to the National Trust, seven have passed into different ownership, two are ruins and four have vanished altogether.

I could not have written this book had it not been for the many kind people who gave me access to papers and permission to quote from them; told me their memories of some of the houses, provided me with information and illustrations and helped me in other ways. On one or more of these counts I would express my gratitude to each of the following, not a few of whom have made my work more enjoyable by giving me hospitality as well as help: The Duchess of Devonshire; the Marquess of Hartington; the Marquess and Marchioness of Salisbury; the Earl and Countess of Dunraven; Lord and Lady Dunsany; the Dowager Lady Egremont; Lord and Lady Monteagle; Lady Mairi Bury; Lord Charles Cecil; Lady Mary Clive; Lady Georgina Forbes; Lady Pansy Lamb; Sir Toby Coghill, Bt.; Sir Christopher Coote, Bt., and Lady Coote; Sir Josslyn Gore-Booth, Bt.; Sir Hercules Langrishe, Bt., and the Hon. Lady Langrishe; Sir John Leslie, Bt., K.M., K.C.S.G.; the late Sir Cecil Stafford-King-Harman, Bt.; the Hon. Bryan and Mrs Bellew; Mr and the Hon. Mrs William Montgomery; the Knight of Glin and Madam FitzGerald; Mr Colin Anson; Mrs Pieter Bairnsfather-Cloete; Mr and Mrs Paul Burton; Mrs N.K. Cameron; Miss Grace Carroll; Mr C.D. Cholmeley-Harrison; Mr Henry Clark; Mr and Mrs Thomas Hal Clarke; Mr George Clive; Mr and Mrs Adrian Cosby; Miss Lydia de Burgh; Mr Nigel de la Poer; Mrs George Dennehy; Mrs Robert Eborall; Mr Tom Feerick; Mr Adrian FitzGerald; Brigadier Denis FitzGerald, D.S.O., O.B.E.; Mr and Mrs John FitzGerald; Mr and Mrs Arthur French; Mr and Mrs Robert Gosling; the late Molly Keane; Mrs Robert Kennedy; Colonel and Mrs Anthony Lawrence King-Harman; the late Captain Robert Douglas King-Harman, D.S.O., D.S.C.; Mr and Mrs Jeffry Lefroy; Miss Melosina Lenox-Conyngham; Mr Thomas McCarthy; Mr and Mrs Henry McDowell; Mr Gordon St George Mark; Mrs Hugh Montgomery; Mr and Mrs Terry Morriss; Mr and Mrs Martin Moyes; Mr and Mrs Pyers O'Conor Nash; Mrs Catharine Okuno; Mr and

Mrs Thomas Pakenham; Mr and Mrs Michael Penruddock; Mr Gavin Perceval-Maxwell; Mr John Perceval-Maxwell; Mr William Power; Prof. Dr. Otto Rauchbauer; Mr Colin Smythe; Mrs Candida Snow; Mr and Mrs Christopher Somerville; Rev. Anthony Symondson, S.J.; the late Major-General E.A.E. Tremlett, C.B.

A special word of thanks must go to Mr Donall Ó Luanaigh and other members of the staff of the National Library of Ireland; to Dr Anthony Malcomson and other members of the staff of the Public Record Office of Northern Ireland; and to Mr David Griffin, Director of the Irish Architectural Archive, and members of his staff; in particular Ms. Anne Henderson, Mr Simon Lincoln and Miss Aisling Dunne. Finally I must express my gratitude to my wife Gillian who, whenever I am at a loss for a word, is always able to come up with the right one.

# Chapter 1

## Adare Manor
### COUNTY LIMERICK

THADY QUIN, who came of the old Irish family of O'Quin, acquired lands at Adare in County Limerick towards the end of the seventeenth century; and he, or his son, built a house here that was typical of its period, with a pediment and a high-pitched roof. It stood on the banks of the River Maigue, close to an old castle, a ruined Franciscan priory and two other medieval monastic ruins, surrounded by a demesne that the agricultural writer Arthur Young admired for its woods. Young, who came here in 1776, was received by Mrs Quin in the absence of her husband and was much impressed by the pictures in the house, some of which had been brought back from Italy by his hostess's son Valentine, who had recently returned from the Grand Tour.

Valentine Quin, who, like his father, was a member of the Irish House of Commons, was raised to the peerage in 1800 as Lord Adare. In 1810 his elder son married Caroline Wyndham, heiress to large estates in South Wales. Caroline came to Adare for the first time in the summer of 1812; she and her husband were met four miles from the house by the tenantry and 'all the common people of the country'.[1] The horses were taken out and the carriage was pulled by forty men; garlands of flowers were borne ahead of them and a band marched in front. A military escort prevented people from getting under the carriage wheels and when they arrived at the house a guard of honour of the Adare Infantry fired a salute. Though Caroline was too tired to walk about very much, she thought the grounds 'most beautiful' and the house 'much better than she expected'.[2] She had clearly expected it to compare unfavourably with Dunraven Castle, her own family home in Glamorganshire. Her father-in-law was sufficiently impressed by Dunraven to take it for his title when he was made an earl in 1822; the family surname was changed to Wyndham-Quin in acknowledgement of Caroline's great inheritance.

The newly created Earl of Dunraven died in 1824 and Caroline's husband became the second Earl, their schoolboy elder son becoming Viscount Adare. One Christmas a few years later, he and three other boys who were staying – the future poet and writer Aubrey de Vere and his two brothers, who lived five miles away at Curragh Chase – set out to climb a hill 800 feet high called Knockfierna, or 'Hill of the Fairies'. Though they were accompanied by the young Lord Adare's tutor and another man, they had not realized what a stiff climb it would be and had brought no lunch with them. By the time they reached the summit, the sun was going down and they felt faint with hunger and too tired to walk home. They managed to reach a farmhouse, where the farmer, though he was unable to offer them any food, gave them each a glass of rough cider. This made them sleepy and after a few minutes none of the boys could walk or stand. The tutor was very upset and he stamped up and down the road exclaiming 'Gracious patience!', his favourite catch-phrase, over and over again. Then he and his fellow-adult also succumbed to the effects of cider on an empty stomach and collapsed into the mud with the boys.

They came to after a quarter of an hour and walked home, arriving back just in time to hear the dressing bell ring. At dinner, the story of their adventure caused much laughter. When the boys told of how, as they were collapsing, each gave his arm to his neighbour, Lord Dunraven said, 'You see, young gentlemen, each of you undertook to support and guide his neighbour, though not one of you could take care of himself. That is the way of Ireland.'[3]

From 1832 onwards Lord Dunraven began rebuilding the house. It was a way of occupying his mind, for though he was only fifty, he was so crippled by gout he could no longer shoot or fish. He and his family continued to live in the old house while new buildings of grey stone in the fashionable Tudor-Gothic style – including a tur-reted entrance tower copied from the entrance to the Cloisters at Eton – gradually went up behind it. To a certain extent, Lord Dunraven and Caroline acted as their own architects, helped by a master mason named James Conolly and making as much use as they could of local craftsmen, notably a talented carver. But they also employed the fashionable architect James Pain, who was based in Limerick.

Despite the building work, which was to continue for thirty years and must have caused a great deal of discomfort, life in the house went on much the same as ever. As Caroline records in her diary, people were always coming to stay. In June 1833 the party included a geologist: 'We had a great deal of geological talk all the evening.' Next day, 'the gentlemen all went off geologising' but Caroline stayed at home with the other ladies and went to a committee that she ran. On the Sunday following, while the rest of the party went off to explore some mines, she went to church and taught her Sunday school and in the evening attended a lecture. Lectures, the committee and the Sunday school loomed large in Caroline's life; during the fortnight following the geologist's visit she attended two more committee meetings and went to three lectures in Limerick given by a Mr Ainsworth; while in September she had the children of the Sunday school examined in the conservatory and gave them tea in the garden with 'a nice little lecture afterwards'.

The geologist was followed that autumn by a guest who brought a telescope and they 'had a great treat looking at some of the Celestial Bodies'. And a few days later they 'did gas experiments in the eve'. However, the guests at Adare were by no means predominantly scientific, but included grandees such as Lord and Lady Caledon and Lord Selkirk as well as country neighbours like Captain Gerald Blennerhassett of Riddlestown. 'We were quite alone except for Captain Gerald Blennerhassett,' Caroline observed, as though having only one guest were rather unusual.[4]

Although Lord Dunraven was himself unable to shoot or fish, the gentlemen guests would go off shooting and fishing in the usual way, as they did when the house party included Sir John and Lady Douglas and their two daughters and two sons. On that occasion there was music after dinner. Caroline was musical; she would go to concerts in Limerick and had lessons from an Italian, whom she refers to as 'the Signor'. In summer there was swimming in the river and there were picnics at the ruined Franciscan priory. The priory provided another occupation for the Dunravens' guests: they would be put to work cutting ivy here or at the old castle in a way that, had it been a century later, would have won the approval of Queen Mary.

As well as the continual house party, people came to luncheon and dinner. Caroline and her husband had luncheon – which she often spoke of in the modern way as 'lunch' – in the middle of the day and dinner in the evening. But when the annual 'book sale' was held at Adare in 1833, dinner was at the old fashioned hour of 4.30. On that occasion, forty-six people dined, and were afterwards given tea in the conservatory; as the evening had turned out wet, it was difficult getting them there. Then there was dancing in the hall, which went on until nearly eleven, when all but a few went away.

Towards the end of 1834 the Dunravens set off on a protracted tour of the Low Countries and Germany. In Antwerp, they bought carvings for the gallery that was being built at Adare under the supervision of James Pain, who came to lunch with them a month before they left. When they returned in June 1836 they 'found glad faces all the way and much love and gratitude'. The village greeted them with illuminations and bonfires; they walked about enjoying it until nearly midnight when Caroline came home very tired, but delighted 'to be once more in my own dear comfortable bed'. She was also 'very much struck with the beauty and grandeur' of the new building and 'admired its style more than any I had seen. The grey stone is, in my opinion, so much handsomer than any other colour . . . the rooms likewise promise to be very comfortable.' Comfortable does not seem quite the word for the gallery, which was habitable though not yet finished; it was 132 feet long and more than twenty-six feet high, with an open timbered roof reminiscent of a Gothic church.

During the next couple of weeks they had a great many visitors, including the young William Monsell of Tervoe, a neighbouring landowner, who came to ask Lord Dunraven for the hand of their daughter Anna-Maria. Caroline approved of him: 'He was very amiable in every respect and I have the comfort of thinking that my dear child has every prospect of happiness and likewise that she will be situated near me.' She and Anna-Maria drove over to Tervoe, which surprisingly they do not appear to have visited before, though it was only about seven miles away, and they 'had the gratification of finding the house and gardens excellent'. The wedding took place in August. Anna-Maria drove through the crowd of villagers to the church having 'passed most of the morning in fervent prayer', as her mother observed. Caroline also noticed how, when the bride was about to go downstairs, having changed into her travelling dress after the wedding breakfast, 'she gave one look up to Heaven that went to my heart; but did not shrink back and was a heroine to the last'. It was more than her mother could bear to see her drive away, so she handed her to her father and her husband and ran off 'to indulge in a flood of tears'.[5]

In that same month, the Dunravens gave a 'grand dejeuner' in honour of the marriage of their son Adare to Augusta Goold, a judge's daughter, which had taken place in Dublin a week after Anna-Maria was married. A breakfast for about 150 people was laid in the unfinished gallery, which was the only room large enough for it. The Adare band played during the meal and afterwards 'Little Supple' played on the piano and everybody danced on the lawn. When it became too damp they returned indoors and continued dancing in the hall; but by ten the people staying in the house, who included Anna-Maria and her husband and the O'Briens from Dromoland in County Clare, were so tired that they went to bed.

It was not until 1840 that the floor of the gallery was finished, and at the same time a 'huge stove' was installed in the central fireplace. Lord Dunraven feared that the room would be too hot; but, as he told Caroline, who was away at the time, this would make up for the other principal room in the new building, the Great Hall, being 'cold enough for anything'. Caroline's future sitting-room, which projected from under the gallery with a splendid view of the river, was also 'very cold', as he somewhat depressingly informed her; though he was 'getting the grate enlarged and new-set, to throw out more heat'. This room was one of a series of private apartments into which the Dunravens planned to move when the old house was demolished to make way for another Tudor-Gothic range. The work of demolition was already starting and Lord Dunraven was having to move from one room to another. Yet he was happy enough: 'I walk, ride, eat, drink and sleep in great perfection,' he assured his wife, which must at any rate have been true as far as eating was concerned, for he had a French cook. Though he wondered how they would ever manage to fill the gallery, which, as he said, 'looks almost like a cathedral'.[6]

Some years later, when the gallery was finished and in regular use, Caroline made it sound friendly and lived-in when she wrote of 'musical instruments and games of different kinds' scattered about and the scent of 'a constant supply of rare and beautiful plants . . . brought in from the conservatory' added to 'the delicious tones of the

The gallery at Adare Manor.

The children of the family playing battledore and shuttlecock in the Great Hall at Adare
Manor in about 1850. A drawing by Miss L.P. Gallwey.

Adare Manor

'organ'. Though it could be heard in the gallery, the organ was in fact in the Great Hall, which Caroline describes as 'peculiarly adapted to every purpose for which it may be required'.

'It has been frequently used with equal appropriateness as a dining-room, concert-room, ballroom, for private theatricals, *tableaux vivants* and other amusements,' she continues enthusiastically. The 'other amusements' included battledore and shuttlecock, played by her grandchildren. And despite her husband's gloomy reports about the temperature, Caroline goes on to make the Great Hall sound almost cosy. 'When only one person is seated at the ample fireplace where on medieval firedogs huge logs are blazing, the *coup d'oeil* is so perfect and the whole room so comfortable, that one could not wish it in any way changed or diminished, notwithstanding its great size.'[7]

For the 'ample fireplace', the monumental staircase and other features of their Great Hall, Caroline and her husband obtained designs from Pugin. They were produced in 1846, when Ireland was in the throes of the Famine. That Christmas, Caroline wrote somewhat despondently that she 'was very busy giving out clothes and getting through Christmas business, but without the usual comfort of feeling one's usefulness – on the contrary, the wants of the people seem so beyond what any one individual could do for them, that really the reflection is a sad one that unordered

The young Lord Adare, afterwards 4th Earl of Dunraven, in the ruins of the Franciscan Priory at Adare in 1850. A sketch by Miss L.P. Gallwey. Adare Manor can be seen in the background.

Charity is really but a drop of water in the ocean'.[8] One of Caroline's efforts in the way of famine relief was to get local girls to do gros point for the seats of the chairs in the gallery.

Lord Dunraven died in 1850 and his son Adare, who was now the third Earl, completed the house by building a Tudor-Gothic garden front where the old house had been, to the design of the English architect P. C. Hardwick. He showed his filial piety by putting up an inscription on his new front proclaiming that 'this goodly house' had been built by his parents 'without borrowing, selling or leaving a debt'. This would have been more of an achievement earlier on in the building of the house than it was after the finding of coal on the Wyndham estates in South Wales.

The third Earl of Dunraven was a distinguished Irish archaeologist, a friend of some of the leading archaeologists of the day such as Stokes, Graves and Petrie, who often stayed with him at Adare where they were able to examine the three old monastic buildings. He employed Hardwick to carry out a second restoration of two of these, namely the Trinitarian and Augustinian abbeys, which had already been restored by his grandfather to serve as the local Catholic and Protestant churches. Having been originally Catholic, the Quins had conformed to Protestantism in the early eighteenth century, but the third Earl, like his friend and neighbour Aubrey de Vere, was a Catholic convert. He tried to persuade his son to follow him, but without success.

The fact that his son refused to adopt the religion of the majority of the local people did not make him any less in sympathy with them. As a small boy he used to drop in on the tenants and they would hoist him on to the table to make a speech; his speech was always the same, concise and to the point, 'I am an Irishman bred and born', and it was greeted with applause. Having acquired his love of Ireland at the earliest age, the future fourth Earl, when he was a little older, acquired another of the loves of his life, which was big-game shooting and exploring; he and his father caught the enthusiasm from a family friend who was a mighty hunter in North America. They put up wigwams in the deer park, shot deer by lantern-light and led the simple life. It was great fun for a boy, though, apart from his father, the grown-ups did not enjoy it so much and were glad to return to the house for their meals.

The fourth Earl of Dunraven, who came of age in 1862 – the drawing-room, library and other reception rooms in the newly completed garden front were brought into use for the celebrations – and succeeded to the earldom in 1871, became famous not only as a big-game shot, but also as a yachtsman, whose ocean-going yachts, notably *Valkyrie*, competed for the America's Cup. He was an artist and had inherited his grandmother's musical talent. He played a part in politics and was chairman of the conference that helped to solve the Irish land question in 1902.

Twenty years earlier, when that question was still unsolved and the country was in a state of unrest owing to the so-called 'Land War', the Viceroy, Earl Spencer – known as the Red Earl on account of his luxuriant red beard – came to stay at Adare for the Limerick Show. Before he arrived, a deputation of the tenants came to Lord Dunraven and said: 'We hope you won't expect us to present a Loyal Address to His Excellency. That would be against our principles. But as your guest, we will give him a hearty welcome and you can tell him that he need not be sending down soldiers and police. We will take care of him,' The tenants were as good as their word; they turned out in force at the railway station, lined the platform, lined the roads, took off their hats and cheered, while the village band played 'God Save the Queen'. Since they were not normally in the habit of playing this tune, Lord Dunraven reckoned that they must have learned it specially for the occasion.[9]

Despite the tenants' assurances, soldiers and police had been sent to guard the Viceroy. That night, a formidable array of constabulary was drawn up outside the house, while inside, in the Great Hall, the police officer responsible for His

Ladies of the family reading and playing the harp in the gallery
at Adare Manor in about the eighteen-sixties.

Excellency's safety entertained him and the rest of the party by singing a rebel song,
'The Wearing of the Green', at the top of his very fine voice. An American journalist friend of Lord Dunraven's who happened to be staying was rather surprised.

Another distinguished figure from the world of politics who stayed at Adare
during this period was Lord Randolph Churchill. At the time, Lord Dunraven
was Under-Secretary for the Colonies and Lord Randolph had until recently been
Chancellor of the Exchequer in the same government, but he had resigned, that fatal
resignation which ended his political career. In the circumstances, he cannot have

A page from the scrapbook of a lady who stayed at Adare Manor in 1892. Between the photographs of the 4th Earl of Dunraven and his wife are details of the game shot during this particular house party. Below the photograph of the house is pasted the Adare Manor letter-head, complete with coronet.

contributed much to what the fourth Earl remembers as the 'fun and jollity' of house parties at Adare, where there was also a great deal of music, as there had been in his grandmother's day. The Irish composer Charles Villiers Stanford was a frequent guest. An eminent personage from a different walk of life who stayed here in the nineties was the war correspondent Sir William Howard Russell.

Among the most illustrious of the fourth Earl's guests at Adare were the Duke and Duchess of York, the future King George V and Queen Mary; they stayed here in 1897 when the house party also included Field Marshal Lord Roberts, who was then Commander-in-Chief in Ireland. The Duke of York's cousin Prince Henry of Prussia, the Kaiser's younger brother, with whom Lord Dunraven went sailing at Cowes and at Kiel, also stayed at Adare. There were other German guests during

The Duke and Duchess of York, the future King George V and Queen Mary, at Adare Manor in 1897. The bowler-hatted Duke stands to the right of the column; with his host, the 4th Earl of Dunraven, standing between him and Field-Marshal Lord Roberts, whose face is partly obscured by the hat of the Duchess of York who sits in front of him, wearing a light-coloured dress.

the last winter before the Great War: a couple who stayed that winter at the hotel in the village for the hunting. Lord Dunraven found them charming and often invited them to dinner, though he was convinced that the husband was a spy and that 'the hunting was, on the part of two evident novices, the thinnest of veils'.[10]

With the coming of the Irish Free State, Lord Dunraven, who had been a moderate Home Ruler, was invited to join the Senate. He accepted, which put Adare at risk, for the Civil War was raging and the chief of staff of the Republican forces had ordered that the houses of all senators should be burnt. Adare, however, survived the conflict; the family believed it had been spared through the influence of one of Lord Dunraven's gillies, who was himself a staunch Republican.

The fourth Earl died in 1926 aged eighty-five and was succeeded by his first cousin. The new Lord Dunraven was getting on for seventy when he came to live at Adare, but he was to enjoy a reign of twenty-six years during which the house was run in the traditional style. A butler and five footmen in livery waited at table; there was an excellent, if temperamental, female cook. The food was delicious and, rather surprisingly, hot, for the kitchen was at the opposite side of the house to the dining-room and at a lower level; a hot cupboard outside the dining-room warmed the food up after its long journey. At breakfast, there was a fine array of chafing dishes as well as a cold table; at luncheon there was a fish course, an entree, a meat course and a pudding, together with cheese and fruit. At tea, there was an immense spread, with scones and hot buttered toast. At dinner, there was soup, fish, a main course, a pudding and a savoury.

Like the food, the bathwater was hot and there were plenty of bathrooms with huge mahogany baths. And while there was no central heating, the house was warm, with a roaring fire in the Great Hall, though people would complain of draughts. The maidservants were as numerous as the men, with a head housemaid named Bridie to whom the family were devoted. She won some money in the Irish Sweep and they tried to persuade her to put it into the bank, but she would not, for she was convinced that the bank was English. 'If they'd steal the Six Counties, they'd steal my money as well.' It is not known whether her views were shared by the reputed saviour of the house, the gillie, who had been a Republican in the Civil War. Lord Dunraven had inherited him from his predecessor, and like most of the Adare staff, both indoor and outdoor, he stayed for ages. He was excellent at his job,

A gathering in the grounds of Adare in 1930. The Countess of Dunraven, wife of the 5th Earl, sits on the left. In the background is the ruined Franciscan Priory.

a wonderful fisherman and very courteous to Lord Dunraven's guests. He and the other gillie wore a livery of moss green, which was also worn by the head keeper and the foresters. Lord Dunraven had a portrait of the head keeper in his livery painted by the eminent Irish artist Leo Whelan, who also painted his own portrait.

Lower down in the outdoor hierarchy of Adare was the army of 'scratchers', old men who earned an honest penny in their retirement by gently scratching the gravel and the edges of the sweep and the drives and paths with hoes. They would spend much of their time leaning on their hoes and talking to each other, but when Lord Dunraven or one of his family approached, they would separate and resume scratching. Lady Dunraven used to complain that there were too many scratchers, but Lord Dunraven was fond of the old men, who were all great characters, and used to have long conversations with them about their families and their ailments.

Lord Dunraven liked nothing better than to walk round the estate talking to the men who worked for him and having a cup of tea with them, as well as looking at his trees, which were his great passion. He loved Adare and much preferred it to Dunraven, his castle in South Wales, where he went every summer out of a sense of duty. Lady Dunraven, however, preferred Dunraven, though she was hardly less Irish than her husband, being a daughter of the Earl of Mayo, who was a highly successful Master of the Kildare Hunt before he became Viceroy of India. But while she may have preferred Dunraven, she was a charming hostess at Adare, a tall, graceful, white-haired figure who contributed in no small way to the happiness of the house, which was always full of laughter and good humour.

Although some of the Dunravens' many guests were people from outside the world of the Irish country house, such as Mr and Mrs James McNeill, the then Govenor-General of the Irish Free State and his wife, and also de Valera, most of them were familiar figures in this scene. There was, for example, the elderly sportsman Sir Hercules Langrishe from County Kilkenny, who was always mercilessly teased on account of the time when he came to stay for a shoot and found he had left his guns behind. There was Lord Muskerry with his strong Irish brogue and his hairy, ginger-coloured Harris tweed shooting suit. A flavour of the theatre in days gone by was brought by the Marquess and Marchioness of Headfort, Lady Headfort being the former gaiety girl Rosie Boote, and by Colonel Richard Charteris of Cahir Park in County Tipperary, who in his youth had been a great 'stage door Johnny' and who had married a red-haired chorus girl known as the 'Copper Queen'.

In the daytime, people staying at Adare usually went out hunting, shooting or fishing, depending on the season, or they went to the Limerick Show or to a local race meeting. Lord Dunraven was not a fisherman himself, but his study overlooked the river and he always knew what was going on there. Once, when a sister-in-law of his naval younger son, Valentine Wyndham-Quin, caught a salmon in the pool

James McNeill, then Governor-General of the Irish Free State, and his wife at Adare Manor in 1930. They are flanked by Colonel Richard Charteris and his wife, a former chorus girl known as the 'Copper Queen'.

A shooting party at Adare in 1931. The 5th Earl of Dunraven stands in the centre with, on his left, the Marchioness of Headfort, who was the former Gaiety Girl Rosie Boote.

The 5th Earl and his wife with the Knight of Glin – a grandson of the 4th Earl – in front of the Great Hall fireplace at Adare Manor in 1934.

below the house, the gillie attending on her looked up at the study window and said: 'His Lordship is taking off his hat to you.'

'Can he really see I've caught a fish?' the lady asked. To which the gillie replied: 'See? He'll know to within an ounce what the fish weighs.'

The house party would forgather in the Great Hall, and in the evening people would sit in the Gallery with fires burning, playing poker or rummy. The Dunravens' granddaughter Mollie, their son Valentine's daughter – now the Marchioness of Salisbury – would prefer, when she had finished her dinner, to tuck up her skirts and go fishing. She and her two sisters, Ursula and Pamela – who when they were grown up were photographed by Cecil Beaton as the Three Graces – loved staying with their grandparents at Adare and regarded Ireland as their home, although they normally lived in England. They loved the hunting and the fishing, the charades and dumb crambo in the Great Hall, the Irish dancing which a woman

The 5th Earl with his wife and others in the Great Hall at Adare Manor in 1934.

came up twice a week to teach them. They loved the long walks with their grandfather who talked to them about trees and wild flowers, teaching them the Latin
names.

They also had their grandfather to themselves when they visited him in the
morning while he was shaving; he would tell them of his campaigns in South Africa
and of Hendrik, his grey charger. The girls heard other memories of Empire from
their grandmother, who had been in India when her father was Viceroy; she had
even shot a tiger – its skin, complete with stuffed head, adorned her sitting-room
next to her bedroom. When the girls were older, their grandfather would talk to
them about wine, on which he was something of an authority, and at dinner he
would give them a glass of his excellent claret.

The girls had many friends among the servants and people on the place. They
were particularly fond of the temperamental cook and always went to the kitchen to
greet her when they arrived; she would make whatever pudding they chose, which
was usually one with spun sugar. They would visit the cottage of the gillie who had
been a Republican in the Civil War. It was always full of children; Lady Dunraven
had tried to persuade him and his wife not to have any more, but without success,
and they eventually had fourteen. The gillie taught Pamela, the youngest of the three
Wyndham-Quin sisters, Irish songs, including the one about how

'On the twenty-eighth day of November
Close to the town of Macroom
The Tans in their big Crossley tender
Came driving along to their doom'.

She sang it to her grandparents and it did not go down well, unlike that other rebel song, 'The Wearing of the Green', when it was sung at Adare in the presence of Lord Spencer more than half a century earlier. It was not the politics of the song which offended, for Lord Dunraven, though he had been a colonel in the British Army and a Conservative MP, took a romantic view of Irish Republicanism. It was the ending:

'And the Irish Republican Army
Made shite of the whole f.....g lot'.

Lady Dunraven told her husband that he should get rid of the gillie, but of course he did nothing of the sort.

While she did not consider the ending of this song as suitable for polite society, least of all coming from the lips of a young girl, and while she herself was totally virtuous, Lady Dunraven was, in fact, quite worldly. She was once talking to some of her guests at Adare when a certain person's behaviour was mentioned. 'My dear,' she said, 'I've lived long enough to know that in this world, nothing succeeds as much as vice.'[11]

Lady Dunraven died a few months after the outbreak of the Second World War. Her death caused her husband to move downstairs to a bedroom nearer his sitting-room. The war brought ration cards and a shortage of petrol, but in other respects life at Adare went on much the same as ever; Lord Dunraven remained vigorous though now in his eighties. Among the people who came to stay during the war years were the British representative to Ireland, Sir John Maffey, and the American Ambassador, David Gray, and their respective wives; there were also a number of young men on leave from active service who went hunting and were exempted from paying the full cap.

Air travellers on their way to and from America, whose flying boat was delayed at Foynes on the Shannon, came to stay at the Dunraven Arms, the excellent hotel in the village, and were often invited up to the house for luncheon or dinner. Prince Bernhard of the Netherlands came to luncheon and dinner when his flying boat was thus delayed, and Lord Dunraven's daughter, Lady Olein Wyndham-Quin, took him blackberrying. On another occasion, Lord Dunraven found a stranger trespassing in the grounds and reprimanded him. He then heard that the King of Greece was staying at the hotel and invited him up for a meal. The King came and Lord Dunraven bowed to the erstwhile trespasser.

At the beginning of the war, Lord Dunraven's fourteen-year-old granddaughter Pamela — now the Dowager Lady Egremont — was sent to Adare with her French governess. They stayed for nearly three years, during which time the governess made

The 5th Earl of Dunraven with his
grand-daughter Pamela Wyndham-
Quin at Limerick Horse Show in 1940.

little headway with Pamela's education, apart from encouraging her love of French literature, because of constant distractions. 'There's a very good meet today. Why don't you go hunting?' Lord Dunraven would say to his granddaughter, and that was the end of the day's lessons. The fortunate Pamela was able to ride the hunters of her uncle, Lord Adare, who lived with his family a few miles away, he himself being engaged in patrolling the countryside looking for parachutists. Once, when she was sixteen, she rode her uncle's thoroughbred hunter illicitly in a local point-to-point. She knew that her father and mother would have objected to her riding in the race, and that her grandfather would have stopped her riding in it had he known about it in time. So she said nothing about it and on the day of the race she left the house wearing a long skirt over her jodhpurs and carrying her hard hat. But she met her grandfather who asked her where she was going. Being honest, she told him, and he was enchanted. He was even more enchanted when she came in third.

The French governess may have resented Lord Dunraven's over-indulgence of her charge, and this may have been the real reason for the scene she made one day at luncheon. Lord Dunraven was talking about de Gaulle and the Free French when the governess suddenly burst out in defence of Pétain. She spoke passionately of Verdun and of '*ils ne passent pas*'; she declared that Vichy was the only legitimate French government. She was, in fact, a staunch Vichyite; she kept a photograph of Pétain in her room. But a few days after the scene at luncheon, Pamela found that the governess had put the photograph of Pétain away.[12]

# Chapter 2

# Ardfert Abbey

## COUNTY KERRY

TOWARDS the end of the seventeenth century, Sir Thomas Crosbie, MP built himself a house a few miles inland from the North Kerry coast at Ardfert, of which his grandfather John Crosbie had been Bishop. The Crosbies, who were descended from the Chief Bards of the O'Mores of Leix — their surname was originally MacCrossan, meaning 'son of the rhymer' — were granted lands in North Kerry by Queen Elizabeth I. Sir Thomas Crosbie's house, which was improved by his grandson Sir Maurice Crosbie in 1720, was very much of its time, with a pedimented centre and a high roof; the main block was extended by lower wings that ran forwards at right angles to make an open courtyard. Inside, the rooms were panelled and there was a staircase of good joinery. The demesne was no less typical of the period, with yew alleys, 'trees cut into an arcade', avenues of beech, lime and elm. A ruined Franciscan friary in the grounds caused the house to be known eventually as Ardfert Abbey.

In 1745 Sir Maurice Crosbie's son William married Lady Theodosia Bligh, daughter of the first Earl of Darnley. He brought her to Ardfert for the first time a few months later, after a journey during which they were troubled by fleas, worst of all in Limerick, where the army turned out and the bells were rung in their honour and a wine merchant and his wife gave them dinner, making the young bride eat 'six great slices of mutton'. On arriving at her future home, Theodosia could not keep back the tears, at which her husband was not very well pleased. She was met at the coach door by her father-in-law, and 'craved his blessing'. She then went up to her mother-in-law, Lady Anne Crosbie, who stood at the door of the house, 'and did the same thing by her, without being sure it was she', having met neither her nor Sir Maurice before.

'I was in pucker enough all dinner time,' Theodosia told her sister Lady Mary Tighe, whom she called 'Bug', which was a little unfortunate when writing about fleas on the journey. 'But I assure you that before we went to bed I was so great with Lady Anne as if I'd been acquainted with her all my life.' She also liked Sir Maurice, though had naturally not seen as much of him as she had of Lady Anne. 'I am, without a joke, quite bewildered with all the kindness and tenderness I meet

Ardfert Abbey.

with, from them all,' she wrote. When she came down to breakfast, she was given a purse of 100 guineas and told to buy herself a present at the local fair. She planned to buy a 'girdle buckle', and having been promised an additional fifty guineas by 'Sweet William', hoped to get 'a very handsome one' – certainly one would think so, considering what the money would have been worth in those days.

In her next letter to 'Bug', Theodosia complains of 'an old, rusty, grunting Bishop who has been here this fortnight, he is such a formal piece. One would think a man would be no trouble to one, but he is as bad to me as any Mrs . . . whatever, for he is so feeble, he can't walk about with the men and so is left upon our hands the whole day long, and a heavy load he is, God knows. I believe I shall never endure the sight of a black gown again, for there is such a regiment here of them, every day, dancing attendance after him, that it quite kills me.'

There were many other 'day visitors', as well as the Bishop's hangers-on. 'Colonel Ponsonby and his wife and her sister . . . came here,' Theodosia reported, 'dressed out in a most surprising manner, in single lappets and their best Castle gowns. You must know how I took a great spite to them from a story I heard, that they sent six miles for a maid to dress them the day they came. This I heard the day before they came and it gave me a strong prejudice against them.'

Theodosia was 'in great dread' of their staying, as she gathered they generally did, though they only lived a few miles away at a country house named Crotto. This time, however, they did not stay. 'But they will come here soon to stay a week when the coast is clear, for it's a flood at present and locusts cover the land.' One of the 'locusts' was Mrs Freke Crosbie, the pretty young wife of a cousin. Theodosia was sure she would have liked her 'wonderfully' had she not used some rather tiresome slang.

They had been 'jaunting about very much', dining alfresco on the strand, which Theodosia found 'really very pleasant'. But she preferred the Ardfert deer park, where they dined the week before: 'on top of a hill, surrounded by trees, all of Sir Maurice's own planting. There, one has a full prospect of the sea and the whole country for miles about, and let me tell you, no ugly one either; though I won't go so far as to say I think it as pretty as my sweet North.' 'Her sweet North' was County Meath, where the Darnleys had their Irish seat.

On the previous Sunday, she had to dress up for church 'in honour of my Lord Bishop'. She wore her 'yellow and silver', and it was one of the only two occasions since she came here when she 'had a rump on' – the other being the wedding anniversary of her husband's uncle, the Earl of Kerry. She grumbled about it, but did it to please Lady Anne. 'Next Thursday the Bishop and his gang decamp, and Friday we are to go to Dingle.'

The week at Dingle was a great success; they shared a house with the Ponsonbys and another family 'besides straggling men'. There was boating and racing and a ball every night; Theodosia 'led up the ball' in the absence of Lady Kerry, who was too grand 'to partake of any country diversion'. She wore her 'white and silver' on the first night, but it was too hot; so for the rest of the week she made do with 'a lutestring nightgown' which was cool to dance in. These 'jovial doings' seem to have continued after they returned to Ardfert, at any rate for her husband, for when Theodosia next wrote to her sister, he was suffering from a hangover 'occasioned by a merry meeting on the strand yesterday'. She confessed that she was 'not charmed' with parties of this sort, 'for they seldom end till every man is completely drunk, but such things must be, at this time, to please the higher powers'.[1]

Theodosia's father-in-law eventually become the first Lord Branden and her husband the first Earl of Glandore. He died in 1781, she having predeceased him. Their son John, the second Earl of Glandore, did not come to live at Ardfert until two years after he had succeeded; the neighbours could not believe that he would settle here. His sister, Lady Arabella Ward, was of the same opinion. 'Brotherkin', as she called Lord Glandore, was described by a contemporary as 'a strange, absent, staring sort of being', and his wife Diana, a daughter of Viscount Sackville – better remembered as Lord George Germain, Secretary of State for the Colonies at the time of the American War – as 'a most dissipated fine lady'.[2] She was a notorious flirt and a gambler whose slowness in paying her debts earned her the nickname of 'Owen Glendower' (Owing Glandore), though to her family she was known more romantically as 'The Fawn'. But while she did not seem much suited to being the chatelaine of a country house in North Kerry, she and her husband did, in fact, settle down at Ardfert, and when the recently created Earl of Portarlington and his wife came to stay in 1785, she had been here for two years 'without stirring'. This, in Lady Portarlington's view, must have been 'penance' for a fun-loving young woman like her.

'We found Lord and Lady Glandore very glad, I believe, to see a new face,' Lady Portarlington reported to her sister. 'For though there are several people in the house with them, yet their neighbourhood is thin. They have no great resources here, it being an old-fashioned place in a very bleak country, with a bowling green surrounded with clipped hedges to look out upon . . . a dismal place, and he is so partial to everything that is old that he is determined not to alter it. The house is also in the same style, small low rooms, wainscotted, and the drawing room perfectly antique, which he won't let her alter. It is with difficulty he has let her fit up a little dressing room belonging to the apartment I am in, which indeed she has made a sweet little place. It is hung with white paper, to which she has made a border of pink silk, with white and gold flowers stuck upon it, and hung the room with all Mr Bunbury's beautiful prints.'

Lady Portarlington admitted that she found Lady Glandore 'much more pleasing' than she expected she would. 'The people here seem to admire her very much.' And for all her faults, she showed herself to have feelings by her genuine distress when, soon after the Portarlingtons' arrival, she learnt of her father's death. One evening, when they were all 'very merry', the post came. Lord Glandore, having glanced at a letter, ran out of the room, at which Lady Glandore's 'countenance changed'. Exclaiming that something must have happened, she 'fell into a violent fit of crying' and ran out of the room after her husband, who returned a few minutes later to tell them sad news. Lord Glandore was 'almost as affected as she was'. The other ladies who were present and the gentlemen 'all went up every minute by way of comforting her', but Lady Portarlington felt it would be kinder to leave her alone.[3]

Some years later, Lady Glandore had a boarding school at Ardfert, which is surprising, since she and her husband had no children of their own. Perhaps it helped to pay for her gambling and her trips to England. She was away in England for rather a long time in 1793, which she feared might have displeased her husband. By 1809 Lord Glandore's finances were in a bad state and he was angling for a well-paid public office. He does not appear to have been unduly worried, for at the same time he was carrying out repairs and other building works at Ardfert. 'I see you in your

The hall at Ardfert towards the end of the nineteenth century.

Two of William Talbot-Crosbie's grandchildren in the hall at Ardfert towards the end of
the nineteenth century.

study surrounded with books,' his sister wrote to him later that year, 'with not a few unopened letters before you.'[4]

On Lord Glandore's death in 1815, the earldom became extinct and the barony of Branden passed to his clerical cousin William Crosbie, who is remembered for having brought an action against the future Prime Minister, Lord Melbourne, alleging the seduction of his wife. Ardfert was inherited by a son of Lord Glandore's sister, who married a Talbot of Mount Talbot in County Roscommon. His son, William Talbot-Crosbie, who lived until 1899, was one of the first breeders of cattle in the British Isles to sell pedigree bulls to the Argentine. He gave luncheons at Ardfert for his cattle sales, which were held in the ruined Franciscan friary. The grander Argentinian buyers were invited to stay in the house, the less grand were put up in the village.

The last member of the family to live at Ardfert was Mrs Lindsey Talbot-Crosbie, the widow of William Talbot-Crosbie's second son, who died in 1913. She herself had Crosbie blood, she and her husband having been first cousins. In 1919 she had two small granddaughters living with her. The elder, who was then aged five, was spoilt and allowed to have dinner downstairs at the big dining table. The younger, who was three, had to stay upstairs in the nursery.

In 1921, Mrs Talbot-Crosbie decided to close Ardfert and move to Dublin. The house was emptied of its furniture which was taken to the railway station in farm carts driven across the fields. In the following year, during the Civil War, the Republicans burnt the house to prevent it from being occupied by Free State troops; nothing now remains of it.

# Chapter 3

# Ardfry

## COUNTY GALWAY

AMONG the many castles held by the Blakes, who were descended from one of the fourteen ancient civic families of Galway known as the 'Tribes', was Ardfry, on a peninsula jutting out into Galway Bay, which Sir Richard Blake garrisoned in the service of Charles I. In about 1770 Joseph Blake built a new house here; it was long and two-storeyed, with a higher, pyramidal-roofed pavilion at each end. The house had a hall with alcoves supported by pairs of columns and another large room next to the dining-room, which in Joseph Blake's time can hardly have been large enough to hold the family and their guests, for when Mrs Herbert, the wife of the Rector of Carrick-on-Suir in County Tipperary and the mother of the diarist Dorothea Herbert, came here in 1787, she was told 'that they seldom or ever sat down to a meal with less than a hundred in family'. In those days 'family' meant the house party and other guests as well as family in the strict sense.

Mrs Herbert was touring County Galway in a party that included Dorothea and her husband's amusing if somewhat eccentric nephew Ned Eyre. It was Ned Eyre – himself a County Galway landowner, though he lived near Carrick-on-Suir – who brought them to Ardfry. They arrived to find 'a large party of grandees', who according to Dorothea were gathered to celebrate the marriage of the son and heir, young Joseph Blake, to Lady Louisa Bermingham, daughter of the Earl of Louth, as well as the forthcoming marriage of Elizabeth, one of the Blake daughters, to a Scottish peer of illustrious birth, the Earl of Erroll. As young Joseph's marriage to Lady Louisa took place about three years earlier, and Elizabeth's to Lord Erroll did not take place until more than two years later, one suspects that Dorothea's memory played her false regarding the reason for the gathering. Though she may have associated it with young Joseph's marriage because his father-in-law, Lord Louth, was present, and she may have heard on that occasion that Lord Erroll was already casting eyes at Elizabeth, whom she describes as 'a great beauty' and also a wit.

Dorothea felt sure that she and her companions were quite a success with the 'formidable set' they found at Ardfry, except for one unfortunate incident. Ned Eyre's dog, Lady Dapper, a very large 'spotted' spaniel of the 'leopard breed' to whom he

Ardfry.

was in the habit of feeding 'the finest ripe peaches and apricots', made a mess in the room and Lord Louth 'blindly' stepped into it. However, they were forgiven and pressed to stay to dinner, but for some reason they declined.[1]

Having represented Galway in the Irish House of Commons for many years, the younger Joseph Blake was raised to the peerage as Lord Wallscourt at the time of the Union. As he only had a daughter, the peerage was granted with a special remain-der, so that after his death it was held successively by two of his nephews. The younger of the two, another Joseph Blake, became the third Lord Wallscourt in 1816. He was a man of exceptional strength who had made a name for himself as a boxer; he had a fierce temper and was often very violent. In 1822, having already squandered most of his fortune, he married Bessie Lock, a celebrated beauty whose family had until recently lived at Norbury Park in Surrey and were friends of Dr Johnson and Fanny Burney. Her father settled £8,000 on her and in 1825, the year in which she was painted by Sir Thomas Lawrence, her husband took her to Ardfry for the first time.

The place was then sadly neglected. The house had been uninhabited for some years and was empty of furniture and very dilapidated. For the time being, the Wallscourts stayed at Renville, a neighbouring country house also on the shores of Galway Bay. 'I spent the whole of Friday in the gardens at Ardfry,' Bessie wrote to her mother soon after their arrival. 'The woods and walks are certainly very pretty

The beautiful Bessie Lock, who married the 3rd Lord Wallscourt. A portrait by
Sir Thomas Lawrence.

and some of the trees very old and remind me of those poor dear old woods at
Norbury, but the house is even in a worse state than I had expected, and you know
I was not prepared to find *grande chose*. The building at a distance looks very well and
is very handsome, but it seems to me impossible anything can be done with it. There
is so much to do, repairing and building, to make it all inhabitable, that I am sure

Wallscourt will not attempt it.' Instead, they planned to move into Prospect Hill, a small house nearby that had belonged to Lord Wallscourt's father.

In the end, they decided to restore Ardfry. Bessie was clearly falling in love with the place; the large, sheltered kitchen garden, the woods, where, although the Atlantic storms had taken their toll, many fine old trees still stood; the views across Oranmore Bay to the far shore and down Galway Bay towards the Atlantic – it was said that in this direction no land lay between Ardfry and America. There was a magic moment one evening when they looked across Oranmore Bay and saw a fleet of seven or eight frigates sailing in for shelter.

'Wallscourt has made a nice road all through the woods for driving, which is a great improvement,' Bessie reported at about this time. 'But the house does not seem to get on much.' However, it was eventually made habitable and even given a few fashionable Gothic touches, such as battlements, and they were able to move in before the end of the following year. 'The rooms look quite comfortable now,' Bessie wrote, 'although they are but scantily furnished as you may imagine. Fortunately there is no temptation to *buy* furniture as there is none of any sort to be had here for any money, so at least *he* cannot spend anything in that way. He has lately bought at a sale a beautiful china dinner set which we really wanted. He got it very cheap and it is very pretty indeed. None of us know the hour, having no clock and none to be got in this part of the country. All our watches but Wallscourt's are stopped or wrong, mine, alas, I have nursed with care but cannot succeed in making it go.'

To celebrate moving in, they gave a ball for the servants and tenants. More than eighty assembled in the hall and in the room next to the dining-room, which had just been floored though was still unfinished. At first the men stood in silence on one side of the room and the women on the other, but then, as Bessie recounted, 'the great decorum and silence gave place to the most violent noise and rioting as they grew merrier, and they danced incessantly to a piper till five in the morning . . . Wallscourt danced an Irish jig with his old nurse and *very well*; it was very dear to see him and gratified her to a degree! She is a fine looking old woman, not old in *years* but in *looks*, she speaks very little English and calls him *Mavourneen*, her darling. I danced too with Wallscourt, but an English country dance.'

Bessie did not stay long at the ball, knowing that the nurse in charge of her own children was 'languishing to be in the midst of it all'. So she went up to the nursery and told her to go and join in the fun. At first she was shy about doing so, but at last 'yielded' while Bessie 'stayed up with the babies'. Having been persuaded to dance, the nurse became the life and soul of the party, 'springing and capering about in a most ludicrous way'. There was a supper consisting of a whole sheep and two or three rounds of beef, and the whiskey, which they called 'the cratur', flowed freely. According to Bessie, everyone went home 'mad drunk' from drinking the health of young Henry, the infant son and heir, who was safely upstairs in the nursery; some of them fell into the sea on their way back. Later in the morning, the piper played for the Wallscourt children and the one-year-old Willy danced 'furiously'. His mother observed that he had 'quite the life of the Irish jig in him'.

A few days later the rooms of Ardfry echoed to music of a rather different kind. An American who had been at Ballinasloe Fair – a great social event in County Galway – came to stay. He was rich and well-born, being a cousin of Marchioness Wellesley, the American wife of the Duke of Wellington's elder brother who was then Lord-Lieutenant of Ireland – through whom, incidentally, Wellington and Napoleon were connected by marriage, the sister of Lady Wellesley's first husband having married Jerome Bonaparte. Bessie was thrilled to find that her American guest was a '*fanatico per la musica*'; he had brought an Italian opera company to New York, the first that had ever been heard there. He was 'a perfect musician himself with a most delightful voice'; while he was at Ardfry, he and Bessie sang '*incessantly all day and all night*' so that in the end she was quite exhausted. 'Sometimes his Italian accent in singing is not quite as perfect as one might wish,' she observed. 'But he has *none* of the Yankee about him in anything.'[2]

Singing Italian opera with the American was a rare treat for Bessie, whose life at Ardfry was normally of a simpler outdoor sort. She and her husband would go sailing; they never went out without meeting two or three large seals. Lord Wallscourt rather unkindly tried to shoot one of them, but it escaped. In summer they bathed; many people came here for the bathing, which was thought to be very good, and took little cottages along the shore. It reminded Bessie of Castellamare, near Naples. While Lord Wallscourt actually swam, she was content merely to have a dip, supported in the water by an old woman. She complained of the bathing cabins, which could not be moved, so that when the tide was low she had to run some way from the cabin into the sea and then back again. This, she thought, was unseemly.

For Bessie, life at Ardfry was inclined to be lonely. She may well have avoided having people to stay on account of her husband's rather odd behaviour. Lord Wallscourt liked walking about the house naked; Bessie managed to persuade him to carry a cowbell when he was in this state so as to warn the maidservants of his approach. But what was harder for her to bear than her husband's oddities was his vile temper. He became increasingly cruel to her; he treated her worse rather than better after their elder son Henry, to whom she was devoted, died at the age of five in 1828. In the following year they lost their other little boy, Willy, who died in London of an infectious fever that nearly killed their daughter Frederica, known as Freddy, who, however, survived, just as she later managed to survive when she was in a boat that capsized in the middle of Galway Bay and could not swim. Eventually the Wallscourts lived apart; he went to Ardfry on his own and she stayed with her parents in England. There was, however, a brief reconciliation that brought another son, who became the fourth Lord Wallscourt.

The journalist and Nationalist politician T. P. O'Connor, when he was a student at Queen's College, Galway in the 1860s, used to admire Ardfry from across the water. 'To me,' he wrote, 'it was a dream castle in which a proud and prosperous member of the landed aristocracy enjoyed all the delights that wealth seemed to offer when one is both young and poor.' But when, later in life, he met the fourth Lord Wallscourt, 'the heroic and gallant figure who had haunted my dreams since my seventeenth year', he saw 'a tiny little man, sad, deprecatory, almost timid in manner'.[3] He was a man beset by money worries, whose finances were made worse by his second wife, who was a gambler. In the early years of this century, she sold the lead off the roof at Ardfry to pay her gambling debts, so that the house gradually fell into ruin. The Wallscourt peerage did not survive the house, becoming extinct on the death of the gambling Lady Wallscourt's stepson in 1920.

# Chapter 4

# Ballyfin

## COUNTY LEIX

IN 1812 Sir Charles Coote bought the estate of Ballyfin, on the edge of the Slieve Bloom Mountains in what is now County Leix but was then known as the Queen's County. Sir Charles was the Premier Baronet of Ireland, the baronetcy having being conferred on his ancestor and namesake Sir Charles Coote, who came to Ireland from Devon in 1600 and was a notable military commander in the Irish wars of the first half of the seventeenth century. Having bought Ballyfin, Sir Charles built a new house here, originally employing an architect named Dominick Madden and then changing over to Sir Richard Morrison and his son William Vitruvius Morrison. Madden and the Morrisons between them produced a Classical house on a palatial scale, with an Ionic portico on the entrance front and a curved bow with Ionic columns in the centre of the side containing the long library. The Morrisons gave the house an interior of great magnificence, with exciting spatial effects and a wealth of rich plasterwork, scagliola columns and inlaid parquetry floors. A great

Ballyfin.

Sir Charles Coote, 9th baronet, with his grand-daughter Caroline de Massingy, in the
library at Ballyfin in about 1855. A water-colour by Sir Charles's son-in-law, the
Marquis de Massingy de la Pierre.

top-lit saloon in the centre of the house was flanked by the staircase and by a domed
rotunda leading to the library. The house was finished in 1826 and Sir Charles filled
it with a splendid collection of pictures and furniture.

Early this century, Ballyfin was the home of Sir Charles's grandson Sir Algernon
Coote and his wife and children. Sir Algernon had three sons and a daughter by his
present wife, who was his second, as well as three sons and a daughter by his first
wife, who died in 1880; when Ralph, the son and heir, married in 1904, he was
nearly thirty, whereas his youngest half-brother Max was only eight. Max was barely
out of the Ballyfin nursery before his half-nephews, Ralph's two sons, came to take
his place. The nursery was above the so-called 'Bachelor Rooms', the rooms given
to single male guests, which were along a passage entered from the service end of the
dining-room. The children used the back stairs, which were also used by the staff.
Ralph's son Thomas rather envied the grown-up members of the family and their
guests who used the grand staircase with its red carpet and polished stair-rods.

Every morning the children would be brought downstairs by their nanny for

Family and friends outside Ballyfin in about 1905. Sir Algernon Coote, 12th baronet, stands at the back, his second wife Ella sits in front of him holding the infant John Coote, son of her stepson Ralph. Ralph Coote, who became the 13th baronet, sits on one of the lower steps at the left, with his wife Alice behind him.

prayers. This was a formal event and it took place in the great saloon with its Corinthian columns, its paintings by Greuze and Murillo and its chairs upholstered in scarlet brocade, said to have been made for George IV when he was Prince of Wales. Sir Algernon conducted a service from a lectern; the guests were expected to join in the responses and in the hymns, which somebody accompanied on the grand piano. The servants knelt at cane-backed chairs behind the columns at the staircase end; the housekeeper, the footman, the under-cook, the five housemaids all neat and starched; only the cook and butler were missing, too busy getting breakfast ready. As young Thomas Coote passed the housemaids on his way to his grander seat with the gentry near the blazing log fire he 'always longed to give their neat bottoms a pinch'.[1]

Morning prayers were followed by breakfast, when the children were allowed to join the grown-ups round the long dining-room table. On the sideboards was a splendid array of swivel-topped silver chafing dishes containing eggs and bacon and kidneys or sausages; hot rolls and boiled eggs were in silver stands on the table covered with well-ironed napkins to keep them warm. Immediately after breakfast, the children disappeared, reappearing when they joined the grown-ups for half an hour after tea in the saloon, where there was plenty of room for them to play with their toys on the floor, until they were 'bidden to withdraw'.[2] In wet weather, when they could not go out, the children were allowed to play with their model railway on the polished floor of the rotunda.

Occasionally, the children went into the billiard room, which was much fre-
quented by the grown-ups. The billiard room and the saloon seem to have been the
rooms most generally in use, though guests also sat in the Red Drawing Room,
which was Lady Coote's sanctum; it was rather dark and cluttered, with heavy red
curtains. Nobody ever sat in the beautiful White Drawing Room and people seldom
went into the library except on their way to the large and graceful Victorian conservatory which opened off it. This was surprising, since the house was usually fairly
full. In 1902 no fewer that 147 people came to stay; in 1904 the number rose to 161.[3]
Guests at Sir Algernon and Lady Coote's house parties included the art collector
Sir Hugh Lane and the great Professor John Pentland Mahaffy of Trinity College,
Dublin.

When he wished to escape from his guests, Sir Algernon retired to his study
which faced across the sweep towards the lake; its windows were fitted with a special
kind of glass through which he could see out without being seen from outside. The
study had an acetylene gas fire. Sir Algernon had a dangerous habit of turning on
the evil-smelling gas, then searching for a matchbox and then, when he had found
one, throwing lighted matches at the fire until it exploded. His grandsons in the
room next door would ask their step-grandmother what the noise was and were told:
'It's only Grandpa lighting his fire.'[4]

The gas was made in an acetylene plant at the entrance to the stable yard. Beside
it was a smelly pile of carbide waste, which the nanny did her best to keep the chil-

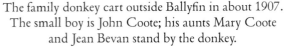

The family donkey cart outside Ballyfin in about 1907.
The small boy is John Coote; his aunts Mary Coote
and Jean Bevan stand by the donkey.

John Coote, who became the 14th baronet,
in his toy motor car outside Ballyfin in about 1907.

dren away from. Near the gas house was a copse in front of which a tree was planted one year on the birthday of each of the two boys, the dates being recorded on iron plaques. One birthday of John, the elder boy, would have been memorable without any tree-planting if things had gone as he and Thomas had intended. They made a container and filled it with petrol, planning to blow it up as a birthday treat; it was carefully hidden the day before in the wild garden between the end of the lake and the house. Unfortunately someone discovered the home-made bomb before it could be exploded, much to the boys' disappointment.

The boys had plenty to amuse them without having to make petrol bombs. They played games in the squash court in the further yard, opposite the place where motor cars were cleaned, Sir Algernon being an enthusiastic pioneer motorist. They visited the old bearded carpenter Keegan and his son in the carpenter's shop in the first yard and saw all the fascinating things they were making. In summer they swam in the lake, where there was even a springboard for diving. They were taught to fish for the giant pike in the lake by Tear the keeper, who was the most important of the outdoor staff.

Another important personage outside the house was the head gardener who brought in the fruit, luscious peaches and nectarines and big purple grapes, and gave it to the butler for the table. Ballyfin in the years before the outbreak of the Great War was particularly well equipped with hothouses; in one of them there was even a banana tree which usually produced two large bunches of bananas every year. As well as the hothouses, the gardeners had a great deal to see to. There were the flower borders along the path from the centre of the walled garden, the vegetables which grew behind the borders and the strawberries and other soft fruit which grew near one of the walls. There was Lady Coote's rose garden. There were the pleasure grounds near the house where the fountain was turned on when guests were staying. The fountain was surrounded by a pitch-and-putt golf course, much used by Sir Algernon's older sons. One of them deliberately drove a ball at the conservatory and scored a direct hit. As an alternative to pitch-and-putt, there was, of course, tennis.[5]

On Sundays, Sir Algernon and Lady Coote with their children and grandchildren and the house party processed down the avenue and along the path across the fields to the family church, where they sat in the balcony. John and Thomas were each given a penny by their mother to put in the plate. Sir Algernon was a pillar of the Church of Ireland and he and Lady Coote did many good works; local meetings were held in the house. He was a generous employer and paid out £3,000 a year in wages – the highest wage bill in the county. At Christmas he and Lady Coote gave presents to the hundred or so men who worked on the estate and also to their wives and families.

One year, the *Leinster Express* printed an account of the Christmas ritual at Ballyfin. 'On Saturday evening the workmen on the estate were brought together, and substantial fare, in the shape of beef, etc., was presented to each. The soothing effect of "the pipe of peace" was also taken into account and each man was given a

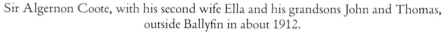

Sir Algernon Coote, with his second wife Ella and his grandsons John and Thomas, outside Ballyfin in about 1912.

supply of tobacco, in the puffing of which they could reflect upon the pleasures of the good things when consumed. Cheers were given for the generous donors by the recipients. Sir Algernon, in addressing the men, wished them a happy Christmas, and expressed the pleasure it gave him to see them all happy and contented. He mentioned that he had been asked to join a Labour League, but he thought the best way to show his sympathy with the labourer was by giving them plenty of employment (hear, hear) . . . The wives and families of the workmen were not forgotten, and among them Lady Coote distributed many useful and suitable gifts of clothing, etc., which were most acceptable'.[6]

Like so many in his position, Sir Algernon was not as rich as he appeared to be; his estate was mortgaged. After his death in 1920, his eldest son, who was now Sir Ralph Coote, had to give up Ballyfin. The widowed Lady Coote went to live in London and the new baronet and his family continued to live in a smaller house on the estate which had been built just before the war, the great Classical mansion being left empty until a purchaser could be found. Sir Algernon had died at the height of the Troubles, but the house came to no harm because Sir Ralph was sensible enough to put in a caretaker who was an ardent Sinn Fein supporter and had been imprisoned by the British at the Curragh Camp. In 1923 Sir Ralph and his family moved to a villa near Dublin, the Ballyfin estate was sold to the Land Commission, and the house was eventually bought by a religious order.

*Chapter 5*

# Barmeath Castle
## COUNTY LOUTH

A N OLD castle, turned into a Georgian house, then made to look medieval again in the first half of the nineteenth century; this could describe the ancestral seat of a number of Irish families and it describes Barmeath, seat of the Bellews in County Louth. Barmeath was acquired in the reign of King Charles II by Sir John Bellew, a clever lawyer of old Norman-Irish stock whose original estates in County Louth had been confiscated under Cromwell. Bellew succeeded in getting the confiscated estates of Lord Carlingford given back to him after the Restoration and Lord Carlingford gave him a part of them, including Barmeath, as his fee.

Towards the middle of the eighteenth century Barmeath was the home of Sir Edward Bellew, the third Baronet – the family had obtained a baronetcy in 1688 – who was married to Eleanor Moore from Drogheda. Eleanor's book of receipts gives us an idea of what the Barmeath table would have been like in those days. Some of the receipts are in French, for example '*pour mariner veau ou venaison et du sanglier*', so we can assume that the Bellews and their friends enjoyed French cuisine. There are receipts for 'The Duke of Norfolk's Famous Punch' – obviously a drink popular in the Catholic world, to which the Bellews as well as the Duke belonged – and for 'The Bishop of Elphin's Beer'. We also learn what remedies Eleanor and her family had recourse to when they were indisposed. For 'a fit of the colic' they took 'a tea-spoonful of gunpowder in a little Genaoca' – an Italian wine rather like Chianti. For other complaints they favoured Tincture of Rhubarb: 'It will not give more than a motion or two which will be over before dinner and need not confine you'.[1]

Eleanor's son Sir John Bellew, who succeeded his father in 1741, was advised to take a supply of Tincture of Rhubarb with him when he went on his travels, also some Powder of Crabs' Eyes which was just the thing 'should his stomach at any time go sour'. Alas, these remedies did not prevent him from dying at the age of twenty-two in 1750. Barmeath passed to his brother, Sir Patrick, who enlarged and remodelled the house, giving it an interior in the best mid-eighteenth-century taste, making a very handsome library on the first floor with a ceiling of rococo plaster-work incorporating Masonic emblems. Sir Patrick was a Freemason and used the

Barmeath Castle.

room for Lodge meetings. When the Papal condemnation of Freemasonry was promulgated in Ireland, he told his former brethren that they could continue holding their meetings here during his lifetime, though he himself would henceforth be unable to attend them.

Francis Bellew, one of Sir Patrick's younger sons, got into trouble for helping a secret society of a very different sort. While they were having dinner at Barmeath during the Christmas season of 1792, one of the guests let slip that a troop of cavalry was going to the Grangebellew crossroads to break up a meeting of Ribbon Men — members of one of the several terrorist organizations that existed in Ireland at this time. After the ladies had gone out, Francis asked one of the footmen to get him a horse and he galloped off and warned the Ribbon Men that 'they would be cut to pieces if they remained'. They duly dispersed and Francis galloped home again, his horse 'in a great sweat'. Unfortunately, there had been an informer at the meeting and he found himself having to stand trial at Dundalk Assizes. He was, however, acquitted, having been ably defended by his brother William, who was a lawyer.[2]

While Francis was accused of being a friend of the Ribbon Men, his father was having trouble with another set of terrorists who called themselves the 'Defenders'. Some of them came to Barmeath asking for arms; Sir Patrick expected them to attack the house and had his guns cleaned so as to be ready to repulse them. After his death in 1795, his eldest son Sir Edward commanded a corps of the volunteer Yeomanry which was raised as a protection against Defenders and United Irishmen as well as to resist a possible French invasion. Sir Edward was prominent among the group of influential Irish Catholics who worked to achieve full Catholic Emancipation. He died in 1827, two years before the Emancipation was granted, but his two sons benefitted from his labours, both becoming Members of Parliament. The elder, who was another Sir Patrick Bellew, also became Lieutenant for County Louth; he was, however, a man of retiring disposition who preferred staying at home at Barmeath to going into society or playing a part in public life. His younger brother, Richard Montesquieu Bellew, was a more active politician and became a Lord of the Treasury. When they were in Ireland, the two brothers lived together at Barmeath, although they both had wives.

Like his grandfather and namesake, Sir Patrick Bellew enlarged and remodelled Barmeath, but while his grandfather made the house Classical, he gave it turrets and battlements. His wife Anna Fermina, who was the daughter of a Spanish admiral, complained in her diary on New Year's Day 1839 that the house was full of workmen and that there was no room to receive anyone, though they did in fact have the local priest, Father Flanagan, with another priest and Mr Darcy, the Chief of Police, to dinner. A couple of days later they gave a dance in the hall; there was 'great dancing' and Eddy, the eight-year-old son of the house, 'excelled himself'. Pat Ward, the coachman, 'came dressed like a wild Irishman with a torn coat and a caubeen' – the latter being a particularly Irish sort of cap. Barney Duffy was 'Primo Violino', Chaffrey the Piper was 'ten times better than the Scotchman'. The 'Scotchman' to whom Anna Fermina refers was the piper who had played at a party given by neighbours the day before; he had been brought by Lord Glenlyon, who was on a visit to County Louth.

Later that January came the dreadful storm remembered as the Great Wind. 'In this demesne, no words can describe the devastation which daylight showed us,' Anna Fermina wrote. 'Poor Sir Patrick wept and the poor labourers seemed to share his grief.' Fortunately the house suffered little, though a great many slates were blown off, but trees were blown down on all sides. Barmeath was worse affected than most places having a great deal of very old timber.

Father Flanagan came to dinner again soon after the storm and cheered them up with 'his droll stories'. The other priest and Mr Darcy came too. In February they tried to raise a fallen ilex tree; it took 150 men, four bullocks and twenty pounds' worth of cable and they do not appear to have been successful. When they returned to their devastated demesne after a visit to County Wicklow, it was some consolation to hear that Viscount Ferrard, who owned one of the largest estates in County Louth, had called while they were away and had been much impressed by the improvements they were carrying out.[3]

Lord Ferrard was one of few peers in the county. In 1848, however, their number was increased when Sir Patrick was raised to the peerage as Lord Bellew. He owed

The 2nd Lord Bellew sitting outside Barmeath Castle with his four sons, some time in the eighteen-sixties. The eldest son Patrick died in a shooting accident; the second and third sons Bertie and George succeeded in turn as the 3rd and 4th Lord Bellew; the youngest son Richard was the only one to have children.

his elevation to his politically active brother, and also, perhaps, to Queen Victoria's desire for more Catholic peers.

His son Eddy, who was at school at Stonyhurst with the ill-fated Roger Tichborne and appeared as a witness in the Tichborne case, became the second Lord Bellew. Although a newspaper account of a meet of the Louth Hunt at Barmeath in the 1870s reports that the fox ran into 'an unknown sewer in the park',[4] there were still no water closets in the house in the second Lord Bellew's time. It was his son Bertram, known as Bertie, who gave the house indoor sanitation after he had succeeded as the third Lord Bellew in 1895. He did so after an unpleasant experience; he visited the old outdoor privy not realizing that the family greyhound was in there, having puppies under the seat; when he sat down he was bitten.

Bertie married Mildred de Trafford, who came of a prominent English Catholic family. They had no children of their own, but the four children of Bertie's youngest brother by his first wife, who had died, spent a great deal of time with them at Barmeath. Having no mother, the children – Edward and Bryan, Guendaline and

The Bellew children, Edward, Guendaline, Ada and Bryan, outside Barmeath Castle in the eighteen-nineties. Immediately inside the door was the water-closet where they annoyed their Uncle Bertie.

Ada – were fairly wild. Bryan shot his aunt's tumbler pigeons with his catapult; she was watching them when they suddenly fell dead. Poor Bertie suffered from loss of memory and the children shamelessly took advantage of this; they all kept telling him that it was their birthday and he kept on giving them presents.

One of the closets installed by Bertie had a partition that did not go right up to the ceiling, as in a school or a club. There was an occasion when one of the boys lifted up one of the girls so that she could look down over the top of the partition at her uncle, who was ensconced here. 'What are you doing, Uncle Bertie?' she asked brightly.

'Go away, little girl,' her uncle snapped back at her. As soon as he was in a position to do so, he went to her father and told him that she must be severely punished.

'What has she done?' asked her father.

'I can't remember. I know it was very naughty.'[5]

Of the four children, Edward and Bryan both eventually succeeded to the

The same foursome with the same pram in the same place about seventy years later. Edward was then the 5th Lord Bellew; Guendaline was the Hon. Mrs Lloyd-Thomas; Ada was the Hon. Mrs Herbrand Alexander. Bryan was to succeed his brother as the 6th Lord Bellew.

peerage. Barmeath is now the home of Bryan's grandson, Mr Bryan Bellew, and his wife and family. Guendaline married an eminent diplomatist; Ada married, as her second husband, a brother of Field Marshal Earl Alexander of Tunis and lived to celebrate her 101st birthday.

## Chapter 6

# Carton

## COUNTY KILDARE

THE LANDS of Carton in County Kildare always belonged to the FitzGeralds, Earls of Kildare, whose chief castle was nearby, at Maynooth; but they were leased in the seventeenth century to the Talbots, who built a house here. In 1739 Robert, nineteenth Earl of Kildare, bought the reversion of lease and made Carton his principal seat. He employed the architect Richard Castle to transform the house into one of the great country houses of Georgian Ireland, a three-storeyed central block with a pediment and many windows joined to flanking office wings by curved colonnades. In contrast to the massive plainness of the wide-spreading grey stone exterior was the rich baroque plasterwork of the great dining-room, which was by the Francini brothers and depicted 'the Courtship of the Gods'.

The rebuilding of Carton was completed in 1747. By that time the nineteenth Earl of Kildare was dead, and it was his son James, the twentieth Earl, who came to live here with his beautiful and talented sixteen-year-old wife Emily, a daughter of the second Duke of Richmond and a sister of Lady Sarah Lennox, whom the young George III wanted to marry, and of Lady Louisa, who was to marry the Kildares' neighbour Tom Connolly of Castletown. Emily immediately fell in love with 'Dear Sweet Carton' as she called it, and she and her husband spent much of their married life decorating the house and improving its surroundings. They made a Chinese bedroom on the ground floor with Chinese wallpaper and they appear to have followed the prevailing fashion and made a Print Room. They planted clumps of trees and dammed a stream to make a lake and a broad serpentine river, turning the demesne into a great landscape park in the manner of 'Capability' Brown, to whom Lord Kildare is said to have offered £1,000 as an inducement to come to Ireland, but without success. As the final touch to her landscape, Emily acquired a herd of spotted cows, for which she had a passion. 'I wish you could see the cows in the garden, they look so pretty,' she wrote to her husband, having returned to Carton in his absence. 'There is a man to watch them who is generally asleep. The butter and cream is excellent; I enjoy it so much after that at Castletown, which is bad. The ale and small beer I have not ventured on.'[1]

Carton.

James, 20th Earl of Kildare, afterwards 1st Duke of Leinster, with his beautiful and talented wife Emily in 1753. Emily is examining the architect's drawing of one of their improvements. A painting by Arthur Devis.

While admiring her cows and enjoying her butter and cream, Emily did not neglect the mundane side of country house life. She inspected the domestic offices and when she found that one of them did not come up to her standard of cleanliness, she herself scolded the manservant responsible for it, rather than leaving this to Mrs Winter, the housekeeper, or to Stoyte, the butler. 'There's a wife after your own heart for you!' she told her husband. She found a woman in the laundry one morning who had no business there and turned her out. And when the children's nurses were going with all the other servants to some races that were being held outside the demesne wall and proposed taking her infant son and daughter with them, she would not allow this but stayed at home with her sister Sarah to look after the two young children.

Emily gave birth to no fewer than fourteen children, so she did not go out into society very much. But people came to stay at Carton. Lady Drogheda brought her schoolboy son who slept on a camp bed in the room next to hers. 'He . . . runs about all day, so he is no trouble to me,' Emily reported. Another visitor was the architect Richard Castle, who while he was here started writing a letter to a carpenter working on the building of Lord Kildare's Dublin house and fell dead; some said his death was caused by drinking, for he was fond of the bottle. In 1759, when she was alone at Carton, Emily had an unexpected caller in the form of Primate Stone, the Church of Ireland Archbishop of Armagh, who was then living at Leixlip Castle nearby. Stone, the virtual ruler of Ireland, was the chief political opponent of Lord Kildare, who supported the popular party. For all his power, he seems to have been in some awe of a countess who was the daughter of a duke; having made conversation, he 'stammered and coloured' and told Emily he had come to request a favour. Would she allow his sister-in-law Mrs Stone to call on her? Emily agreed, though wondered whether she ought not to call on Mrs Stone, and wished her husband were there to advise her. A couple of days later Mrs Stone turned up unexpectedly; Emily, back from taking the air after dinner, found her in the Print Room. She was very awkward and Emily felt confused. 'I am really ashamed with myself for having profited so little from *les usages du monde,*' she told her husband. However, they 'fell by degrees into a chatty conversation enough'.

In 1761 a house party at Carton performed *The Beggar's Opera*. Viscount Charlemont, who later became famous as the Volunteer Earl, played Peachum and Emily's sister, Lady Louisa Connolly, was a success as Lucy. Emily herself also took part together with her brother-in-law Tom Connolly and Viscount Powerscourt.

Life at Carton was less to Emily's taste when she returned here alone in December 1762. The house, normally warm, had been unoccupied for some time so was bitterly cold; not even the cherry brandy, sent by her husband's aunt, Lady Inchiquin, could cheer her up. Her winter rooms were being redecorated; the Print Room was comfortable enough, but the way to it was perishing. The stairs and passages were 'running with wet'. It was necessary to have fires everywhere and not be sparing of the coal; but the maids were 'exceedingly so of their trouble'.[2]

Lord Kildare, who had been raised to a marquessate in 1761, was made Duke of Leinster in 1766. He died in 1773 and was succeeded by his eldest son William Robert, who married two years later. The new Duke and Duchess lived almost the whole time at Carton, for he was keen on farming and she loved the country and hated London and only went to Leinster House in Dublin when she was expecting a baby. Compared to Emily and her husband, people found them a little dull; yet life at Carton in their time was far from being bucolic. 'Everything seems to go on in great state here,' Lady Caroline Dawson wrote when staying at Carton soon after her marriage in 1778. 'The Duchess appears in a sack and hoop and diamonds in an afternoon; French horns playing at every meal; and such quantities of plate, etc., that one would imagine oneself in a palace. And there are servants without end . . . It is not the fashion at Carton to play at cards. The ladies sit and work, and the gentlemen lollop about and go to sleep — at least the Duke does, for he snored so loud the other night that we all got into a great fit of laughing and waked him. They asked me if I liked cards and I pretended I did, much more than I really do, for the sake of getting a card table; for when there is a good many people sitting in that manner it's very tiresome, so I had a party at whist every night; but they seemed to think it very odd that a young woman should like cards. Yesterday, before we set out, we went to church with them. They have a very comfortable gallery with a good fire. I forgot to mention to you the Duke's chaplain lives in the house with them and reads prayers every morning, which all the ladies of the house attend very devoutly, but I can't say so much for the gentlemen.'[3]

A young lady named Miss Sandford who came to stay a year later also mentions the French horns, which must have sounded ravishing beneath the lofty baroque ceiling of the dining-room; and she tells us more about the actual meals. 'We breakfast between 10 and 11, though it is called half-past nine. We have an immense table — chocolate, honey, hot bread, cold bread, brown bread, white bread, green bread, and all coloured breads and cakes. After breakfast, Mr Scott, the Duke's chaplain, reads a few short prayers, and then we go as we like; a back room for reading; a billiard room, a print room, a drawing room, and a whole suite of rooms, not forgetting the music room. We dine at half-past four or five; courses upon courses, which I believe takes up two full hours. It is pretty late when we leave the parlour. We then go to tea; so to cards about nine; play till supper-time — 'tis pretty late by the time we go to bed.'[4]

Miss Sandford also reported that the house was crowded, with many comings and goings; that there were 'all sorts of amusements' and that the gentlemen were out hunting and shooting all the mornings. Yet the company at Carton in the time of the second Duke and his Duchess was not limited to peers and country gentlemen and their womenfolk, but included such people as Dean Marlay, the future Bishop of Waterford, who is remembered more as a wit than as an ecclesiastic, and Robert Jephson, nephew of the dramatist, as well as the actor John Henderson and the actress Mrs Fanny Abington, who came here when she was appearing in Dublin in *The School for Scandal*. When Emily Duchess heard that Mrs Abington had stayed a night at Carton, she raised her eyes.

While the second Duke was farming and entertaining an endless succession of guests, his younger brother, Lord Edward FitzGerald, was in Paris, absorbing revolutionary ideas. Having married the beautiful Pamela, reputed to be the natural daughter of Madame de Genlis and Philippe-Egalité, he returned to Ireland where he became a leader of the United Irishmen. In May 1798 he planned for his friends in County Kildare to march on Dublin; but before this could happen he was arrested and he died in prison of the wounds he had received when trying to resist arrest. A regiment of Scots Fusiliers was sent from Dublin to occupy Carton; they arrived and piled their arms in the colonnades. The Duke was in England at the time, but some of his daughters were at home and one of them, Lady Elizabeth FitzGerald, wrote immediately to the Chief Secretary, Lord Castlereagh, so that the troops were withdrawn to the nearby village of Maynooth before they could do any damage. The butler took the precaution of walling up the family plate.

For a time after the death of the second Duke in 1804, Carton was deserted; his son Augustus Frederick, who became the third Duke, being only thirteen when he succeeded. 'Carton, once the scene of youthful joy, now the scene of desolation,' lamented Lady Sarah Napier, the sister of Emily Duchess.[5] But the young Duke brought Carton back to life after he came of age. Having sold Leinster House in Dublin in 1815, which left him with money to spare, he employed the Irish architect Sir Richard Morrison to enlarge and remodel the house. Morrison replaced the curved colonnades with straight ones behind which were wings containing additional rooms, including a new dining-room with a barrel-vaulted ceiling and screens of Corinthian columns. It came at the end of the enfilade along the principal front, which also included the former dining-room, now the saloon, and a drawing-room where the entrance hall had been. Since this front faced south, it now became the garden front and the entrance was moved to the north front, the former music room becoming the hall.

The Duke also installed hot, cold and 'vaporous' baths. 'I am sure there is in no private house so magnificent a cold bath,' declared the Earl of Donoughmore, who came to dine at Carton in 1822. Lord Donoughmore, who was accompanied by a nephew and also by Mr and Mrs Austin, the Church of Ireland clergyman at Maynooth and his wife, with whom they were staying, was much impressed by the general magnificence, the grand rooms, the excellent servants; also by the 'easy and interesting manners of the Duke and Duchess'.

They dined at 6.30. As well as the party from the Glebe, there were three other guests, the clergyman brother of Earl Talbot, who had been Viceroy of Ireland until the previous year, the Duke's cousin, Colonel FitzGerald de Ros, and a Mr Mitchell. After dinner, the Duchess played on the fine organ in the drawing-room; Lord Donoughmore was told that it had cost the Duke 2,000 guineas. Mrs Austin sang, being accompanied by the Duke on his double bass as well as by the Duchess. The Duchess, who like the Duke's grandmother Emily was English, a daughter of the third Earl of Harrington, was, as Lord Donoughmore observed, 'again obvious in a family way'; she already had 'two very fine children'. Lord Donoughmore considered her 'not handsome but most interesting' and thought that 'to all appearances the Duke could not have made a better choice'.[6] The Duke and Duchess were both serious musicians; they brought many volumes of music to the library at Carton, the works of great composers of the past as well as of contemporaries such as Rossini, Clementi and de Bauval – who dedicated his *Martiale Divertimento* to the Duke.

The diarist Thomas Creevey stayed at Carton a few years after Lord Donoughmore's visit. He was greeted on his arrival by the Duke's 'two fine boys' and their French tutor. Then the Duke appeared. 'He was all kindness and good humour, as he always is,' Creevey recalled. 'He conducted me himself to my bedroom, and would not have minded brushing my coat if I had wanted it.' Creevey had been given the Chinese bedroom: 'French to the backbone in its furniture, gilt on the roof, gilded looking-glasses in all directions, fancy landscapes and figures in panels, a capital canopy bed,' was how he described it.

There were five other male guests in the drawing-room before dinner, including the Duchess's brother Augustus Stanhope and two young lordlings, the Duke of Somerset's son Lord Seymour and the Earl of Gosford's son Lord Acheson. Then the Duchess herself entered. 'From the prettiness of her manner it was quite impossible not to feel at home with her from that moment,' Creevey wrote. 'But she is not nearly so pretty as I expected.'

As when Lord Donoughmore was here, dinner was at 6.30. The Duchess was taken in to dinner by Lord Seymour and Lord Acheson, who sat on either side of her; Creevey, however, managed to put himself on the other side of Lord Seymour and talked across him to the Duchess until they all went to bed at 11.30. In a letter he wrote next morning, he excuses himself for having dominated the conversation by saying that the Duchess enjoyed a good laugh and did not get one from the two 'demure, negative striplings' on either side of her.

'What a difference it makes when one has a room to write in with all one's little comforts about one,' Creevey remarks in the same latter from Carton. 'I never, to my mind, had one so made for me as my present one ... my own escritoire in a recess with paper *lighters* before me of all colours, and in another corner of the room another recess that shall be nameless, through a door, quite belonging to itself and to no other apartment; the whole to conclude with a charming fire which woke me by its crackling nearly an hour ago, whilst my maid thought, of course, she was making it without waking the gentleman.' To add to Creevey's satisfaction, when he went to breakfast at 9.30, he found 'the nobility sprigs still mute and everything to be done by Mr Thomas'.[7]

The Chinese bedroom was occupied by more illustrious guests in 1849 when Queen Victoria came to Carton accompanied by Prince Albert. A large party had been invited to meet the royal visitors; the country people danced jigs on the lawn to the music of Irish pipes, which delighted the Queen. She was also struck by how different the Irish yells of welcome were from English cheers.

The Queen was driven about the place in the Duke's jaunting car, which was unusually large and drawn by two horses instead of one; it must have resembled one of Bianconi's Long Cars. She liked it so much that the Duke ordered one to be built in Dublin and sent it to Windsor for her; which inspired the following verse:

> Shure when the Queen was over here she said she'd like her health to thrive,
> So the darlin' Duke of Leinster thought he's thrate her to a dhrive.
> She got on his outsidher, and before she had gone far,
> 'Be me sowl' says she, 'I like the joultin' of yer Irish jauntin' car'.
> So he had one made in Dublin, and he wrote to Mister Maher
> To send out Larry Doolan for to dhrive the jauntin' car.[8]

'Darlin' Duke of Leinster' is appropriate, for the third Duke was known affection-ately as the 'Good Duke'. He was an admirable landlord, having, like his father before him, an extensive knowledge of farming. He worked hard as a magistrate and was broad-minded in matters of religion; though he and his family belonged to the Church of Ireland, he took a keen interest in the college for Catholic clergy at Maynooth, which his father had helped to found. He kept a small Catholic missal, in Latin and English, at Carton, presumably for the use of his Catholic guests.

The last of the Good Duke's improvements to Carton was the installation of a magnificent new organ in the saloon in 1857. Its ornate baroque case, spanning the doorway to the anteroom and dining-room, was designed by his second son, Lord Gerald FitzGerald, an officer in the Scots Guards who as well as being an artist was himself a musician; some of his compositions, such as *Paris Polka*, *Ariadne Quadrille* and *Crinoline Galop*, were published.

Not long after Lord Gerald's elder brother succeeded as fourth Duke in 1874, Carton had another royal visit: Queen Victoria's soldier son, the Duke of Connaught, came to stay. He would have felt very much at home, for the new Duchess of Leinster was a daughter of the Duchess of Sutherland, who had been

The Duchess of Leinster, wife of the 4th Duke, in her pony cart outside the garden front of Carton in about 1880.

his mother's Mistress of the Robes and one of her closest friends. While he was here, the Duke of Connaught attended a meet of the Kildare Hunt at Maynooth, accompanied by a son and daughter of his host. What a journalist described as 'the beauty and chivalry' of Meath and Kildare had turned out in force and a special train from Dublin had brought half the garrison, 'its hunting half at least'. The Marquis and Marchioness of Ormonde had come from Kilkenny, Viscount Powerscourt from Powerscourt. It was a beautiful sight as the cavalcade wound its way along the avenue towards Carton, bright sun lighting up the mass of vividly red coats.[9]

King Edward VII and Queen Alexandra, as Prince and Princess of Wales, came to Carton in 1885, though not to stay. Two years later, the fourth Duke was succeeded by his son, who was married to Lady Hermione Duncombe, daughter of the first Earl of Feversham, who lived in Yorkshire. Hermione was as beautiful and talented as Emily Duchess had been; but she was less fortunate. She and her shy and rather dull husband were not happy together. The Duke would be sitting in the library, cataloguing his books, and Hermione would come to him with some plan which he would turn down. 'Hermione, I have settled it,' he would say, walking out of the room. When she took up sculpture, her husband did not approve; and he would not let her go up to her studio until she had performed her household duties, written her letters and practised for an hour on the organ; and he would not allow her to have a fire in her studio.

A page from the scrapbook of a lady who stayed at Carton in 1893, with photographs of
the beautiful Hermione Leinster and her husband the 5th Duke as well as of the house.

Hermione found consolation not only in sculpture and painting and indeed
music – for all her disgust at having to practise the organ to order – but also in
making a wonderful garden at Carton. She built a pergola, the first ever to be seen
in Ireland; she planted snowdrops everywhere, wild violets and daffodils by the lake.
But the lake, where on summer afternoons she went among the pink water-lilies in
her boat, was to be associated in her mind with loss. She adored her sister Helen and
she was devoted to her friend Sir Edgar Vincent, that brilliant young man who ran
the finances of the Ottoman Empire. The two of them were staying at Carton when
they became engaged. As she watched them walking towards the lake, Hermione
'made a little movement with her hands' and said sadly: 'There go two of the people
I love best in the world and they have taken each other away from me'.[10]

Another important young man who came to Carton was Hermione's cousin
Lord Houghton, a rich and handsome widower who was then Viceroy of Ireland.
His entertainments at Dublin Castle were being boycotted by the Unionists who
regarded him as a traitor because of the Home Rule policy of his government. 'I
receive you as cousin, not as Viceroy,' Hermione said as he came in. And she did
not give him a curtsey.

Hermione had received Lord Houghton's politically acceptable predecessors
with suitable state (while engaging in a minor feud with Lady Zetland who on one
occasion had accused her of being unladylike when she whistled a tune for the

orchestra to play), and she had entertained on a grand scale when the Papal Nuncio visited Ireland. But she was happiest with a small and devoted coterie of friends who came often to Carton. They included Lord Cloncurry's brother Freddie Lawless who played the organ, and his sister, the poet and prose writer Emily Lawless, a figure of the early Celtic Revival, as well as the Earl of Dunraven and the lively Countess of Fingall, known as Daisy. On her visits to Carton, Daisy was usually given the Chinese bedroom and she would have her breakfast in the state bed surrounded by a vision of Cathay in blue and gold. Since the room was on the ground floor, some of the other guests would gather at the window and talk to her while she ate her bacon and eggs and drank her coffee.

Once when she came to stay at Carton she arrived late for dinner and was shown straight into the Chinese bedroom. She hurriedly did her face and, in order to see better, propped up a Queen Anne mirror on the back of the dressing table. Somebody came to tell her she was late and, being already fussed, she made a clumsy movement and knocked over the mirror which fell and broke. When she went in to dinner, for they had started without her, she sat down beside the Duke and told him of her disaster with the mirror. 'It means seven years' misfortune for me, doesn't it?'

'Not for you, Lady Fingall,' he assured her, smiling. 'This misfortune is for the house in which it happens.' Within less than seven years, the Duke and Hermione were both dead; the Duke died of typhoid in 1893, Hermione of consumption in 1895, aged only thirty-one.

Daisy Fingall has left a picture of Hermione during her brief widowhood. On arriving at Carton to stay with her, she would find her amidst the white and gold baroque splendours of the saloon. 'She would have been sitting at her grand piano perhaps, playing, and would take her lovely hands from the keys as I came in and smile, that smile of hers that always seemed to light a room. The windows of that room looked out over the formal garden to the park and the Dublin and Wicklow mountains were always blue against the sky.' At night, after she had undressed, Hermione would come to Daisy's room 'with her lovely brown hair loose about her shoulders and sit talking by the fire, turning her feet up to the flames'.[11]

While Emily was the first Duchess of Leinster to live at Carton, Hermione was, as it turned out, the last. She and her husband left three young sons; the eldest, the sixth Duke, was mentally unstable and died unmarried; the second, Lord Desmond FitzGerald, a young man of great promise, also died unmarried, killed in the Great War. The youngest, who eventually became the seventh Duke, was a spendthrift; while his two elder brothers were alive, he was foolish enough to sign away his expectations to Sir Harry Mallaby-Deeley, the 'Fifty Shilling Tailor', in return for ready money and an annuity. As a result of this unhappy transaction he was in financial difficulties for the rest of his life and unable to live at Carton, which was occupied by his bachelor uncle, Lord Frederick FitzGerald. Lord Frederick was here during

The saloon at Carton as it was when Daisy Fingall would find Hermione here. 'She
would have been sitting at her grand piano perhaps, playing, and would take her lovely
hands from the keys as I came in and smile, that smile of hers that always seemed to light
a room'. The grand piano can be seen in the left foreground.

the Troubles when a dozen or more men carrying lighted torches rang the hall doorbell and said politely to old Staples, the butler, when he opened the door: 'Will you
please tell his Lordship that we are obliged to burn the house.' Staples went and told
Lord Frederick who took the portrait of Lord Edward FitzGerald off the dining-
room wall. He carried it out of the hall door, confronted the intruders with it and
said: 'Have you come to burn the house of Lord Edward FitzGerald?' They crossed
themselves and went away.[12]

After Lord Frederick's death in 1924, Carton was occupied by his sister, Lady
Nesta FitzGerald. Shortly before the Second World War she decided to go and live
at Kilkea, an old castle in the south of County Kildare which was the dower house
of the family. Carton was shut up and eventually the decision was taken to sell it. In
1947, just before it was sold, the family came into residence for the last time when the
seventh Duke's son, the Marquess of Kildare, opened up the house for a horse show
party. Lord Kildare found a certain amount in the cellar, including a bottle of
poteen, which he and his guests drank while they were making themselves bacon
and eggs after coming back from a dance. One of the party, not knowing that poteen
can have an unfortunate effect when mixed with water, had a drink of water after
going to bed and then went raging about the passages.

*Chapter 7*

# Castle Forbes
## COUNTY LONGFORD

JUST EAST of the Shannon, where it widens into Lough Forbes, but screened from it by the woods of its demesne, stands Castle Forbes, on first appearance a solid nineteenth-century castle of grey ashlar dominated by a round corner tower. In fact it incorporates two earlier wings, as well as part of a medieval castle. The castle acquired its present name after being granted in 1628 to Sir Arthur Forbes, a Scottish soldier, who built a new house adjoining it: a house typical of its period, with mullioned windows, hipped roofs and tall chimney stacks. It kept the protection of the castle bawn, which was fortunate when the rebellion of 1641 broke out. By that time Sir Arthur was dead, having been killed in a duel in Hamburg where he went with his regiment to assist Gustavus Adolphus of Sweden in the Thirty Years' War; but his widow Jane, a Scot like himself and a lady of great ability and courage, defended Castle Forbes on behalf of her eighteen-year-old son, who was away raising troops for her.

To withstand a siege, Lady Forbes stocked the castle with arms, ammunition and provisions, as well as recruiting a garrison from among those of her tenants who were English or Scottish settlers. She was joined by Sir John and Lady Seaton, a neighbouring landowner and his wife, together with some of their tenants, so that there were now about 250 people in the castle, whom she had to feed at her own expense. She put the castle on a defensive footing and she and her son kept watch and ward.

Eventually the castle was besieged by a force of some four or five hundred, from out of the nearby county of Leitrim in Connaught. The garrison made several sallies as well as firing at the besiegers from the castle, killing or wounding about eighty of them. The besiegers killed several of the defenders by firing at the windows of the castle, and they also shot some of the garrison who were manning the walls. Then they captured the well that supplied the castle with water and, having hanged and disembowelled a Scotsman, they 'threw him into the well where he lay until the dogs devoured him', as one of the garrison, himself a Scot, wrote in his account of the siege. When the defenders were nearly dying of thirst, they dug a hole forty feet deep in the castle bawn and struck water, which 'refreshed them much'. Having been refreshed, they 'went out privately to seek relief'. Whether it was their sense of delicacy – with Lady Forbes keeping watch and ward – or their regard for hygiene which prevented them from doing so within the bawn, it was unfortunate; for the besiegers 'did from time to time murder and leave them to be devoured by dogs or fowl'. The author of the eyewitness account went on to say that 'the rebels often called the Protestants of the castle Puritan dogs and heretics, traitors to God and the King'. Such was the confusion of the times that so-called Irish rebels claimed to be fighting the English and Scottish settlers in the name of King Charles.

Hopes rose among the garrison when government troops were reported to be only ten or twelve miles away. But then it was heard that they were not coming to relieve Castle Forbes but were returning to Dublin. As the siege dragged on, the defenders 'were forced to eat the stinking cowhides that had lain on stinking dunghills in the bawn from Christmas or Holytide last', Lady Forbes having given 'all her great horses to the poor to eat'. Lady Forbes and Lady Seaton sent a letter to the besiegers begging that the garrison should be allowed 'to go into the garden or before the castle gate to eat the grass that was growing there'; but the besiegers replied that they would keep them shut up in the castle 'till the ravens did eat their guts'. To show that they meant it, they shot at two children who went out to eat weeds and grass, killing one of them and wounding the other. But at least two of the besiegers, one of them an officer, showed some humanity by smuggling food into the castle on dark nights; they continued to do so for eight weeks, but were eventually found out and hanged.

When the siege had gone on for nine months and they were starving, Lady Forbes and her garrison managed with some difficulty to come to terms with the besiegers, who allowed them to march away, taking with them nothing but the clothes they stood in and the arms they wore, together with ten muskets. The besiegers were to have the rest of their arms and ammunition; however, before he left, the Scotsman who wrote the account of the siege hid all the remaining powder in a deep hole. Having abandoned the castle, Lady Forbes and her companions endured 'many dangers and miseries'; but they eventually made their way to Dublin.[1]

Castle Forbes was again besieged during the Williamite wars, but Lady Forbes's son, who had become the first Earl of Granard, managed to hold out, though by then he was nearly seventy. Like his father, he was a soldier, having fought in Scotland under Montrose; this military tradition was carried on by subsequent Earls of Granard. The third Earl had a naval as well as a military career and was also a diplomatist. He was envoy to the Empress Anne of Russia, who liked him so much that she offered him the command of the Imperial Russian navy, an offer he declined.

The sixth Earl of Granard, who became a general, married Lady Selina Rawdon, the sister of Lord Rawdon, as he was then, one of the ablest military com- manders on the British side in the American War of Independence. Soon after his return from America in 1781, Lord Rawdon recommended a cook to his sister, who had recently come to live at Castle Forbes, she and her husband having spent most of their time since their marriage in 1779 travelling on the Continent. Selina was still only in her early twenties and would not have had much experience as a chatelaine; though according to her mother, Lady Moira, she had 'an amazing turn for business'. Lady Moira, however, was not very encouraging about the cook: 'What professed cook would come from England to you?' she asked her daughter. On the other hand, she believed that even the best of Irish cooks were 'old-fashioned in their bills of fare in respect to the English tables'.

Lady Moira, who was herself English, does not appear to have given Selina any further advice on the relative merits of English and Irish cooks. Instead, she sent her some 'ornaments' for her dessert table. 'There are four dome circles for the ends, which you must bend to fit the ovals, four long straight pieces for the middle and four shorter straight ones,' she told her daughter. 'I am afraid you may not like them, but I could not get better or cheaper, for I thought it necessary to have them rich and full.' Lady Moira also sent her daughter seeds and cuttings from Moira Castle, the Rawdons' family seat in County Down, as well as some sweet chestnut trees, of which she wrote: 'As the trees are habituated to the climate so as to produce fruit, I think in the friendly soil of Castle Forbes it would become very fruitful.' A benefaction of a different sort was Mills's *Catalogue of Honour* and another work of genealogy which Lady Moira sent Selina for her library. She had bought them at an auction: 'They cost little, because that science is disregarded here.'[2] Being herself the daughter of the ninth Earl of Huntingdon, of the ancient and illustrious family of Hastings, Lady Moira clearly felt that, at Castle Forbes at any rate, 'that science' ought not to be disregarded.

In 1798, when her husband commanded the Longford Militia at the Battle of Castlebar and gallantly attempted to rally his regiment when it ran away, Selina remained at Castle Forbes. Her brother Lord Rawdon congratulated her on the good example she set by her decision to stay, rather than going to Dublin. But he spoke of the 'danger' that hung over her and of pillaging 'banditti'. In the event, Castle Forbes came out unscathed from '98. After the Union, when Lord Granard, no longer having a seat in the Irish House of Lords, retired from politics and devoted himself to his estates, there were plans to embellish and modernize the castle, which was still basically the early seventeenth-century house with two later wings running back from it. Lady Moira promised to consult the great Irish architect James Gandon; Selina obtained a design and an estimate for a surprisingly modern-looking water closet from her neighbour, the inventor Richard Lovell Edgeworth of Edgeworthstown.

In May 1806 there were great celebrations at Castle Forbes for the coming of age of the Granards' son and heir, Viscount Forbes. On the afternoon of his birthday, three rooms in the castle were 'thrown open' and the tenantry from County Longford and County Leitrim, together with the Newtown Forbes Corps of

Cavalry and Infantry and a number of visitors, 'sat down to a most plentiful and hospitable entertainment', as a Dublin newspaper described it. 'In each room one of the branches of the family presided with the utmost attention to the guests; the greatest good humour and harmony prevailed.' The Band of the Royal Longford Militia 'played appropriate tunes' and numerous toasts were drunk, including one to the young Lord Forbes's grandmother, 'the venerable and respectable Countess of Moira'. At seven, the guests went out into the park, where the Yeomanry drew up and fired a *feu de joie*. 'The lawn was thronged with the labourers and neigh-bouring peasantry who were regaled with an ox and several sheep roasted whole, with abundance of strong beer, etc.' Then groups of dancers appeared and there were bonfires and fireworks. Five days later there was a dinner followed by a ball and supper for the neighbouring gentry.[3]

Chief among the neighbouring gentry were Richard Lovell Edgeworth of Edgeworthstown and his family, which included his talented daughter Maria; and, from a little further away, the young Earl of Longford and his mother, who lived at Pakenham Hall across the county boundary in Westmeath. The Edgeworths were among those who came to Castle Forbes in the autumn of 1813 for a theatrical enter-tainment. Three farces were performed, *Bombastes Furioso*, *Of Age Tomorrow* and *The Village Lawyer*. The company at Castle Forbes was varied and civilized; there was good conversation with a taste for literature.

At the end of the Napoleonic Wars, Lord and Lady Granard went to live in Paris and Lord Forbes, who was still single, lived at Castle Forbes. He was there on the night in November 1825 when the castle caught fire. But for Pilot, his springer spaniel, who pulled him out of his bed, he would have been burnt to death or suf-focated. Pilot afterwards had his portrait painted, with the burning castle in the background.

Once out of bed, Lord Forbes showed great presence of mind, carrying out a quantity of gunpowder from a closet into which the flames were already entering and then helping to rescue the family papers and pictures. Another gentleman was somehow endowed with superhuman strength and in the midst of the fire wrenched a fine marble bust of Cromwell from the iron spike with which it was fixed to its pedestal; he carried it downstairs and threw it on to the grass. Next morning, he found he could not lift it; nobody else who tried could so much as get it to budge.

Some valuable prints and books were lost, since the room in which they were kept was locked and in the excitement the key could not be found. Other books in the library were also lost, for the servants imagined the largest volumes to be the most valuable, so wasted their energy carrying out folios of *Irish House of Commons Journals* and *Statutes*. In three hours, the early seventeenth-century castle was reduced to the bare walls, though the later wings survived.

These wings were extended in a Gothic style by the Cork architect John

Hargrave to make a house for Lord Forbes, with a long gallery as the principal room. The work was not yet finished when Lord Forbes married the daughter of a Suffolk squire in 1832. In September 1834, when Lady Forbes was away, Captain John Hart, a friend of the family, wrote to tell her how things were progressing. 'C. Forbes is such a different-looking place at this season of the year to the time you have seen it, you would hardly fancy it was the same place . . . They are still working at the long gallery. The flooring is finished and the studding is nearly completed. The enlarging of the two windows in the nursery makes it a nice room and it has now abundance of light, and I think the enlarging of the windows rather improves exter-nally the appearance of that part of the house. Your flower garden looks clean and neat, new sashes have been put into the greenhouse, new stands for the flower pots and the floor has been new tiled, and it looks really respectable – also new wooden receptacles for the orange trees.'[4] Lord and Lady Forbes now had an infant son, hence the enlarging of the nursery windows.

Early in the following year, Lady Forbes had a report on Castle Forbes from her husband, who was there on his own. 'I never saw the garden in such order, except-ing the pines. They are crowded and can never come to any size. The house is very clean. I sleep in the bedroom and dress as usual next the library. The long gallery is beautiful – the shutters carved oak and brass ornaments.' A few days later the cata-strophe of 1825 came near to repeating itself. 'The house has just been on fire,' Lord Forbes told his wife. 'It broke out in the outside hall. Luckily it was only 3 o'clock . . . no harm is done. It was lucky it was not at night that it took place.'

For Castle Forbes at that time there were worse dangers than fire. Both Lord Forbes and his father Lord Granard were in financial trouble. The family estates were heavily in debt; Lord Granard was being threatened with eviction from his lodgings in Paris for not paying his rent and was putting pressure on his son. 'I may be ruined if Fitzgerald loses influence over my fool of a father, who has neither head nor heart,' Lord Forbes lamented to his wife.[5] Hamilton Fitzgerald was a helpful in-law who, as well as trying to make Lord Granard see sense, tried to get Lord Forbes to economize by giving up his establishment at Castle Forbes and letting the demesne. If the consumption of meat and poultry at the castle in a week in February 1833 is anything to go by, the housekeeping must have been on the lavish side. During that week, 194 pounds of beef were consumed, together with 71 pounds of mutton, 25 pounds of pork, 21 pounds of bacon and ham, two turkeys and two chickens.[6]

In 1836 Captain Hart, who became such a habitué at Castle Forbes that two rooms were kept specially for him, joined with Hamilton Fitzgerald in urging Lord Forbes to make economies: 'As you are not likely to come here this year, they will be no kind of inconvenience to you.'[7] The family's absence was due to the unrest in Ireland known as the Tithe War. 'You have no idea in what a disturbed state this

Castle Forbes.

neighbourhood is,' Hart wrote in February of that year; and he sent the silver and some of the books from Castle Forbes to England for safe keeping. In November Lord Forbes died suddenly of an apoplectic stroke at the age of fifty-one. His body was taken back to Castle Forbes, where Hart feared that the coffin would be stripped of its lead by the 'disaffected' if it were left above ground until a suitable mausoleum could be built.

There followed a sad period when the family affairs were taken over by the Court of Chancery, while Lord Forbes's son, who became the seventh Earl of Granard in 1837, was still a minor. The Chancery receiver proposed to live at Castle Forbes, claiming that he needed a residence on the estate in order to be able to manage it and that there was no other house available that was worthy of him. The widowed Lady Forbes was naturally indignant at the suggestion, for she was anxious to live at Castle Forbes herself; although she spent a considerable amount of time away from Ireland having become a Lady of the Bedchamber to the young Queen Victoria.

Lady Forbes was no less indignant when the family solicitor in Dublin allowed the furniture at Castle Forbes to be sold off by auction for less than £500; she reck-oned it would cost her son £2,000 to replace when he came of age. For the young seventh Earl of Granard, who inherited a debt of nearly £200,000 accumulated by his father, grandfather and previous generations, prospects were not bright; but in 1858, four years after coming of age, he managed to save the situation by marrying a rich wife, Jane Grogan Morgan. She came from the impressively turreted and bat-tlemented Johnstown Castle in County Wexford, which her father had built, and a few years after their marriage she and her husband commissioned the architect James Joseph MacCarthy to enlarge Castle Forbes in the same style. The new block, with its round corner tower and square entrance tower and its pitch-pine baronial interior, very much overshadowed the older parts of the castle.

The fact that MacCarthy was the architect of many Catholic churches may have appealed to the Granards, who were themselves converts to Catholicism. Their conversion brought Lord Granard a letter from the local Church of Ireland clergyman in November 1867 seeking confirmation or denial of rumours that he and Lady Granard had attended the local Catholic church; Lord Granard rather unkindly told the clergyman that his letter was 'an intrusion and a piece of studied impertinence'.[8] The fourth Earl of Longford referred to the Granards as 'the heretics' after being entertained at Castle Forbes in 1868. He describes Lord Granard on this occasion as 'swelling visibly under pretence of a cold, he toasts himself at the fire and keeps himself up with luxurious food'.[9]

The Granards only had daughters; when Lady Granard died in 1872, her money went to them. Lord Granard's second wife Frances Petre, whom he married a year later, gave him five sons but no money. She came of a great English Catholic family, being a daughter of the twelfth Lord Petre. But while Lord Granard was now

Family group outside the hall door of Castle Forbes in the eighteen-eighties. The 7th Earl of Granard stands on the left, his second wife Frances sits on the right, with their seven children in front of them; the eldest boy Viscount Forbes, afterwards the 8th Earl, stands on Lord Granard's right. On Lord Granard's left is his nephew George, son of his brother the Hon. William Forbes, who stands on the right.

The 8th Earl of Granard shooting at Castle Forbes soon after his marriage to Beatrice Mills, who sits behind him.

The 8th Earl of Granard shooting at Castle Forbes in the period immediately before the Great War; his wife Beatrice sits behind him, flanked by his sisters Lady Margaret and Lady Eva Forbes.

Beatrice Countess of Granard with her sisters-in-
law Lady Margaret and Lady Eva Forbes at the
same shoot.

prominent in the Catholic world, becoming the first president of the British
Association of the Order of Malta when it was set up in 1875, his financial position was not much better than it had been before his first marriage. The trustees of
Maynooth College, the Irish Catholic clerical university, obliged him by consoli-
dating his various borrowings in a single mortgage. When, during the agrarian troubles in the 1880s, the Land League tried to stop his rents, it brought down upon
itself episcopal wrath.

After the seventh Earl's death in 1889, there was a danger that Maynooth might
have foreclosed; but the mortgage was taken over by the wealthy third Marquis of
Bute, who was a distant relation of the Granards and had become a Catholic at
about the same time as the seventh Earl and his first wife had. If Lord Bute played
a major part in saving Castle Forbes, so too did the widowed Frances Lady
Granard, who kept the place intact and the family solvent while her eldest son, the
eighth Earl, was making his way in the army and in politics.

The eighth Earl of Granard was a Liberal and supported Home Rule. In 1906
he joined Campbell-Bannerman's government as Assistant Postmaster-General
and in 1907 he became Master of the Horse to the King. Two years later, the family
fortunes made a spectacular recovery when he married Beatrice Mills, a very wealthy
American heiress. Castle Forbes was refurbished and soon boasted every luxury,
including a French chef.

In 1922 Lord Granard was nominated by W. T. Cosgrave to the original Senate
of the Irish Free State. This put Castle Forbes at risk, for the Civil War was raging

Lady Moira Forbes, elder daughter of the
8th Earl of Granard and his wife Beatrice,
on her tricycle in about 1914 with Castle
Forbes in the background.

Lady Moira and Lady Eileen Forbes and
Arthur, Viscount Forbes, three of the four
children of the 8th Earl of Granard and
his wife Beatrice, in about 1918. Arthur
became the 9th Earl of Granard; Eileen
became the Marchioness of Bute.

and the chief of staff of the Republican forces had ordered that the houses of all
senators should be burnt. On a night in February 1923, when Lord and Lady
Granard were away in London, raiders arrived and planted two land-mines in the
castle, one in the hall and one in another of the rooms. Fortunately the one in the hall
failed to explode; but the explosion of the other mine broke every window in the
village of Newtownforbes outside the demesne and was heard seven miles away.
Had both mines gone off, the castle might have been completely destroyed; as it was,
very considerable damage was done. Following the attack, Cosgrave put a continu-
ous guard on the castle which went through the remaining months of the Civil War
without any further incident.

Repairing the damage provided Lady Granard with an opportunity to carry out
an extensive remodelling of the interior. Employing a London architect, F. W.
Foster, and decorators from London and Paris, she gave the castle an English
Palladian drawing-room in the manner of William Kent and a dining-room and

The 8th Earl of Granard with his son Arthur, Viscount Forbes, canoeing on Lough Forbes sometime in the nineteen-twenties.

library with rich *boiseries* and painted ceilings. During the 1920s and 1930s, these rooms were the background to many house parties at which the guests were drawn not only from the Ascendancy and the *beau monde* of Britain and abroad, but also from the new Ireland. Thus when the young sixth Earl of Longford, who was to give Dublin its second theatre company, came to stay, the other guests included Cosgrave and his Minister for Agriculture, Patrick Hogan. As a senator who was also Master of the Horse, Lord Granard was a unique link between Buckingham Palace and the men who now ruled in Dublin. He came near to being appointed Governor-General of the Irish Free State.

One memorable house party at Castle Forbes during those years between the wars was predominantly Ascendancy. The guests included the fourth Marquess of Headfort from County Meath and his wife, who was the former gaiety girl Rosie Boote; and Sir Cecil and Lady Stafford-King-Harman from Rockingham in County Roscommon. For some reason there had been a feud between the Granards and the Headforts, who had been invited on this occasion in an attempt to make it up. The atmosphere was at first rather stiff, with the Granards and Headforts being over-polite to each other. After dinner there was bridge, Lord Headfort and the delectable Rosie being at different tables. They had not been playing for long when Rosie suddenly threw her black silk knickers across the room to her husband with a shriek of: 'My dear, look what's happened!' She claimed that they had fallen off, though everyone was sure she had done it on purpose. At any rate, it completely broke the ice.

# Chapter 8

# Castle Leslie (or Glaslough)
## COUNTY MONAGHAN

T HE SEAT of the Leslies in County Monaghan, where they have lived since Bishop John Leslie, known as the 'Fighting Bishop', came here from Scotland in the seventeenth century, is called Castle Leslie. But it is more usually known as Glaslough, 'Green Lake' in Gaelic; for the house faces across a blue-green stretch of water half a mile long, the home of giant pike, to the Big Wood on the far shore, a primeval forest where the rooks gather in their thousands. The house, a gabled Victorian pile of grey stone, its somewhat dour exterior relieved by an Italian Renaissance cloister in the garden front overlooking the lake, was built in the 1870s by Sir John Leslie, who was made a baronet in 1876. It replaced an earlier house to which his wife, Lady Constance — a sister of the fourth Earl of Portarlington and a daughter of Mrs Fitzherbert's protégée Minnie Seymour — took a dislike; and she was a woman who usually got her way.

Castle Leslie from the lake.

Castle Leslie. The cloister.

The hall at Castle Leslie.

The gallery at Castle Leslie, with Sir John Leslie's frescoes.

He employed the Belfast architects Sir Charles Lanyon and William Henry Lynn. Lynn would have been responsible for the interior, except for the cloister, where one can detect the hand of Lanyon, as one can in the interior of the house, with its rich Italian Renaissance flavour. One can also detect the hand of Sir John Leslie himself, who had travelled much in Italy. He was a talented artist who had the distinction, when a subaltern in the Life Guards, of winning the Grand Military Steeplechase and painting a picture that was hung in the Royal Academy in the same year; he was able to display his artistic talent in his new house by painting frescoes of rather pre-Raphaelite angels, as well as of himself and his family, in the top-lit gallery behind the cloister. The house was lit by petrol gas and had a bathroom with running water pumped up from the lake. When a lever was pulled, water gurgled into the bath through a hole in the bottom, together with water boatmen and other forms of aquatic life. Neighbours unused to such marvels would be shown the bath working.

In 1884 the Leslies' only son, Jack, married Leonie, the youngest of the three beautiful daughters of Leonard Jerome of New York and a sister of Lady Randolph Churchill. They were married in the United States, and when they came to London after the wedding, Sir John and Lady Constance were slow to receive their American daughter-in-law, or more likely it was Lady Constance who was slow. They left their London house and retreated to Ireland. But they – or she –

unbent sufficiently to summon the newly married couple to Glaslough for Christmas. When they arrived, Jack's twelve-year-old sister Olive came running down the stairs and stopped dead at the sight of the 'lovely lady' in the hall. 'She looked more elegant than anyone I had ever seen,' Olive later recalled. Even Lady Constance could find nothing to criticize in her except that she 'would overload the Christmas tree'.[1] As well as being elegant, Leonie in due course did what was expected of her by presenting her husband with no fewer than four sons. The eldest, born almost exactly a year after his parents' marriage, was christened John by the local clergyman, who once distinguished himself by falling into the fountain outside the hall door on his way to church; he arrived in time to preach his sermon wearing a pair of trousers borrowed from the Leslies' butler.

Leonie taught her boys to walk on the drawing-room sofa, above which hung a large painting in which 'sunburned satyrs carry off white-thighed Bacchantes with obvious intent'. 'But what are they all doing?' each of the boys asked his mother. 'Having a lovely picnic, dear,' she would reply.[2] When they were older, the boys were introduced to the delights of real picnics by their grandmother. They were held on the far side of the lake in full view of the house. Two footmen, in the family livery of dark blue and canary yellow, carried the hampers; the children crossed the lake in a boat and Sir John, more spectacularly, pedalled across on a sort of floating bicycle consisting of a seat perched on two canvas canoes with a paddle wheel. Lady Constance would drive round to the picnic place in an open carriage known as a 'sociable', arriving there when all was ready and the tablecloth spread over a big tree stump. 'Tell everybody, Herbert, that I am very pleased,' she would say to the first footman.[3]

When not assisting at picnics, Herbert waited at table and cleaned the silver; while his colleague Walter, the second footman, in addition to waiting at table, fed and talked to the parrot who lived in the saloon. The two footmen came under Mr Adams, the white-haired, bushy-browed butler, who as well as presiding in the dining-room would iron the newspapers – which was done in those days not just for the sake of appearances but to kill possible germs – and bring in the post. In the evening, he would light the gas-burners while Herbert drew the curtains and carried in the oil lamps that provided the light necessary for reading. Just as he sometimes exercised his discretion as to the year of the port that he took up to the gentry, so did Mr Adams keep two barrels of beer of two qualities for visitors below stairs, who were given the strong or the small beer according to how they rated in his opinion. To any beggar who called, Mr Adams, on his master's instructions, gave a shilling.

As well as Mr Adams and the two footmen, the domestic staff included the 'odd man', who did odd jobs assisted by the 'odd boy'; and there were about seven women, headed by the housekeeper and by Mrs Grey the cook. The maids were mostly called Annie and were known as Long Annie, Little Annie, Deaf Annie or whatever was appropriate. For reasons of propriety, the younger maids slept in a room that could only be reached through that of the head housemaid, a duenna of forty summers or more; while the menservants' rooms were in a separate wing with its own staircase. Despite these precautions, there was the occasional scandal.

The outdoor staff included the head gardener, Mr Bryce, if indeed he could be called outdoor, for to Lady Constance's chagrin he spent much of his time in the house, arranging flowers. Or else he spent his time in the hothouses, gathering lilies which filled the drawing-room with scent or tasting the grapes and the peaches to see if they were ready for the table. He was invariably dressed in a smart suit with a gold watch-chain and he wore a panama hat.

Another important personage was Weir, the coachman, who had worked for the Leslies since he was twelve. As he approached the lodge entrance on the box of the brougham with one or more of the family inside, he would shout 'Gate!' A woman would come out of the lodge and tug at the gates which squeaked as they opened, curtseying as the carriage went past. Weir's daughter Lily became a housemaid to Queen Victoria at Windsor.

To the Leslie boys, particularly to John and Norman, the two eldest, far the most important people on the place were Bob Gilroy, the head forester, and James Vogan, the head gamekeeper. John, who would one day achieve distinction as the writer Shane Leslie, attributed his knowledge of forestry and his lifelong love of trees to Gilroy. And he remembered Vogan as 'a magnificent red-bearded Celt, devoted to the Leslie family as not distantly related to the Holy Trinity . . . a perfect shot and fisherman, acquainted with the ways of fur, feather and fin'.[4] The boys were happy to do their lessons if they knew they were going out with Vogan afterwards; they also enjoyed the tea parties, followed by 'the wildest games', which Vogan gave in the woods for all the children of the estate.

Lady Constance used to say that Vogan was her grandsons' real governess, though they had a mademoiselle and a fraülein. The latter, when not attempting to teach the boys German, went tobogganing with their Aunt Olive in hip-baths down the hill to the lake. For this sport, Olive and the fraülein wore Jack Leslie's old riding breeches, so they had to take refuge in the boathouse whenever Lady Constance appeared. Apart from the immodesty, Lady Constance may not have liked to see the hip-baths misused in this way, for they were still very much required for their proper purpose. Sir John's famous bath, being inconveniently situated on the top floor, was mainly used for washing dogs. It also served as an aquarium to amuse the boys; one of them was even allowed to fish in it.[5]

The children had luncheon in the dining-room with the grown-ups, but at a sep-arate table. Mr Adams, having struck the great gong to summon the family, gov-ernesses and guests, would carve, scolding the two footmen while he did so. After luncheon Lady Constance would set off in the sociable with earthenware jars containing soup and the remains of the childrens' pudding which she took to people who had suffered some misfortune. Having done her good deed for the day, she would most probably retire to her boudoir and write endless letters with a scratchy quill. While she was thus occupied, her husband would be standing on the steps outside the saloon feeding the white pigeons, or wandering along the loggia. Or else playing Mozart or Rossini on the organ in the distant organ room; a little shakily, for he was over seventy.

His daughter-in-law Leonie, if she was at Glaslough, might also be making music, and with more vigour, practising Wagner on her Bechstein in the drawing room. Or she might be in her bedroom, reading and smoking, causing her mother-in-law, with whom she usually managed to maintain a surprisingly amicable relationship, to register a gentle protest. Lady Constance would appear at her bedroom door and say: 'May I come in, Leonie? I thought I smelt something burning.' When Leonie admitted to her cigarette, she would say, sweetly: 'My dear Leonie, but of course you must do whatever you wish, but not − I pray − before the children.' Having said this, she would leave her daughter-in-law in peace to read and perhaps light up once again.[6]

As a *grande dame*, Lady Constance was surpassed by her much younger neighbour, the Countess of Caledon, who lived with her husband and four sons at Caledon, a magnificent Georgian house of which the demesne marched with that of Glaslough, though it was across the county boundary in Tyrone. Lady Constance, when she drove out in her carriage, had a liveried footman on the box; Lady Caledon had postillions in white buckskin breeches. Only once did Lady Caledon appear at a disadvantage; she turned up unexpectedly at Glaslough just before dinner in evening dress and satin slippers, having walked all the way from Caledon after her husband had done something to offend her. She was welcomed by Lady Constance, given dinner and put into the best guest bedroom for the night. Next morning a contrite Lord Caledon came for her in a pony trap, waiting at the inner gate until she chose to join him.

The four Alexander boys, sons of Lord and Lady Caledon, almost exactly matched up in age with the four Leslie boys. When a Glaslough cricket XI was started, Leslies played against Alexanders in the Caledon XI. The second-youngest of the Alexanders, a boy known as Tubby whose real name was Harold, made most of the runs.

The Caledons' distant kinsman Primate Alexander, the Church of Ireland Archbishop of Armagh, was a frequent visitor to Glaslough; once he brought Archbishop Benson of Canterbury with him. The Primate's wife was the Mrs Alexander who wrote 'All things bright and beautiful' and other well-known hymns; the Leslie boys were expected to recite some of her hymns to her and after much rehearsing just about managed 'There is a green hill far away'. Another leading light of the Church of Ireland who stayed at Glaslough was the great Professor John Mahaffey of Trinity College, Dublin, who often invited himself for the snipe shooting. At the end of dinner he would coolly demand the best port: 'I think I remember some excellent port here; there should still be a bottle left.' Nobody grudged it him, for he was such wonderful company. Once, out shooting, young Norman Leslie's gun went off unexpectedly and shot the 'Great Mahoof's' clerical hat off his head, though he was otherwise unscathed. He remained calm but said solemnly: 'If that shot had been half a foot lower, it would have blown half the Greek out of Ireland.'[7]

There was an occasion when two brilliant talkers were staying at Glaslough at the same time: Leonie's brother-in-law Moreton Frewen and Sir Horace Plunkett. Both were full of schemes for Ireland, so there should have been a fascinating discussion; but to everyone's dismay they would not speak to one another owing to a feud that went back to the days when they both ranched in Wyoming. Among other great talkers who came to Glaslough was that redoubtable sailor Lord Charles Beresford, a nephew of Sir John's, and, of course, Leonie's young nephew Winston Churchill.

The most illustrious visitor during this period was Leonie's friend the Duke of Connaught, who came for the first time in 1902 when he was Commander of the Forces in Ireland. He was accompanied by the Duchess and their two daughters, Princess Margaret and Princess Patricia. In anticipation of this royal visit, Leonie gave her sons the following injunctions: 'Never sit down while THEY stand, never start the conversation, never change the subject, never ask a question – and don't touch the Bar-le-Duc jam!'[8] When the royal train pulled into Glaslough station, the first familiar face the Duke saw on the platform was that of Lily Weir, the housemaid at Windsor.

In 1906, Sir John and Lady Constance celebrated their golden wedding: there was a large house party and a garden party for the neighbourhood. They then handed over Glaslough to Jack and Leonie and went to England for good; the move, needless to say, being at the instigation of Lady Constance. Some of the people on the place were said to have wept for a week after Sir John had visited them for the last time. Leonie was able to redecorate the house and put in bathrooms, central heating and electric light; the twelve or more indoor servants were reduced to seven. Among those who went was Mr Adams; his squeaky shoes as he walked round the table with the wine were getting on Leonie's nerves and he was given honourable retirement. Another departure was that of the parrot, who was given away.

The house parties became more fashionable and more fun. They were also more relaxed, except, of course, when Leonie entertained royalty in the person of the Duke of Connaught. When the Duke came this time, a waiter had to be hired from Belfast to assist Mr Adams's successor. He arrived having had a few drinks and

Sir John and Lady Constance Leslie with members of their family at their Golden Wedding in 1906. Their son Jack stands with his hand on Lady Constance's chair, with his wife Leonie standing to the right of him. John, the eldest son of Jack and Leonie, who was to become well-known as the writer Shane Leslie, stands on the far left; two of his three brothers are also in the group, Seymour standing behind Sir John and Lionel, the youngest, sitting on the ground wearing a sailor suit; for some reason Norman, the second oldest of the brothers, was not present. Olive, now Mrs Murray Guthrie, the youngest daughter of Sir John and Lady Constance, who as a girl went tobogganing with the Fräulein in hip-baths, stands between her nephews John and Seymour; the boy in the kilt is her son Patrick Guthrie.

imagining that now was his chance to talk to a member of the Royal Family. At luncheon, when there was a gap in the conversation, he suddenly said to the Duke: 'Your Royal 'ighness there's 'am and cold rabbit pie on the sideboard.' He then went on to thank the Duke for visiting Loyal Ulster, assuring him that the blinds were still down in the town of Portadown 'in mourning for Your Royal 'ighness' Ma'. And when passing round a soufflé, he said: 'Your Royal 'ighness, will you try the Puff?'[9]

When they were at home, Leonie's house parties were enlivened by the presence of her three eldest sons, who were now grown up. The second son, Norman, a dashing subaltern who was rather too attractive to the ladies, found himself challenged to a duel by a wronged husband when he was serving in Egypt. Though duelling was, of course, forbidden by English law, it was decided that he was honour bound to accept the challenge. His challenger was one of the best swordsmen in Europe; so for several weeks after returning home to Glaslough, Norman practised swordsmanship on the lawn outside the house with his father, who had fenced for the Army. The duel eventually took place in France and lasted over an hour; both parties drew blood and honour was satisfied. Norman had the distinction of being the last serving officer in the British Army who fought a duel.

The Leslies' eldest son showed literary talent. He became a Catholic and a Nationalist and took the name of Shane instead of John in order to be more Irish. His father, who was a staunch Ulster Unionist, showed forbearance with regard to Shane's political views, while refusing to have Winston Churchill at Glaslough after he espoused Home Rule. When, during the Home Rule crisis, Jack Leslie was going out of the house in the evening to review his own regiment of Ulster Volunteers, he would meet Shane, who was slipping quietly out to inspect the local regiment of Irish Volunteers. Writing to her friend Lady Londonderry in June 1914, Leonie described the martial activities at Glaslough. 'The Volunteers are very keen and Jack now has 1,800 men in the two battalions and 1,600 of them are fully equipped! They look splendid with their new hats and bandoliers. We had a very impressive out-of-door service for them on Whit Sunday and the Bishop of Clogher preached a fine sermon. I am just finishing a second nursing course . . . Now we are going to present colours to the battalions.'[10]

The threat of civil war in Ireland receded with the outbreak of the Great War. In October 1914 Norman Leslie was killed in action. James Vogan, the game-keeper, saw him standing on the terrace at Glaslough looking down at the lake. Not yet knowing he was dead and imagining that he had returned unexpectedly from the front, he called out, 'Master Norman, Master Norman!' Vogan never recovered from his death, nor for that matter did Norman's father. Shane Leslie's wife Marjorie, who like his mother was American, also believed that Norman's spirit returned to Glaslough after his death; she heard his unmistakable footstep on the stairs going up to the empty room that had been his and his brothers' nursery.

The two elder children of Shane and Marjorie, Anita and Jack, came to Glaslough for the first time at the end of the war, having spent their earliest years in the United States. On the morning after they arrived, they were woken by a 'pink-faced housemaid' called – needless to say – Annie, who said, 'Look at the rooks waking.'[11] From then on, Glaslough was always associated in their minds with the cawing of rooks.

After America, the house seemed to them rather cold. The central heating system that their grandmother had put in before the war provided only for radiators in the reception rooms; and these grew tepid when the wood with which the two garden-ers fed the furnace was damp. The temperature of the house did not, however, matter very much to the children as they spent all the time they could out of doors, in the woods and by the lake. They got to know the people on the place, several of whom had been here when their father was a child, notably the red-bearded James Vogan.

Weir had retired as coachman but was still around aged nearly ninety. His successor, Willie Dawson, who had come to Glaslough as a stable boy in 1898 and risen to being second coachman – taking time off to join the Irish Guards when the regiment was first raised in 1900 and serving as groom to Field Marshal Lord Roberts – was now the chauffeur.

The children acquired pets. When Lady Leconfield, a grand but childless and rather sad peeress from Sussex, came to stay, she asked Anita to sit by her and tell her about herself. Anita dared not move because her pockets were full of white mice. Lady Leconfield also encountered the droppings of Jack's pet kid in the drawing-room. 'It looks as if some sheep have been on the sofa!' she exclaimed in horror. Like Anita's mice, the kid was not allowed in the house; but like the mice, it would somehow get in.

In wet weather, the children played in the attics. While 'soft rain pattered on the attic roof',[12] they opened cupboards, pulled out trunks and in an atmosphere of camphor, lavender and dust examined the finery of other days: hats decked out with roses and ostrich plumes, a ball-gown of heavy rose-coloured satin embossed with flowers which their grandmother had worn at Viceregal Lodge in the 1880s, a dress of bright orange corded silk made by Worth for their great-aunt Jennie, Lady Randolph Churchill, in 1876.

Like most children, they liked exploring unfamiliar rooms. But one room in the house frightened them. This was their Uncle Norman's bedroom, at the end of a passage on the top floor. Their grandmother kept it exactly as it was when he left it for the last time in 1914. As Anita, who was to become a distinguished writer like her father, recalls, 'a curious sad atmosphere lingered in this room . . . on the walls there still hung trophies of his army days in India – the hooves and antlers of animals he had shot – and on tables stood those yellowing photographs of his sweet-hearts and his polo ponies'.[13]

Every year on his birthday his mother would spend long hours in solitary vigil here, and she would lay a bunch of dried flowers with rosemary for remembrance on his pillow. But while a part of her was with her dead son, Leonie had not lost her zest for life. She continued to entertain. Some of her guests were survivors from the Edwardian world like Count Mensdorff, who was Austrian Ambassador in London before the war. He came to Glaslough in about 1924 and would go for walks along the avenue in white spats, wearing one or other of his two overcoats which he called 'My Windsor' and 'My Sandringham'. A younger guest was the fascinating Vittoria, Duchess of Sermoneta. Shane Leslie, who was at home at the time, took her to call on the local Catholic Bishop; she curtsied graciously to him and told him that her family had given two Popes to Holy Church, for she was by birth a Colonna. The Bishop, somewhat taken aback, coloured but said nothing.

An even younger friend of Leonie's who came several times during the 1930s was

A shoot at Glaslough in about 1930. Anita Leslie, Shane Leslie's daughter, stands next to her Aunt Olive Guthrie; whose loader, footman and chauffeur Archie McCall can be seen at the back against the fence.

Prince Pierre, son-in-law of Prince Louis of Monaco and father of Prince Rainier. He arrived in a long cream-coloured car with a chauffeur, and when he left after one visit he gave Wells, the butler, a pair of gold cuff-links with his coronet and cipher on them. Coming back from a walk, he asked if the moss by the side of the avenue was planted or natural. 'These foreigners are strange people,' old Jack Leslie, now Sir John, remarked. 'He asked me if the moss was planted.'[14]

Prince Pierre was taken to visit the Duke and Duchess of Abercorn at Barons Court and also to Caledon. Lady Caledon, long widowed, was as formidable as ever. She would drive over to tea at Glaslough in her carriage; her son Harold, when he was at Caledon, would walk over. He was now married and doing well in the Army, but his mother, who continued to call him Tubby, treated him as if he were still in the schoolroom; she treated her other married sons in the same way. Her eldest son Eric, now the Earl of Caledon, was unmarried. He had a lady-love, a marchioness with a husband and children; his mother would not have her at Caledon, so when she came to visit him she stayed at Glaslough, being given the best guest bedroom, the mauve room. Unfortunately for the Leslies she injured her leg motoring while she was here and was laid up in the mauve room for weeks, with the lovesick Eric walking over for every meal.

In the year of Munich, Anthony Eden, who had recently resigned as Foreign Secretary, came to luncheon on his way to stay with Lord and Lady Erne at Crom Castle. Having expressly forbidden her family to talk politics with him, Leonie proceeded to take him for a walk along the terrace and round the walled garden, hoping to hear all the latest political news. Shane's wife Marjorie ignored her mother-in-law's injunction to the extent of sitting with Eden on the terrace and arguing with him as to whether Germany or Russia constituted the greater threat. 'There's nothing to fear from Russia,' Eden said blithely. 'The last thing she wants is to expand. Look at little Estonia and Lithuania.'[15] Leonie forgot to ask him to sign the visitors' book, so Willie Dawson was made to drive to Crom with it, sixty miles there and back, to get his signature.

Willie Dawson, never entirely at home as chauffeur, was soon able to return to his true place on the box of the brougham when the Second World War made petrol unobtainable. Petrol was needed for the electric light generator as well as for the motor car, so the Victorian paraffin lamps had to be brought back into use. Then there was no paraffin and it was back to candles. At least there was plenty of wood, and there were still six servants to keep the flickering wood fires burning; but with no coal the lofty Victorian rooms became arctic. Wraps were kept on indoors; fur rugs and hot-water bottles were taken into the dining-room.

Old Jack Leslie and Leonie, who were now in their eighties, still dressed for dinner every night. They were waited on by Wells, the butler, who was very English; though Glaslough was in neutral Eire, he wanted to impose a blackout such as prevailed a mile or two away in Northern Ireland. He had to be content with painting the windows of the top storey dark blue.

The Leslies' neighbour Lady Caledon had died soon after the declaration of war; when told the news, she had just said: 'Tubby will be there.' While Lady

Anita Leslie, still in uniform, with her brothers Jack (right) and Desmond, on a side car at Castle Leslie in the summer of 1945.

Anita Leslie's wedding to Commander William King, DSO, DSC, in 1949. The bride and bridegroom and their two pages are photographed in the conservatory at Castle Leslie, beneath a stone Madonna and Child by Campagna acquired in Italy by Sir John Leslie and subsequently bought by Sir John Pope-Hennessy for the Victoria and Albert Museum.

Caledon did not live to see her favourite son leading the Allied armies to victory, Leonie was able to enjoy the reflected glory of being Winston Churchill's aunt during his finest hour. She wrote frequent letters to her nephew after he became Prime Minister, sending them off from a post office on the northern side of the Border to which she drove in the brougham. On these drives, after America came into the war, she would see some of her countrymen: the GIs who did sentry duty along the Border between the demesne walls of Glaslough and Caledon. She would greet them as she passed by putting out an elegant hand through the carriage window and making a 'V sign'.[16] A guest at Glaslough during the war years was John Betjeman, then press attaché in Dublin; Jack Leslie told him how, as a child, he had met Edward Lear.

Leonie died in 1943 and her husband a few months later; Glaslough was inher-ited by their grandson Jack, who was then a prisoner-of-war. Their son Shane Leslie succeeded to the baronetcy; though based in London and elsewhere, he was often to be seen at Glaslough in the years that followed. When he arrived for one of his visits, he would be out of the house in no time, an impressive kilted figure striding across the great sweeping lawn in the direction of the lake to look at his beloved trees.

# Chapter 9

# Coole Park
## COUNTY GALWAY

I**N A ROMANTIC** and heavily wooded demesne in County Galway, at the end of a long, straight avenue that passed under a dark arch of ilexes, stood Coole Park, the white, three-storeyed Georgian house of the Gregorys. From the house, one could see the mountains of the Burren, in the neighbouring county of Clare; but woods hid the grey lake at the edge of the demesne where lived the wild swans. The house showed signs of having been altered at various times; the entrance front, with its central feature of a Diocletian window above a Venetian one, was not quite symmetrical. The original entrance door was hidden by a later porch; a pair of early Victorian bows had been added to the garden front.

The house was built in about 1770 by Robert Gregory, a wealthy East Indian 'nabob' who became chairman of the East India Company and a Member of Parliament. Robert the Nabob's great-grandson William Gregory was also in Parliament, being elected as Member for Dublin in 1842. At about that time the young Anthony Trollope, who was then a post office official stationed at Banagher, some forty miles away, came to stay with him at Coole. William Gregory had been a schoolfellow of Trollope's at Harrow, though younger than him and not a particular friend; now, as well as giving him hospitality, he gave him copy for the novels he was hoping to write by regaling him with social and political gossip. At Coole, Trollope met Charles Lever, who had given up a successful medical career in favour of literature; he had already published two of his popular novels of Irish life.

William Gregory went on to become Governor of Ceylon and was knighted. In 1880, as a childless widower of sixty-two, he married the twenty-seven-year-old Augusta Persse, daughter of a neighbouring landowner. Despite the difference in age, he and his bride, with her lively, observant brown eyes, had much in common; they shared a love of books and pictures, of architecture and travel. And she had that capacity for service which was a characteristic of the Gregorys; Sir William's father had died of fever working for the poor during the Great Famine.

Augusta, Lady Gregory was widowed in 1892, after twelve years of marriage. 'I returned to Coole, to the empty house and the tenanted grave,' she wrote after her husband's death. For consolation she had the eleven-year-old Robert, their only

Coole Park, in about 1890.

child, who was home for the holidays from his school in England. The boy was mostly out with his two new dogs and a new gun given to him by their friend and neighbour Edward Martyn. One evening he did not come in until nine, having rescued a hedgehog, which the dogs had discovered, and carried it back in his hat to a place of safety in the garden.

A year later, Lady Gregory was still finding her life at Coole lonely. 'The arrival here is always sad and depressing,' she wrote. 'The silence, and one's responsibili⁄ ties coming on again – but work is the best cure.'[1] Her responsibilities were consid⁄ erable, for she was not all that well off and determined to keep the place going for Robert. And then there were her responsibilities to the tenants and dependants, to the inhabitants of the hamlet of Kiltartan outside the gates and to the people around. She gave school feasts for more than a hundred children and parties for the inmates of the workhouse. Though she and her family were Protestants, she gave flowers to the local Catholic church; at the time of the Corpus Christi procession there was never a flower left in the garden, for she allowed the inhabitants of Gort to come and take them to bedeck the town. So cordial were her relations with the local Catholic clergy that one old priest asked her to write to the Pope on his behalf.

Like most Irish country houses in those days, Coole gave occasional sustenance to a following of people who were not exactly beggars, in that they did not actually ask for help, but who turned up from time to time knowing that they would be given something if they did not ask too often. They included tramps and itinerants as well

Corley the Piper outside Coole. Also in the picture is Lady Gregory, with Yeats on her right.

Yeats and George Moore at Coole.

as characters like Corley the Piper. Lady Gregory never gave them money, because she was sure they would just spend it on drink; but she gave them sandwiches, apples and perhaps a pot of jam. And when they called, she would always go out and have a word with them.

These and other callers, as well as the people in the cottages, provided a valuable source of folklore for William Butler Yeats when he came to stay. Lady Gregory's friendship with Yeats gave a new dimension to her life; she became interested in the theatre and together with Edward Martyn, George Moore and Yeats himself founded the Irish Literary Theatre in Dublin, the precursor of the Abbey, which she was to direct with such energy and ability. She also began writing successful plays, as well as stories and poetry.

Yeats's first visit to Coole was in 1897. He had not been well and Lady Gregory cosseted him, sending him up cups of soup when he was called in the morning and trying to prevent him from working too hard. She encouraged him to do a little painting and invited other leading spirits of the Irish literary movement, such as 'AE' and Douglas Hyde, to keep him entertained. A result of this Celtic influx was that young Robert, who was coming to the end of his school holidays from Harrow, expressed a wish to learn Irish. A teacher could not be found so he began with a primer and got on quite well with the exercise, checking the pronunciation with one of the men on the place, until the partridge shooting proved too great a distraction. On this and subsequent visits Yeats stayed about two months. He worked in the library, a room almost entirely lined with books, while Lady Gregory did her writing in the drawing-room, which was rather imposing with its red-and-gold

Lady Gregory at her desk in the drawing room at Coole.

Yeats, J.M. Synge and George Russell ('AE')
fishing on the lake at Coole. A drawing by
Harold Oakley.

wallpaper closely hung with pictures, including two by Canaletto. It was not much
used at other times, except when there was a party, or when there were a number of
people staying. As Lady Gregory sat at her typewriter in the drawing-room, Yeats
would suddenly burst in with some new idea. 'I treat you as my father says, as an
anvil to beat out my ideas on,' he would tell her.[2]

His work would also be interrupted when Lady Gregory called him out to talk
to somebody at the door, whether it was a tramp or a farmer or a woman selling fish,
or indeed Corley the Piper. Yeats came to regard his summers at Coole as the most
productive period of his year. When not working in the congenial surroundings of
the library, or going round the cottages with Lady Gregory in search of folklore, he
would wander in those parts of the demesne immortalized in his poetry – in the
Seven Woods and by the lake.

Young Robert, who had grown up to be an artist as well as a horseman and a
cricketer, came of age in 1902. The servants and the workers on the place presented
him with a silver inkstand, which was inscribed 'From his well-wishers inside the
gates of Coole'. Lady Gregory was on very friendly terms with the servants, chat-
tering away with them incessantly. Chief among them was Marian, the house-par-

Lady Gregory.

lourmaid, a woman of vast bulk and formidable temper, who could cope with anyone and anything. Marian did not share her mistress's veneration for Yeats, and when at table he sat with his chair pushed too far out, as was his wont, she always pretended to trip over it, which made him pull it in. But in the summer of 1908, when Yeats, in the throes of composition, did not feel equal to venturing even as far as the library but kept to his bed, she and the other maids had to tiptoe along the passage in which thick rugs had been laid for some distance on either side of his bedroom door to prevent the slightest sound from reaching him. They took him trays of what was said to be beef tea or arrowroot, though Lady Gregory's kinsman General Ian Hamilton, who was also staying at the time, was certain that he once distinctly smelt eggs and bacon.

Hamilton never set eyes on Yeats during that stay; he offered to go to his room and cheer him up by having a chat, but Lady Gregory received the idea with horror. A more convivial visit was in 1911 when Yeats and Douglas Hyde were staying at the same time; the two of them and an American who was also staying would sit up talking into the small hours. Yeats had just finished his poem 'The Seven Woods of Coole' and was so pleased with it that he kept murmuring it over and over again:

> 'I have heard the pigeons of the Seven Woods
> Make their faint thunder and the garden bees . . .'

George Bernard Shaw at Coole in April 1915.

By 1911, Robert had married. His wife Margaret, whom he had met when they were both art students at the Slade, was rather tiresome. She was half American and half Welsh; 'One thing to be said in her favour is that there's not a drop of English blood in her,' Lady Gregory had declared at the time of the marriage.[3] The marriage made little difference to Lady Gregory's position as chatelaine of Coole, particularly after Robert had gone off the fight in the Great War.

Lady Gregory noted how, on St Stephen's Day 1914, the Wren Boys, who came round on that day, instead of carrying the traditional dead wren – the wren being supposed to have laughed when St Stephen was being stoned – brought one of their number dressed as a German soldier and fired imaginary shots at him with a holly bough. For Lady Gregory's two small granddaughters, Anne and Catherine, the war meant that, when they were at Coole, they were only allowed jam *or* butter, not both together, 'to help the troops'.[4] George Bernard Shaw shocked the girls by putting butter on one side of his bread and jam on the other. He also shocked them by cheating when he played Hunt the Thimble with them: he would look between his fingers to see where the thimble had been hidden. Yet they loved him all the same. When the Shaws were staying here in 1915, Mrs Shaw lamented that her husband had never been painted by a good artist. Augustus John was then living not far away, so Lady Gregory suggested getting him over. Before he came, Shaw went into the town of Galway to have his hair cut; unfortunately he allowed too much to be taken off while the hairdresser was telling him of how a German warship had sailed into

Shaw standing with Lady Gregory outside Coole during this same visit. Lady Gregory's small grandson Richard is at the wheel of the motor car and her two small grand-daughters Anne and Catherine are at an upstairs window.

Galway Bay. Shaw and Augustus John were among those of Lady Gregory's guests who were allowed to carve their initials on the trunk of the great copper beech in the pleasure grounds, along with Yeats, Synge, AE and Ian Hamilton – who, at the time when John came to paint Shaw's portrait, was commanding the Allied Forces at Gallipoli. Near the copper beech was a catalpa, under which Yeats and George Moore quarrelled over the play *Diarmuid and Grania*.

In 1917, the year when Yeats married and wrote his poem 'The Wild Swans at Coole', Robert came home on leave from Italy, where he was serving with the Royal Flying Corps. As he stood with Margaret at the hall door one day that autumn, waiting for the carriage that was to take him to the station on his way back to the war, they occupied themselves by seeing who could squeeze the most water out of a wet cloth which the house-parlourmaid Marian had with her, while Anne and Catherine watched from an upstairs window. Then the carriage came and he drove off, sitting upright in his uniform, not looking back nor to right nor left. Margaret did not wave, but stood looking in the direction of the carriage as it disappeared down the avenue. The fat Marian made the sign of the Cross.

Early in the New Year, Lady Gregory went to look at the work she was having done in one of the woods. Some spruce were being thinned so that the blue hills would show through them, an effect she knew would appeal to Robert. She knew

he would also be pleased with the broom and the flowering trees that she was planting. She decided she would spend the whole of the next day in the wood, taking a
sandwich and driving herself there and back in the donkey carriage. Before setting
out, she went into the drawing-room to write a letter. While she was there, Marian
came in very slowly. She was crying and had a telegram in her hand. Lady Gregory
knew at once that it was bad news about Robert. He had died in Italy, when his
plane crashed.

It seems that, as he drove down the avenue in the carriage on that day in the previous autumn, Robert knew that he would not see Coole or his wife and children
again. And he certainly foresees his death in the poem that Yeats wrote about him:

> I know that I shall meet my fate
> Somewhere among the clouds above:
> Those that I fight I do not hate,
> Those that I guard I do not love;
> My country is Kiltartan Cross,
> My countrymen Kiltartan's poor,
> No likely end could bring them loss
> Or leave them happier than before.

With Robert no longer there to enjoy Coole, Lady Gregory began to wonder
whether it was worth the struggle to keep the place going. She thought of selling it,
or at any rate selling some of the land, or perhaps letting the house until her schoolboy grandson Richard came of age. But she decided to carry on; though her daughter-in-law Margaret had little interest in the place and would have been happy to have
seen it sold, she wanted Richard to have a chance of keeping it. 'For Ireland's sake
also I keep it,' she wrote in her journal in 1921. 'I think the country would be poorer
without Coole.' Yeats agreed that she made the right decision. 'There is no country
house in Ireland with so fine a record,' he told her. But he feared that not having
enough money would be a worry.[5]

Lady Gregory's decision to stay on at Coole was made at the height of the
Troubles when many of her County Galway neighbours were leaving. By way of
protection during those months the gamekeeper moved into a room in the house,
though it was felt that he would not have been much use in the event of a raid. More
reassuring was the fact that John Diveney, the coachman, took to carrying a gun. In
the event, he did not have to use it. The nearest the Troubles came to Coole was one
day when Lady Gregory's two granddaughters were stalking a rabbit in the woods
and they came upon two young men in hiding, who pointed rifles at them. Then,
recognizing them, the men walked back with them to the garden gate. They seemed
nice enough and told the girls to stay away from the woods for at least three days,

because a lot of men on the run were hiding there. One of them said: 'Tell Her Ladyship that we wouldn't hurt a hair of anyone in Her Ladyship's family.' When the girls told this to their grandmother they were 'rather horrified' because they thought she was crying, but she said that she had a cold coming on.[6]

Not long before this incident, their mother had come near to losing her life when the motor car in which she was driving with an RUC District Inspector and his wife and two young army officers was ambushed; her four companions were shot dead, though she escaped unhurt. For a week after the ambush, she made Anne and Catherine sleep with her in her four-poster bed. '*How* we hated it,' they recalled afterwards. 'It was all so embarrassing – the nearness of this astral being – clad in a nightdress, and – oh horrors – snoring.'[7]

As a result of the ambush and the encounter in the woods, the two girls were taken to London for six months by their mother; but then they returned and life went on at Coole as before. Though money was short, the house was still in good condition; the rooms were dry, there were no damp patches on the walls; and while it was a long time since any of them had been redecorated, they were not at all shabby. There was a happy atmosphere; to the two young granddaughters, Anne and Catherine, none of the rooms felt creepy. Robert's old bedroom was not left empty and full of memories like Norman Leslie's bedroom at Castle Leslie, for Lady Gregory had moved into it after he was killed. The large bedroom where she had formerly slept remained unused, but it never felt cold.

In some respects, the house was old-fashioned; there was still no electric light, only oil lamps; no telephone and no heating except for fires. On the other hand, it was unusually well equipped with bathrooms; there were no fewer than four, with huge baths encased in mahogany that had been there for as long as anybody could remember; there were also mahogany-clad water closets, each of them up a couple of steps. The water gushed into each bath through a common opening for both hot and cold. There were inclined to be leeches in it, for it came up from the lake. It was pumped to the house by a horse who walked round and round tethered to the arm, stepping over the turning shaft each time he went round. The horse continued to step over an imaginary turning shaft when he was pulling the brougham, the victoria or the side car; only getting out of the way of doing so when they had gone some distance along the road to Gort. Carriages were still the only form of transport at Coole, where there was no motor car until young Richard was given one for his twenty-first birthday in 1930.

The fat Marian was getting old, though she continued to reign over the household. The other dominant figure was Mary Burke the cook, who when younger had been a real Irish beauty. She and the coachman John Diveney were courting, though nobody was meant to know this. Anne and Catherine would, however, tease John by looking at the prominent birthmark on his forehead and asking him 'Did Mary hit you again?' John's language was inclined to be pungent and the girls would come out with words like 'bugger' which they had picked up from him. It was so like children that they should pick up such words rather than a little Irish, which would have pleased their grandmother. Lady Gregory had herself become fluent in Irish, thanks to her friendship with Douglas Hyde; she tried to teach Irish to Catherine, who did not even try to learn it, reducing her grandmother to tears.

Catherine's attitude to the Irish language was rather like that of herself and her sister with regard to Yeats; they just found him boring. On one occasion, when he brought his young son Michael to stay, the girls stuffed the small boy's ears with horse dung. Their grandmother was naturally furious.

Yeats continued to be a regular visitor to Coole, together with other leading figures in the Irish literary and theatrical world. In 1925, Lady Gregory invited the playwright Sean O'Casey to stay, having been sent his play *The Plough and the Stars* with a view to its being put on at the Abbey. When old Marian saw O'Casey, who was without collar or tie, she said with disgust: 'A man dressed like that doesn't come into this house.' Lady Gregory managed to persuade him to put on a kerchief and look a little more presentable; but Marian still felt that he should not be allowed into the dining-room.

Apart from having one or two people to stay, there was not much entertaining at Coole in those days. The local clergyman and his wife would come to luncheon; old Lady Gough would come over for tea. Occasionally people would drop in, such as Mary Studd from Issercleran who drove up one afternoon when Yeats was staying, bringing two Oxford undergraduates and the fiancée of one of them. They were all Yeats enthusiasts, so Yeats recited some of his poems and 'talked of clairvoyants and of religion, the need of an intellectual belief'.[8] Once there was a party with dancing in the drawing-room, which was a great success. The guests wore fancy dress borrowed from the well-stocked dressing-up chest which Coole, like so many country houses, possessed; in fact it was not quite fancy dress, but things like old uniforms of the Galway Militia and womens' dresses left over from Victorian days. A lady from County Clare put on a dress with a bustle; Anne and Catherine, who with their brother were allowed to be present, though it was officially meant to be a grown-up party, asked her why she was not in fancy dress. When the lady replied that she was, the girls said: 'But you always look like that.'[9]

In 1927 Lady Gregory decided that there was no hope of Coole remaining in the family, so she sold it to the Forestry Department. She continued, however, to live in the house as a tenant. At about the time of the sale Marian had a stroke and retired. Her place as Lady Gregory's mainstay was taken by Ellen, who was known as the nursemaid, though there were no longer any children in the nursery. Though Marian had gone, Mary the cook and John Diveney the coachman were still there and still courting; while Corley the Piper continued to pay his periodic visits. When he came in 1929, he was very pleased with himself, having been received by royalty – Princess Mary and her husband Lord Lascelles, who were on a visit to Portumna, the estate in County Galway that Lord Lascelles had inherited.

After Lady Gregory's death in 1932, the family left Coole for good. The house stood empty until 1941 when it was demolished. Anne came back on a visit with her husband just after the war; she expected to find only a ruin, but when they reached the end of the avenue, she found that the house had disappeared altogether. There was literally nothing left. Yeats's prophesy, when he sang of Coole in 1929, had come true:

> Here, traveller, scholar, poet take your stand
> When all those rooms and passages are gone,
> When nettles wave upon a shapeless mound
> And saplings root among the broken stone . . .

# Chapter 10

# Curragh Chase
## COUNTY LIMERICK

ABOVE a reed-fringed lake in West Limerick, with woods stretching away to distant hills, stood Curragh Chase, the many-windowed Georgian house of the de Veres. The house had two adjoining fronts which, though of the same style, were of different periods. The shorter of the two was eighteenth-century and by a Limerick architect; the longer entrance front, rising from a terrace with a broad flight of steps leading up to it, was probably added in 1829 by Sir Aubrey de Vere to the design of an English architect named Amon Henry Wilde. Sir Aubrey, a poet who wrote *Julian the Apostate* and *The Duke of Mercia*, took the surname of de Vere on account of being descended in the female line from the de Veres, Earls of Oxford, the family name having originally been Hunt. Sir Aubrey's father, Sir Vere Hunt, was made a baronet in 1784; his seventeenth-century ancestor Vere Hunt was a Cromwellian officer from Essex who settled at Curragh Chase in 1657.

Better known than Sir Aubrey as a poet was his third son, Aubrey de Vere, most of whose childhood was spent at Curragh Chase shortly before the house was enlarged. 'My earliest recollections are of our Irish home,' Aubrey de Vere wrote towards the end of his life, 'and I always see it bathed as in summer sunshine.' He remembered how, on Sunday evenings, the family and their guests would go down the long ash avenue to join the country people dancing at the gates; when with 'gay, though half-bashful confidence . . . some rosy peasant girl would advance and drop a curtsy' before one of the party from the Big House, 'that curtsy being an invitation to dance'. There was also an open space in the woods where the neighbours danced and to which, as a little boy, he once ventured; only to be picked up and to his annoyance carried home to bed by one of those 'merry maids whose tresses tossed in light'.[1] Like many of the Irish gentry of those days, Aubrey's family mixed easily with the ordinary people, while keeping up considerable state; his grandmother used to drive about the demesne of Curragh Chase with four greys and an outrider.

Aubrey de Vere spent his boyhood at Curragh Chase, taught by a tutor, having returned at the age of ten after three years in England. At dusk one evening in 1829, when he was fifteen, he climbed to the top of the column on the hill opposite the

Curragh Chase.

house and waved a lighted torch to celebrate Catholic Emancipation. Though he and his family were Protestants, they rejoiced with the Catholics who lit bonfires on all the surrounding hills.

Three years later, Aubrey went to Trinity College, Dublin where he made friends with the mathematician Sir William Rowan Hamilton, Astronomer Royal for Ireland. Hamilton stayed frequently at Curragh Chase and Aubrey would sit up with him in his room until nearly sunrise, listening to him, such was his gift for language. In fact it seemed to Aubrey that to have known Hamilton made up for never having known Coleridge. He would take Hamilton for long walks in the demesne and listen to him talking; they were once going along a road that was flooded and he went on talking about transcendental philosophy until the water was halfway up to his knees. Then he said 'What's this? We seem to be walking through a river; had we not better return to the dry land?'[2] When there were a lot of people in the house, the only way Aubrey could have the benefit of Hamilton's talk was to get him alone; for in a room full of noisy company he would sit reading Plato in the original Greek.

In 1846 Aubrey's father Sir Aubrey de Vere died. Aubrey was away in London when he was taken ill. He returned to Curragh Chase; the coachman met him at the gates, pale and weeping, and told him to make haste. Up at the house, he found all the family standing, kneeling or sitting in his father's room. His father saw him, raised himself up, threw his arms around him and exclaimed: 'O my dear Aubrey, do I see you again? I am so happy.'[3] After Sir Aubrey's death, his room was filled with the poor of the neighbourhood who came to pay their respects.

Aubrey, who never married, continued to live at Curragh Chase after his father's death; first with his mother and then, after her death, with his eldest brother, Sir Vere de Vere, and his wife. He continued to sleep in the little bedroom overlooking the deer park which he had occupied as a child; but he took his father's place at the desk in the library, a room completely lined with books. He had already published *The Waldenses and other Poems* in 1842 and *The Search after Proserpine and other Poems* in 1843; now he wrote 'A Year of Sorrow', a poem about the horrors of the Famine, which had the country in its grip. While his brother Stephen sailed to Canada as a steerage passenger in an emigrant ship in order to see at first hand what the Famine emigrants had to endure, Aubrey threw himself into the work of the Famine relief committees. And showing no less of a talent as a prose writer than as a poet, he wrote *English Misrule and Irish Misdeeds,* a book upholding the Crown and the Union yet intensely Irish in sympathy.

In 1848, the year in which this book was published, Tennyson stayed at Curragh Chase for six weeks. He imposed various conditions for his stay, to which Aubrey agreed; these included having breakfast alone, being allowed to smoke in his room, and being left alone for at least half the day. One night he and Aubrey turned his poem 'Day Dream' into a charade which they and other people acted. The part of the Sleeping Beauty was given to a beautiful girl whom Tennyson used to call 'that stately maid', Tennyson himself taking the part of the Prince. While he was here Tennyson wrote his poem 'Clara Lady Vere de Vere'.

Tennyson was not the only great poet among Aubrey's friends. He also knew Wordsworth and, later in his life, Browning, and also the two Catholic poets Coventry Patmore and Gerard Manley Hopkins. And he had friends in the artistic world as well as the literary, including Ruskin and the painter George Frederick Watts. When Watts came to stay at Curragh Chase he drew figures of Dante and Beatrice on a wall of the staircase. Unfortunately, a housemaid of a subsequent period took it upon herself to scrub away the picture of Dante and, by the time she was discovered, not much was left.

Among the poets who were friends of Aubrey, mention should also be made of the churchman John Henry Newman. Aubrey first met him when he visited Oxford in 1838, seven years before Newman's conversion to Catholicism. In 1851 Aubrey himself became a Catholic, on a journey to Rome in the company of another convert clergyman and future cardinal, Henry Edward Manning. Some of his later poems were Catholic hymns, notably a rousing hymn about the Church – 'Hers the Kingdom, Hers the Sceptre' – which is now, alas, seldom if ever heard, being no doubt regarded as 'triumphalist'.

When Newman came to Dublin as Rector of the newly founded Catholic University, he appointed Aubrey to be Professor of Political and Social Science. But the post carried no duties with it and did not take him away from Curragh Chase, where he continued to lead the life of a literary country gentleman, reading and writing in the library and wandering for hours on end in the demesne. There were numerous paths through the pleasure grounds which his father had laid out; one of them, which went down to the lake and into the woods, was his favourite walk in the evening and became known as the Sunset Walk. There was a particular mound where he would sit and meditate and perhaps get ideas for his poetry, which takes the reader to Curragh Chase again and again:

> O that the pines which crown yon steep
> Their fires might ne'er surrender
> O that yon fervid knoll might keep
> While lasts the world its splendour!

If the weather was bad, he would walk up and down the hall, a tall, spare, clean-shaven figure wearing the black Inverness cape that he wore out of doors. The hall was one of the two grand rooms in the house, the other being the saloon. It had a classical frieze and was adorned with sculpture, including a cast of Michelangelo's Moses, a reclining figure of Niobe and a bust of Newman.

Sir Vere de Vere died in 1880, leaving no children. His brother Stephen, who succeeded to the baronetcy, lived mostly on an island in the Shannon estuary; so that Aubrey remained for the rest of his life at Curragh Chase, where he was now to all intents and purposes master of the house. Writing of his home as an old man, he speaks of it as 'haunted ground'. It seemed to him 'a sort of enchantment. The present becomes almost nothing – a mere vapour – and the past becomes so distinct that I recognise the steps of the departed as well as their voices. The most trivial incidents rise up before me wherever I go; and in every room of the house and every walk of the garden or woods I see again the old gestures, expressions of faith, even accidents of dress . . . the old jests are repeated, but with a strange mixture of pathos and mirth.'[4]

Aubrey died at the age of eighty-seven in 1902, in the same small room that he had always occupied. On the death of his brother Stephen two years later the baronetcy became extinct, and Curragh Chase passed to his sister's grandson Stephen, an O'Brien of the Inchiquin family who had taken the name of de Vere. Stephen de Vere was in the Colonial Service and he continued with his career as the Curragh Chase estate did not pay its way. During the long periods when he and his wife Isabel were abroad, the house was looked after by the English cook-housekeeper Mrs Egglestone, who was North Country and a great character. He and her daughter were here through the Troubles, from which the house emerged unscathed; when some men came with cans of petrol to burn it, the locals dissuaded them, telling them how good the family had been to everybody in the past.

Aubrey de Vere aged eighty-seven.

When the family was at home, two maids and a boy were recruited to assist Mrs Egglestone. They were fed on large legs of mutton, milk puddings and tarts and unlimited milk, just as the servants had been fed in former times; though the servants' hall beneath the saloon, with its carpet and comfortable chairs, was now seldom used. The laundry, further along the basement passage from the servants' hall, was likewise no longer used, for the washing was now sent out; but the dairy near the kitchen remained cool and spotless with pans of milk waiting to be skimmed and once a week the noise of the wooden churn could be heard. The lamp room was also very much in use, for the house was never wired for electricity and the large brass paraffin lamps had to be trimmed, cleaned and polished. For a time there had been acetylene lighting, the gas being made by a plant in the yard; but at about the end of the Great War the pipes had become unsafe and the paraffin lamps had been brought back into use.

As well as having no electricity, Curragh Chase in the 1920s still had no motor car. On Sundays, Dinny the ploughman would put on his Sunday best and drive the family to church in the brougham, which was drawn by the two farm horses specially groomed for the occasion. During the service, Dinny would put the horses into a stable adjoining the Church of Ireland church and go off to Mass. Once, when they were driving back from church, they met the family dog running across a field with the Sunday joint in his mouth, chased by an irate Mrs Egglestone. As well as the brougham there was a governess cart pulled by a donkey, in which the de Veres' daughter Joan, often accompanied by Mrs Egglestone's daughter, would drive into the village of Adare, five miles away, for messages.

Joan spent her childhood at Curragh Chase during the Great War and afterwards. She was an only child but never lonely here, happy roaming the woods with the birds, the rabbits and the squirrels as her playmates. She looked for wild flowers which were more plentiful than they had been now that the grounds were not so well kept up. She had many secret places where she could hide from parental authority; though it was not possible to hide all the time and she would be sent on errands taking food, clothes and medicine to the people living in the cottages on the place. Once, when she was about ten, she took a bottle of medicine to an old retired gardener. To her alarm, he drank the whole bottle at once, saying 'That'll do me good!' He had not noticed the label which said 'Take a dessertspoonful three times a day'. However, it seems that he was none the worse; indeed, the medicine may have effected a lasting cure, for she was never asked to take him another bottle.

When not roaming the demesne or going on errands of mercy, Joan did her lessons in the schoolroom off the back stairs, which had a cupboard full of old toys and was sometimes called the office because it had been used by Aubrey de Vere's brother Stephen when he came over from his house on the island to collect his rents and see to the estate. Further up the stairs was a lavatory in which young Joan would lock herself as she enjoyed looking down on the comings and goings between the yard and the kitchen door.

Joan's bedroom was known as the Green Room and had a four-poster bed. It was haunted; many years earlier, a child's coffin with a skeleton inside had been found beneath the floorboards of the adjoining room. When, as a child, Joan walked upstairs to bed, holding her candlestick with its flickering candle, she would feel that she being followed. Having reached the safety of her room, she would pile furniture against the door as a precaution. Then, as soon as her head touched the pillow, there would be three sharp knocks on the door. She would sit up and say 'Come in' and the knocking would stop. This would happen several times each night. She never experienced anything when she slept in this room as a grown-up; although a doctor who was given the room when he came to stay woke up one night and saw a female figure leaning over him; he was so scared that he left first thing next morning.[5]

There were various strange occurrences elsewhere in the house. Perhaps the most remarkable was the periodic disappearance of all the umbrellas and walking sticks in the hall stand; they would be found eventually in some out-of-the-way place upstairs. In spite of ghosts, the house had a very happy atmosphere; though people

A shoot at Curragh Chase in January 1936. Isabel de Vere's neighbour Hon Charles
Spring Rice is third from the left with his wife third from the right. Near her stands their
nine-year-old son Gerald (afterwards Lord Monteagle), who when he came here would
be given a glass of whiskey which he thought revolting.

The beaters at the shoot at Curragh Chase in January 1936.

spoke of a curse and also of bad luck because the steps leading up to the terrace were
thirteen in number.

    After Stephen de Vere's death in 1936 his wife Isabel lived on at Curragh Chase.
A neighbour ran the shoot for her; when his nine-year-old son came here he would
be given a glass of whiskey, which he thought revolting. An American lady once
came to the shoot to watch and when they had finished shooting one of the guns
asked her if she had ever fired a twelve bore. She said she had not so he handed her
his gun to have a try. They were standing by the marshy edge of the lake and she fired

Looking down to the lake where the
American lady threw the gun.

at a bulrush; then, frightened by the bang, she hurled the gun away from her. It landed in the mud barrels first, its stock sticking up into the air.

The place was becoming run down, the flat roof of the house gave trouble, there was a damp patch in one of the bedrooms. But Isabel de Vere cared for it as best she could and managed to preserve what one of her guests, the young British writer and authority on country houses James Lees-Milne, called 'the wonderfully undisturbed flavour of peace and meditation'.[6] The library was left exactly as it was in Aubrey de Vere's lifetime, though it was used as the family room in winter since it was impossible to heat most of the other rooms.

It was in the library, one night in December 1941 shortly before Christmas, that the fire started. Isabel de Vere was alone in the house with two maids who were sleeping downstairs. They woke in time to get out but since there was no telephone the fire brigade did not arrive until the roof was on the point of falling in. People looking towards the lake, which was lit up by the blaze, thought they saw a shadowy figure moving and the cry went up: 'The Lady walks.' One person watching the house burn down said 'Now the curse is gone!'[7]

Among those who mourned the passing of Curragh Chase was James Lees-Milne. Yet he admitted to 'a sense almost of satisfaction in the particular brand of fate' that had 'befallen this truly enchanted place'. For it seemed to him that 'a lingering, mouldering end' would have been 'far, far sadder'.[8]

# Chapter 11

# Drishane
## COUNTY CORK

DRISHANE, a weather-slated Georgian house with a fanlight, looks out between Reen Point and Horse Island to the Atlantic from above the entrance to Castlehaven in West Cork. It was built in about 1790 by Thomas Somerville, a successful merchant and shipowner whose ancestor had come to Ireland from Scotland a century earlier. Thomas's son, another Thomas, was foolish enough to back a bill; with the result that, after his early death in 1811, the bailiffs came to Drishane and stripped the house of its contents, apart from what the Somerville children managed to take up to their mother's bedroom, for there was a law that bailiffs were not allowed to enter the bedroom of the lady of the house. While this was going on, the children's mother lay helpless in her bed, awaiting the arrival of her tenth child.

The eldest of the children, who was called Thomas like his father and grandfather and known as Tom, grew up to be extremely handsome. His two cousins, Harriet and Eliza Townshend, who lived with their parents at Castle Townshend a little further up the harbour, both fell in love with him. They were about ten years older than him, but were both considerable beauties; so that he responded and fell in love with Harriet. He and the two sisters went out hunting together; Harriet was flung over her horse's head and lay unconscious. Eliza galloped up to find Tom on his knees whispering words of love in Harriet's ear, having restored her to consciousness. Such was Eliza's jealousy that she made her parents object to their marriage; and she never forgave her sister when, in 1822, despite her efforts to prevent it, the marriage took place. Henceforth, when visiting Harriet, she would walk up to Drishane with a footman ahead of her carrying a tray with her lunch; for she refused to eat her sister's food.

When Harriet died, Eliza, who made a rather unsatisfactory marriage at the age of sixty, was living in a house in the nearby village of Castletownshead close to the two venerable sycamores known as the Two Trees. Her only acknowledgement of her sister's death was to have her blinds drawn on the day of the funeral. Eliza's heartlessness was made up for by Harriet's husband Tom, who after her death would sit up for hours by his bedroom fire thinking of Harriet and grieving for her

Drishane.

and looking for consolation in his Bible by the light of a candle in her own special candlestick. He would burn two candles every night which Mrs Kerr, the house-keeper, would leave out for him. Then he started to complain, night after night, that he could not find the second candle. Mrs Kerr told his granddaughter Edith what she believed had happened. 'My dear child, *the candle was there*! For I always put it on his table myself! It was Herself that took it, the way your Grandpapa should go to his bed and not be sitting there all night, breaking his heart.'

Mrs Kerr and Travers, the butler, ruled the Drishane household; both were Northern Protestants, Protestantism being, as Edith puts it, the 'established religion for higher officials of the servants' hall'; though in fact the family did not mind what religion the servants were so long as they went to their respective churches. 'Old Tra', as he was known, was with the Somervilles for forty-two years. 'A more ruthless and implacable tyrant never bullied the children of the house, or ground pantry-boys to plate-powder,' Edith wrote of him many years later. Though occasionally Travers had his 'softer moments' when he would bestow on Edith and her cousin Ethel Coghill 'pepper-mint lozenges of dreadful intensity' inscribed with mottoes like 'waste not, want not' and 'wine is a mocker'. Edith and Ethel thought they were horrid, but were too gratified by this rare civility to refuse them.[1]

Mrs Kerr sat at one end of the row of chairs provided for the servants and Travers at the other during the prayers that took place every morning punctually at nine in the hall. Tom Somerville read the prayers standing at a small table, for he never knelt, not even in church. His son, yet another Thomas, and his granddaughters stood beside him; his daughter-in-law Adelaide and his grandsons stood at right angles, facing the servants.

The hall where morning prayers took place was at one end of the house, where the entrance had been moved from the principal front. The original entrance hall, with its fanlighted doorway, had become a library between the drawing-room and dining-room. When Edith was a child, the hall had panelling grained 'hot yellow brown' in imitation of oak. Above the panelling was a mud-coloured wallpaper, with a pattern of Gothic arches. During the half-century since the house was stripped by the bailiffs, more furniture had been acquired, including the black mahogany tables in the hall, on one of which reposed a very early edition of Bradshaw's railway guide, handsomely bound in brown leather. Tom Somerville was a magistrate and when the police brought cases to be summarily dealt with by him, he would swear the deponents on the Bradshaw as though it were a Bible, partly through laziness, partly from 'a certain impishness of character and a love of playing on ignorance'.[2] Under the table with the Bradshaw was a small and very realistic stuffed terrier called Susannah, an object of hatred and terror to all visiting dogs, which eventually disappeared and was thought to have been eaten by a foxhound puppy.

Country people wanting a word with Himself used to frequent the hall doorsteps, as did beggars and travelling musicians, with whom the Somerville children were able to chat unbeknown to their elders. The hall was a room in which the children could play; they were allowed to have games of battledore and shuttlecock here. The drawing-room, with its curtains of deep red maroon and its white-and-gold satin wallpaper hung with portraits of ancestresses – ancestors were relegated to the dining-room, 'a more suitable environment', as Edith supposed, 'for the thirstier sex' – was, by contrast, 'a place of great sanctity wherein the foot of a child never trod except by special invitation (or command, which came to the same thing)'.[3]

When Edith was very young, she was invited or commanded to the drawing-room to be inspected by visitors. When she was older, the invitation or command was 'to exhibit my prowess on the Erard'. In either case she would lurk in agony behind the tall threefold screen by the door, having been pushed into the room by her nurse. Apart from the screen and the Erard piano, the room was furnished with chairs which Edith remembers as having been 'dour and upright as a black Protestant' and sofas 'upholstered in something cold, and pink, and polished, and harder than a plank-bed'.[4] The principal feature of the drawing-room was a marble chimneypiece that was suffering through the attempts of several village masons to exhume the corpses of rats and mice from under the hearth stone, where there was what Edith's uncle Sir Joscelyn Coghill called a 'mouseoleum'.

Tom Somerville died in 1882 and Edith's father, who like so many of the Somervilles and their relations was a colonel, succeeded to Drishane. Three years later Tom's sister-in-law Eliza died at the age of ninety-five. Soon after Eliza's death, a nephew of her unsatisfactory husband came to dine, a stout middle-aged gentle-man 'with a fat, pink, hairless head and a face like a dissolute baby'. He told doubt-ful stories in a high treble squeak 'and was, in short, the best of bad company'.[5] In the middle of one of his stories he laughed so much that he lolled his bald head against the breast of Minnie Townshend, who was sitting next to him at dinner, declaring that he thought he would die of laughing. She was not amused.

Minnie was the wife of Colonel Harry Townshend, a cousin of the reigning Townshend of Castle Townshend and also, of course, a cousin of Colonel Somerville; she and her husband lived nearby. Other Townshend and Somerville relations settled in the vicinity; as did Adelaide Somerville's brothers, the County Dublin baronet Sir Joscelyn Coghill and the Indian Mutiny veteran Colonel Kendal Coghill. Eventually, the village of Castletownshead and the shores of the harbour became inhabited by a large cousinhood centred on Drishane and on the Castle – as the ancestral home of the Townshends was known to distinguish it from the village.

Edith Somerville first acted as mistress of Drishane when her mother Adelaide was away. 'I go through the magnificent form of ordering dinner every morning, and

The young Edith Somerville (left) and her cousin Violet Martin take the oars when boating in Castlehaven. In the bow, with one of the two dogs, sits Edith's brother Boyle Somerville, who became an admiral.

Mrs Kerr's extreme servility appals me,' she reported to her mother. 'I spoke to her with extreme severity upon the loathsome state of the kitchen range which looked as if she had been sick over it.'[6] When Drishane was inherited by her eldest brother Cameron Somerville after the death of their father in 1898, Edith kept house for him, their mother having died three years earlier. Cameron, like Edith, was unmarried; and being, like his father, a soldier, he was away a great deal so that she was left in charge. Her life was not solitary; another of her brothers, Aylmer, and his wife, came to live with her for a time and shared expenses; her younger sister Hildegarde, who was married to their cousin Egerton Coghill, the son of Sir Joscelyn, lived close by and managed the farm for her. And then, in 1906, her friend and cousin Violet Martin, from Ross in County Galway, who under the pen-name of 'Martin Ross' was her collaborator in the great literary partnership of Somerville and Ross, came to live with her permanently at Drishane.

At Drishane, Edith's will was law, even when her brother Cameron was at home. Edith was the dominant member of her family, though Cameron and her other military brother Jack became colonels and her two naval brothers Boyle and Hugh both became admirals. Colonels and admirals were all very well, but she was an admired author; between 1889 and 1915 she and Violet Martin published fourteen books in collaboration including the immortal *Experiences of an Irish RM*. She was Master of the West Carbery Hunt, having revived the pack some years before and revived it

A meet of the West Carbery Hunt at Drishane in the eighteen-nineties. Edith Somerville is mounted, third from the left, next to her brother Aylmer Somerville (with moustache). The small boy standing in front of the group on the steps is Aylmer's son Desmond, who inherited Drishane in 1942.

again after an outbreak of rabies made it necessary for the hounds to be shot. She was a suffragette who became President of the Munster Women's Franchise League; though one feels that she herself could have managed perfectly well without women's rights by the sheer force of her personality.

She was also a talented artist and exhibited her paintings in the United States and elsewhere. When her parents were still alive, she made a studio for herself in a room over the hall door; her mother used to call it a 'filthy purlieu' and it was known as 'The Purlieu' for ever more, just as the nursery passage was known as 'Cockroach Alley'. Later, she made herself a studio in a room in the wing near the stables. It was not a very comfortable room, with a very small fire, but it was handy for seeing to the horses, having a door going out into the open. Tinkers and beggars used to knock on this door at all hours, just as they used to come to the hall door in Tom Somerville's time; Edith, who got on well with everybody, used to chat with them, making them a present of whatever came nearest to hand, however unsuitable.

She could ill afford to be over-generous, for she and Cameron were both chron-ically short of money. To help their finances, Drishane was let for a few weeks each summer, Edith retreating to some smaller house in the neighbourhood, just as Lucia and her friends do in E. F. Benson's novels. Edith has herself recorded her feelings when Drishane was let for the first time and she called on the English couple who had taken it. 'It was a strange and not agreeable thing to ring the bell and be asked by a scorbutic-faced English maid, "What name shall I say, please?"'

Her own people felt even more strongly about the interlopers than she did. One of these, Mrs Crowley, said: 'I'd *hate* to see them in it! I'd twice sooner it was empty!' And Mrs Leary, the laundrymaid, would seize her hand and kiss it whenever she met her, which she did most days when Edith went up to see the horses. The first time she went up after the house was let, Mrs Leary rushed out of the laundry and asked: 'When are yer comin' back, my darlin' lady?' And 'in the blackest of con-spiratorial whispers' she said: 'Send me up yer washin'! I'll do it here for ye!' This meant, as Edith was fully aware, 'an alien's soap and hot water, but I should be expected to ask no questions and assume she did it in her own house'.[7]

The two other maids, Margaret and Delia, ran out to greet Edith when she went round to the stables. She asked Margaret for a bit of sugar to give to one of the hunters and 'instantly about half a pound of the English people's sugar' was brought to her 'furtively but very respectfully in a dining room saucer'. Normally, when Edith asked Margaret for sugar for the horses, she would bring her just a lump or two in her fist.[8]

In spite of being short of money, Edith and Cameron managed to carry out some improvements to Drishane. Cameron, who served in China, gave the hall door a surround of Chinese design; and he put a new chimneypiece, also Chinese, into the drawing-room in place of the battered marble, thereby getting rid of the 'mouse-

oleum' for once and for all. But while Edith 'loved the house passionately' and spent
more than she could afford on improving its amenities, 'little things like dusting and
polishing, mendings and repairs were dull and so passed over; they were also never
noticed', as Moira Somerville, the wife of her nephew Desmond, remembered.

Moira Burke Roche, as she was then, came to Drishane for the first time in
January 1918, as Desmond Somerville's fiancée. On her arrival, she was shown into
the 'white dressing room', where she noticed that 'the curtains over the window were
a pair of old bed-sheets hung by means of safety pins' and that there were two panes
of glass missing in the window 'through which a howling westerly wind blew'.
One leg of the iron bedstead had gone through the floor and the mattress 'felt as
though it had just been lifted off the sea-shore'.[9]

All this and the absence of a cupboard in which to hang her clothes could not
take away from the beauty of the view or from the warmth of the welcome given her.
Moira was greeted not only by Edith but by ten or twelve other members of the
family who were gathered in the hall, accompanied by numerous dogs, 'to look me
over', as she put it. 'The hall was lit by one oil lamp and warmed by a closed
anthracite stove, beside which tea was spread out on a beautiful mahogany table,
cakes, loaves of soda bread, pound pots of jam and in the middle a large kettle on a
spirit lamp which soon boiled over onto the mahogany. The dogs drank tea from the
large slop bowl and were served first.'

Moira could never forget Edith as she saw her on that January afternoon, 'presiding over the tea things in the hall, her little dogs on her lap, the light of the oil
lamp on her thistledown hair, her china-blue eyes, so like a child's, fixed on my face.
From that moment I loved her.'[10] The love was reciprocated; Edith, who was
devoted to her nephew Desmond, took to his fiancée immediately, treating her as an
equal, despite the difference in age. To have gained so sympathetic a niece would
have helped to console Edith, who had not yet recovered from the crushing blow of
Violet Martin's death two years earlier.

One evening during Moira's first visit to Drishane she and Edith were alone
together in the study after hunting. A south-westerly gale was rattling the windows.
Suddenly, Edith laid down her pencil. 'I am so tired, I can't get through to Martin,'
she said. 'It's always bad in stormy weather. Come here, child, and put your hand
on the pencil, you are so young and should have more power.' Moira took the pencil
between her hands, 'placed as in prayer'. The pencil started to move across the page
and wrote a message in a 'cursive Italianate script'. Then, in another handwriting,
it wrote, 'I am with you always, Alexis.' Alexis Burke Roche was Moira's late
father, but Moira would never for one moment have thought of trying to contact him
in this way. The incident left her 'unconvinced but bewildered'; but Edith believed
that it was indeed a message from her father.[11] Encouraged by Geraldine Cummins,
a friend who was a professional medium, she had turned to the occult as a means of

making contact with Violet Martin. She believed that her dead friend still collabo-
rated with her and the name of Martin Ross still appeared as co-author on most of
the books she published after Violet's death. In the first of these, *Mount Music*, published in 1919, two of the characters, 'Mrs Dixon' and 'Robert Evans', are, on her
own admission, based on Mrs Kerr and Travers, the housekeeper and butler at
Drishane in the years of her childhood and youth.

Edith's 'automatic writing' and the nightly disappearance of Tom Somerville's
second candle were not the only supernatural occurrences at Drishane. There were
also the ghostly footsteps heard one night by Edith's sister Hildegarde and someone
else staying in the house after Edith and her brother Jack had thrown away the collection of Indian junk left to their father by a great-aunt and known as Aunt Fanny's
Museum; it had been kept in dusty obscurity on top of the pantry press in a small
glass-fronted cupboard which they now wanted as a china cupboard. Aunt Fanny
presumably forgave them, for her footsteps were not heard again. But when
Drishane's most famous possession, the Fairy Shoe, was sent away to the bank for
safe keeping and bad luck followed, it was wisely decided to bring the Shoe back
and it has remained in the house ever since. The Shoe, which came to the
Somervilles from the Coghills, was picked up on an Irish mountain early in the
nineteenth century; it is exactly like the shoes worn by adults at that time and shows
signs of wear, but it is only about two inches long.

In 1919, Cameron Somerville retired from the Army and came back for good to
live with Edith at Drishane. He remained a bachelor, though many hopeful ladies
came to stay; a romantic path in the grounds was nicknamed 'The Widows' Walk'.
Cameron and Edith were joined two years later by their sister Hildegarde, following the death of her husband Sir Egerton Coghill, as he had become. Hildegarde
brought her personal maid Molly with her. She was deaf and dumb but very sharp-
witted; if Edith wanted her gun she would send for Molly and stamp her feet and
the gun was immediately produced.

Although Cameron was head of the family and Drishane belonged to him, he
still had to defer to Edith. He liked shellfish but was not allowed to have it because
Edith and Hildegarde did not like it. He was, however, king in his own room, a
former bedroom which he had made into an upstairs sitting-room for himself. Here
he kept his books and other treasures. Nobody was allowed in, not even the housemaid, so that the room became more and more dusty.

While Cameron's stronghold was his sitting-room, Edith's was her studio, where
she worked all morning, painting or writing, having not come down to breakfast.
She came down to luncheon and sat at the head of the table with a plate on the floor
beside her for scraps for the dogs; then she went for a ride, which changed to a drive
in her pony-cart after she became lame as a result of an old hunting injury. Rising
costs had forced her, much to her grief, to give up her hounds soon after the Great

Edith Somerville in her studio at Drishane in the late nineteen-twenties.

War; but her former huntsman remained with her to break in the young horses and he would accompany her in the pony-cart. Any guest who was staying would be invited to share in 'this somewhat penitential drive, bumping over bohireens with muddy dogs on one's lap . . . as the greatest treat hospitality could offer'.[12] Though her uncle Kendal Coghill had been an enthusiastic pioneer motorist in his eighties, she never took to motoring. In fact the only time she was known to have ridden in a motor car while at Drishane was one day when a cousin arrived in his car and told her that some men were about to cut down the Two Trees in the village. She immediately got into the car with him and he drove her down to the village at speed, so that she arrived on the scene just in time to save the trees. But she preferred to walk back.

Having returned from her ride or drive, Edith held court in the hall, presiding at the tea table. It was often very draughty and cold, despite the anthracite stove, but the spread on the fine mahogany table was as tempting as it was on that afternoon when Moira Somerville came here for the first time; as well as the cakes and soda bread there would be a freshly baked Sally Lunn, a barmbrack and scones. The company would include various members of the cousinhood and other neighbours such as Sergeant Sullivan, the last Irish sergeant-at-law, who defended Roger Casement in 1916.

Until the Second World War, everybody changed for dinner at Drishane, whether or not there were guests. However, what was perhaps the most illustrious

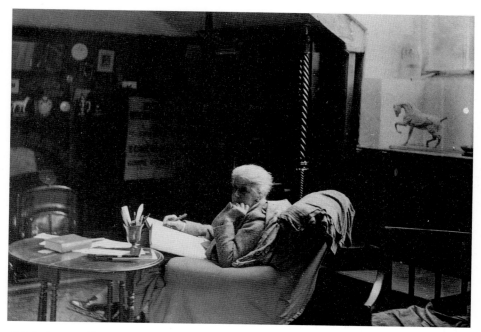

Edith Somerville in her studio at Drishane shortly before the outbreak of World War II.

party that Edith ever had to entertain came not to dinner but to luncheon. 'I am in ten mothers of forty fusses, as Mrs Penrose has dispatched from Lismore a perfectly damnable luncheon party of six Dukes and Duchesses, and they may be here at any moment now,' she complains in a letter to a friend written in April 1919. 'It is a fine day, for which with all reverence and gratitude I thank God, but to have to give up the whole blessed day to "serving tables" when my work is hanging over me like a nightmare is rather trying. If the book ends in misanthropic gloom you will know the reason why.' Mrs Penrose was her cousin Ethel Coghill, now married to the agent at Lismore Castle in County Waterford, the Irish seat of the Duke of Devonshire who, together with his Duchess, presumably led this ducal invasion. To make matters worse, the kitchen boiler had gone wrong and 'the filthy plumber and all his filthy tools' were under the feet of the 'unhappy' cook.[13]

Other distinguished guests at Drishane in Edith's time included George Bernard Shaw and his wife Charlotte, who was a Townshend and therefore a cousin. Edith used to tease Shaw about his vegetarianism, which he took in good part. A writer of a very different stamp who also came to Drishane was the Catholic and cosmopolitan Maurice Baring, whom Edith met when he was staying at Killarney with his sister the Countess of Kenmare. They had a great mutual friend in Ethel Smyth the composer, who like Edith had been a suffragette.

Ethel Smyth often stayed at Drishane and after dinner she would sit down at the piano and insist that everybody sang a part in her latest opera or oratorio. 'Boyle can sing tenor!'

'Nonsense, I can't sing tenor,' Edith's sailor brother Admiral Boyle Somerville would protest. But she usually got her way.[14]

Boyle Somerville and his wife lived in a house in the village. Early in 1936 he was shot dead on his own doorstep in the presence of his wife. His murderers left a card accusing him of being a British recruiting agent; in fact all he had done was to give advice and references to young men of the neighbourhood wishing to join the Royal Navy. The crime was attributed to the extremist organisation calling itself the IRA which W. T. Cosgrave, the then Prime Minister of the Irish Free State, had declared illegal in 1931.

A memorial to Boyle was put up beside the gates of Drishane, with an inscription in Irish, for he had been a keen student of the Irish language. Edith had also studied Irish, though with less success. Her attitude towards Irish national aspirations was, like that of so many of the Ascendancy, ambivalent. When she was young, soon after the Fenian rising, she and her friends 'turned rebels' and 'howled the "Shan Van Voght" and the "Wearing of the Green" in the teeth of English-bred cousins'.[15] Later, she and Violet Martin campaigned for the Unionist Party. Later still, she became a moderate Nationalist; and she wrote many letters to the papers calling for mercy for the insurgents of 1916. She went into the nearby town of Skibbereen to hear Michael Collins speak; it was the last speech he made before he was killed. She disliked de Valera.

Cameron Somerville died in 1942 and Drishane passed to his and Edith's nephew Desmond, the son of their brother Aylmer. Edith continued to live at Drishane, for Desmond Somerville was then away in the Army; and when he retired as a brigadier in 1945, he and his wife Moira not only insisted that she should live here with them, but that she should keep her place at the head of the table. Moira remembered her sitting there, 'doling out the pudding in huge spoonfuls' or 'seated in the grandfather chair by the drawing room fire cheating outrageously at backgammon'. She also depicts her 'clinging to the banisters' as she went upstairs, 'dragging her lame leg, an oil lamp at an angle of forty-five degrees in her right hand'.[16]

It was the graceful Georgian staircase of Drishane, rising round three sides of a staircase hall behind the hall where she presided at tea, which finally drove Edith out of her old home. By the end of 1946 she could no longer climb the staircase, so she went to live with her sister Hildegarde in the village. Here she was able to have a bedroom on the ground floor near her studio, with a door to which her pony-cart could be brought. She went out in her pony-cart on the day before she died at the age of ninety-one in 1949.

As she left only a few hundreds, Desmond and Moira were faced with the task of restoring and modernizing Drishane on very little money. The house had to be reroofed, wired for electricity, redecorated. It was a struggle, but they managed and their son and daughter-in-law have continued to make improvements to the house and also to the garden and grounds since they took over in 1976. Unlike Coole Park and Edgeworthstown and most of the other literary Irish country houses, Drishane has survived as the home of its family and is probably in better condition now than at any other time in its history. Edith Somerville once said: 'If I am ever allowed to return to earth it will be to Drishane that I shall come.' If she were allowed to come now, she would certainly be pleased with what she found.

# Chapter 12

## Edgeworthstown
### COUNTY LONGFORD

TOWARDS the middle of the eighteenth century, Richard Edgeworth, whose family had come to Ireland in the reign of Queen Elizabeth, built himself a house on his estate at Edgeworthstown in the east of County Longford. He built it on the site of an earlier house, so it did not have much of an outlook, but was hemmed in with yew hedges and screens of clipped elm trees and hornbeam. It was also rather old-fashioned for its time, with small windows and low, wainscotted rooms. This is surprising, for Edgeworth, though he lived in a poor and remote part of Ireland, cannot have been entirely out of touch with contemporary ideas; he was a Member of Parliament, his wife was English, he sent his son, Richard Lovell Edgeworth, to Oxford.

Just before the young Richard Lovell Edgeworth went to the university, his sister Mary married a neighbour, Francis Fox of Fox Hall. There were great festivities; Richard and his new brother-in-law hunted every morning and danced all night for three nights running, Richard's favourite dancing partner being the daughter of the curate who taught him his grammar. Late one night when the dancing was over and the young people were enjoying what was then called a 'raking pot of tea', one of the boys, as a joke, put a white cloak round his shoulders to look like a surplice and pretended to marry Richard to the curate's daughter; a door key served as a ring and the words of the marriage ceremony 'with much laughter and playfulness were gabbled over'.[1] When Richard's father heard about the 'mock-marriage', he went to the trouble of having it annulled in the ecclesiastical court. The affair did no harm to the girl's reputation; soon afterwards, she was properly married to another and no less suitable young man.

Like the curate's daughter, Richard Lovell Edgeworth married young, soon after he came down from Oxford, to a girl from Oxfordshire. Under the influence of his friend the writer Thomas Day, who was an admirer of Rousseau, they went to live in England so as to be able to bring up their son according to Rousseau's theories; Richard would himself become well known as a writer on education. In 1768 Richard took Day to Edgeworthstown for a long visit; he also took his son, but left his wife and their infant daughter Maria in England. Though Day was a good con-

Edgeworthstown.

versationalist, his untidy black hair and bad table manners did not go down well with Richard's father and his sister Margaret. Yet Margaret responded favourably when, towards the end of the visit, Day declared that he had fallen in love with her; she agreed to marry him if in a year's time he was of the same mind and had made himself look more presentable, as befitted his station in life, for he was a man of means. In the event, they decided that they were not suited to one another and the marriage did not take place.

Richard inherited Edgeworthstown from his father in 1770; he and his second wife Honora came to live here four years later, bringing some English servants with them. Finding the house dilapidated, they carried out repairs; and they started cutting down the yew hedge and the clipped trees to let in light and air and open up a view of parkland. The estate was likewise in a bad way, with signs of poverty all around; Richard, who had gained experience of land reclamation when travelling in France, set about improving it, so as to better the condition of the people. One morning, when she was watching thirty or forty men levelling a field, Honora dropped her wedding ring. She did not miss it until she was at dinner, when she leaped up from the table and hurried back to the field. Having offered the men a reward if the ring was found, she made them walk one behind the other sifting the newly turned earth until they found it.

Three years later Richard and Honora went to England on a visit and decided to

Richard Lovell Edgeworth.

stay there. It was not until 1782, after Honora had died and he had married her sister Elizabeth as his third wife, that Richard came back to Edgeworthstown for good and really got down to the work of improving the estate. And, over the years, so as not to exceed his income, he remodelled the house, making it large enough to accom/modate his growing family in comfort. It had been what his daughter Maria remem/bered as 'a slice of a house' but now it became much deeper; and a third storey, crowned with a pediment, was added to the centre of the principal front which was brought forward on either side on the ground floor in order to make the rooms more spacious. As well as being an improving landlord and a writer, Richard was an inventor. He filled the house with labour/saving devices: sideboards on wheels, pegs for footwear in the hall, leather straps to prevent doors banging, complicated locks, a water pump that automatically dispensed a halfpenny to beggars for each half/hour they worked it. But while in many respects the house was in advance of its time, it still relied for its heating on fires of bog/turf. When Maria, now a young lady, came back from staying with relations in County Meath, Kitty the maid said, on waking her: 'Dear ma'am, how charming you smell of coals! Quite charming!'[2]

Kitty may have found the smell of the Meath coal fires a nice change from the smell of turf smoke, but the fact that it still clung to Maria could have been a reflection on the soap that her ingenious father made from a receipt in Nicholson's *Chemistry*. Richard also made his own ink. More ambitiously, he constructed a hotair balloon; and he made a telegraph between Edgeworthstown and Pakenham Hall, the seat of the Earl of Longford, some twelve miles away to the east across a desolate stretch of bog covered with yellow weed which someone called 'the Yellow Dwarf's Country'. Pakenham was one of the two country houses in the neighbourhood which provided intellectual society; the other being Castle Forbes, the Earl of Granard's seat, which was to the west and more easily reached.

When Richard returned in 1794 from a visit to England, it looked as if his telegraph might be needed. Disturbances were breaking out; the country was becoming infected with the fever of the French Revolution, which was at its height. Louis XVI had been guillotined in the previous year, attended on the scaffold by Richard's Catholic cousin, the Abbé Edgeworth, who called out to the King as he climbed the ladder, '*Fils de Saint Louis, montez, montez au ciel!*' In July 1794 Edgeworthstown seemed peaceful; the only disturbances were to do with the local fair, the house being close enough to the village for Maria to hear 'the noise of pigs squeaking, men bawling, women brawling and children squealing', as she reported in a letter.[3] In August, however, they were putting bars on the windows following an attack on a house only half a mile away and many of the householders in the village were bringing their arms to Richard for safe keeping. Maria's brother and one of her half-brothers were camping outside the gates trying to send telegraphic messages by night.

For the time being things quietened down. Even in the summer of 1798, the Edgeworths were thinking more about Richard's fourth marriage – which took place at the end of May, Elizabeth having died six months earlier – than about the Rising, which had so far passed them by. But in late August came the news of the French landing at Killala and early in September rebel pikemen were seen marching in the direction of Edgeworthstown. So Richard decided that he and his family should take refuge in the garrison town of Longford. They were offered a lift on a passing ammunition cart, but were not quite ready so it went on without them. This probably saved their lives, for when the cart had gone a little way it exploded and most of the people on it were blown to pieces.

They left an hour or two later, some of them in a carriage and some on horseback. There was not enough room in the carriage so, at her own insistence, the English housekeeper stayed behind. After they had started out, Richard remembered that he had left the list of his yeomanry corps on the table in his study; fearing that the people whose names were on the list might be victimized if it fell into rebel hands, he galloped back at some danger to his life to burn it and then rejoined his family. Maria and Richard's new young wife were also among those who went on horseback rather than in the carriage. They passed the place where the ammunition cart had exploded, with the grisly spectacle of the trunk of a dead man and the severed limbs of horses.

Having reached Longford without further incident, they went to an inn. Then Richard was mistaken for a French spy by an unruly loyalist mob and hit on the neck with a brickbat; surprisingly he was uninjured. Five days later they returned safely to Edgeworthstown where, although the rebels had done a great deal of damage to the village, the house was just as they had left it. A map that they had been looking at before they left was still spread out on the library table; a pansy in a glass of water was still where they had left it on the chimneypiece. To some extent, they owed their good fortune to Richard's popularity as a landlord, but it was also thanks to the English housekeeper. Before the Rising, she had lent a small sum of money to one of the rebels, a tenant farmer, who had shown his gratitude by coming and stand-ing guard over the house, armed with his pike, threatening to kill anybody who set foot in it and assuring the housekeeper that 'not a twig should be touched, nor a leaf harmed'.[4]

By November, life had returned to normal and Richard was busy making a theatre in a room over his study with an elaborate mechanism for changing the scenery. When it was finished, the family put on a comedy entitled *Whim for Whim*. They had written it themselves; Maria must have had to take time off from writing *Castle Rackrent*, her first great novel of Irish life, which was published anonymously in 1800.

One of Maria's half-brothers, Sneyd Edgeworth, put on a more spectacular per-formance in 1805 to celebrate their father's birthday. He organized 'a pretty little *fête champêtre*' and managed to keep it as a surprise. After dinner, he sent the family out on horseback and in the chaise for an airing. When they returned, they heard the sound of music 'and as if by enchantment, a fairy festival appeared'. An amphithe-atre of foliage decorated with the scarlet streamers of Richard's yeomanry had been put up on the lawn and in it danced 'a company of youths and maidens in white, their heads adorned with flowers'.[5] The 'good Kitty' passed round cakes and syl-labubs; while Richard's schoolboy son William, who was then going through a craze for anything to do with electricity, invited the dancers into the study to be given electric shocks. It was a shame that young Lovell – only son of Richard's second marriage who was now the heir, his son by his first wife having died – was not here to join in the fun, for he was in captivity in France.

After eleven years in captivity, Lovell came home in 1814. That year was also notable at Edgeworthstown on account of the heavy snow and rapid thaw. Maria writes of 'wet pouring in at all parts, and tubs and jugs and pails and mops running about in all directions'; a state of affairs that seems to suggest an Irish country house in the late twentieth rather than the early nineteenth century. Having been reunited with his son and heir, Richard Lovell Edgeworth died aged seventy-three in 1817.

Maria Edgeworth when young.

Edgeworthstown was inherited by Lovell, but since he was unmarried his step⁄mother continued to be the official mistress of the house. But the real mistress of the house was Maria, who lived on at Edgeworthstown being also unmarried; though she let Lovell take over the management of the estate, for which she had been respon⁄sible during her father's later years, and she deferred to her stepmother, who was in fact younger than she. Maria was now in middle age, plain, very short and described as 'the remains of a blonde'; but the vigour of her mind and the brilliance of her conversation made her fascinating. More people came to Edgeworthstown to see her than had come to see her father, who, clever though he was, must have been a bit of a bore, as Byron discovered when he met him with Maria in London.

When some English friends were staying in 1819, Maria took them on 'a tour of the tenants'. Driving home, they came upon the country people dancing by the road⁄side. The dancers 'in all the vivacity and graces of an Irish jig delighted our English friends,' Maria wrote appreciatively, 'and we stood up in the landau for nearly twenty minutes looking at them.' She was writing with less enthusiasm of Irish rural life a few weeks later; there had been a terrible row in the kitchen between the cook and the kitchenmaid as a result of which the cook had been dismissed on the spot: 'such a scene of lying and counter⁄lying'. She may have had this and other domestic alter⁄cations in mind when, on a visit to Paris in the following year, she engaged a deaf⁄

and-dumb French washerwoman for the new laundry that was being built at Edgeworthstown. Maria described her to her half-sister Lucy as 'an elderly woman with a very good countenance, always cheerful and going on with her own business without minding other peoples'.

Poor Lucy, who was young enough to be Maria's daughter, was ill for several years, though she eventually recovered. The Archbishop of Tuam, after sitting with her in her room, said how impressed he was at seeing 'such an example of patience and resignation in so young a person'. In a letter written at the time of the Archbishop's visit, Maria gives an account of a typical day in her life. At about eight o'clock, two of her other young half-sisters, Fanny and Harriet, came and read Mme de Sévigné's letters to her. 'I almost envy Fanny and Harriet the pleasure of reading them for the first time.' After breakfast she took her little table into Lucy's room and wrote there for an hour. Lucy liked having her in the room, though she only heard the 'scribble, scribble'. But she did not need entertaining as she was happy with her reading and with her algebra – not, one would have thought, a very stimulating occupation for a sick girl. Maria spent the rest of the day walking, talking and reading, though she did not read as much as she used to because it hurt her eyes; she was taking rather a long time to finish Southey's *Life of Wesley*.[6]

Maria was not always occupied with things of the mind; in August 1821 she was making a sewer and a footpath in the village, reckoning that this would give employ-ment to twenty men for three weeks. Then came the happy day when her half-brother Francis arrived back from Charterhouse, where he was at school, telling them all about his journey at tea, while his younger brother Pakenham Edgeworth – named after his godfather Lord Longford – stood beside him 'feeding him with red cur-rants well-sugared'. In the following year, when both boys were at home, the young people sprung a surprise on Maria and Lovell, who 'were sitting in the library one day after tea when they were suddenly given play bills and invited to go into their stepmother's dressing room on the ground floor to see *Catiline: A Tragedy in Two Acts*'. Francis and Pakenham played Catiline and Cato; Harriet played a male part as Caesar; Fanny and Sophy were Julia and Aurelia. Lucy, who was still an invalid, lay on the sofa with her feet towards the conservatory; there was a half-circle of chairs for the rest of the audience, who sat with their backs to the wardrobe. 'Candlestick footlights, well shaded with square sofa-cushions standing on end' – surely a con-siderable fire hazard – separated the audience from the performers, who had gone to a great deal of trouble over their costumes. Francis, as Catiline, had been dressed by his sister Fanny with the help of Kennet's *Antiquities* and an old rag-bag: 'a more complete little Roman figure I never saw', was Maria's verdict on the result. Cato wore a black velvet cloak and an old wig found in an attic; Aurelia 'looked extremely classical and pretty', draped in Maria's French crimson shawl.

Having had the Church of Ireland Archbishop to breakfast, the Edgeworths had the local Catholic Bishop to dinner, when he came for the confirmations in the summer of 1824; he was fed on what Maria called a 'God-send haunch of venison'. Lucy was now in the dining-room, lying on a bed by the open window where she could smell the roses on the trellis outside and the freshly cut hay. Other visitors at about this time included a number of young Oxford men and Maria's publisher.

That her publisher came all the way from London to see her is a sign of Maria's fame as an author. Such was her standing in the world of letters that in August 1825 Sir Walter Scott came to stay at Edgeworthstown, fulfilling a promise he had made two years earlier when she stayed with him at Abbotsford. He brought quite a retinue with him: his son and daughter-in-law, his daughter and her husband John Gibson Lockhart and a friend. After dinner, the local school band serenaded the great Sir Walter with Scottish airs by moonlight; and he was delighted by the spectacle of the boys playing leap-frog. Next day they took him to visit the village school and he was very favourably impressed. Religious instruction was going on, the Catholics with the priest in one room, the Protestants with the Church of Ireland clergyman in the other. 'More delightful conversation I have seldom in my life heard than we have been blessed with these three days,' Maria wrote at the end of Scott's visit, describing him as 'most benignant as well as most entertaining; the noblest and gentlest of lions'. Scott and his party went on to Killarney and Maria and her half-sister Harriet accompanied them.

Another literary lion who came to Edgeworthstown was Wordsworth. Maria was ill at the time, confined to her sofa, but she enjoyed 'snatches' of Wordsworth's conversation. 'I think I had quite as much as was good for me,' she said after he had gone.[7]

Not being her father's daughter for nothing, Maria enjoyed the company of distinguished scientists as much as that of great novelists and poets. In 1826 the chemist Sir Humphry Davy came to stay; Maria found him one morning at breakfast with 'a countenance radiant with pleasure and eager to tell me that Captain Parry is to be sent out on a new Polar expedition'. A few months later, she and her family were amusing themselves by saying who, among literary and scientific celebrities, they would most like to have here next day. Francis said Coleridge. Maria settled for an astronomer, the younger Herschel. Next day, when she was returning from her morning walk, Maria met one of the maids who was looking for her with a letter. She opened it and found, to her amazement, that it was from Herschel, who was at the local inn having travelled all night on the mail coach in the hope of seeing her. She lost no time in getting him up to the house and he delighted everybody with his conversation, which was not only informative but full 'of humour and playful knowledge' – he told them of the live camelopard 'twelve foot high if he is an inch, ma'am'. After twenty-four hours of his company, Maria declared that if some fairy were to ask her again whom she would most like to see, she would all the more eagerly say, 'Mr Herschel, ma'am, if you please.'[8]

In 1828, the year after Herschel's unexpected visit, the house caught fire; it was the usual trouble, a chimney. Luckily there was no shortage of water and thirty men were quickly mustered to go up the long ladder with a succession of buckets. They had to bore holes in the hall ceiling to prevent the weight of water bringing it down. Meanwhile Maria and her half-sister Honora – one of Richard Lovell Edgeworth's children by his third marriage – were having papers and valuables carried out; title-deeds and leases and their father's portrait. But after three hours the fire was brought under control.

By the time of the fire, Maria was once again in charge of the estate, her half-brother Lovell having been unable to cope with difficulties arising from a financial crisis in 1826. She managed to weather the storm and eventually bought Lovell out with the money she had made from her writing. But while she thus became the real owner of the estate, she insisted that Lovell should still appear to be the owner. As a landlord, she was as popular as her father had been; she carried out many improve-ments in the neighbourhood, selling some diamonds that she had inherited from a relation in order to build a market house in the village.

It may have been her duties as a landowner as much as her age which prevented Maria from writing any more novels after *Helen*, which was published in 1834; for though she was sixty-seven at the time of *Helen*, she was still vigorous and was to live another fifteen years. *Helen* was a worthy conclusion to her literary career, the most elaborate of her novels and regarded by many as the best. When she had finished writing it, the family took it in turns to read it aloud, starting at eleven in the morning and continuing, with breaks, until dark. It was June; after the reading of *Helen* came to an end one evening, Sneyd Edgeworth and Harriet walked round the lawn. The owls were shrieking and flitting by in pursuit of bats; clouds in endless varieties moved across an unsettled sky. Through the windows of the house they could see the library, its walls and pictures in the lamplight. The library was where Maria worked, though everybody else tended to sit there.

In the 1830s, a number of Americans came to Edgeworthstown, precursors of the transatlantic visitors who were to be a familiar feature of Irish country life in years to come. George Ticknor, Professor of Modern Literature at Harvard, stayed for seven days in August 1835 and was impressed by the hospitality; sometimes twenty or thirty friends turned up unexpectedly. He found the house very comfortable and convenient; though in his opinion it lacked 'English exactness and finish'. He admitted that this was a mere trifle 'in the midst of so much kindness, hospitality and intellectual pleasures of the highest order'. Ticknor noticed the bells and other gadgets put in by Richard Lovell Edgeworth and the American authoress Mrs Farrar remarked on one of his locks, which she found on her bedroom door; she dared not shut the door for fear of not being able to open it again.

Some of Maria's American admirers sent her 150 barrels of flour during the Famine, when she was working hard to relieve the sufferings of the people, though she was then nearly eighty. The barrels were addressed to 'Miss Edgeworth for her poor'; the porters who carried them ashore refused to be paid. So she sent each of them a woollen comforter that she herself had knitted. During the Famine, the young Anthony Trollope published his first novel, *The Macdermots of Ballycloran*, and in it he pays tribute to Maria, recounting how, as the coach from Boyle to Dublin passed through to the village of Edgeworthstown, 'the guard pointed out to the Englishman the residence of the authoress of whom Ireland may well be so proud'.

Maria spent her literary fortune in order to keep Edgeworthstown in the family; but it passed out of the family a century later when it was sold by the granddaughter of her half-brother Francis. It was eventually bought by a community of nuns for use as a nursing home. The exterior of the house was much altered and the interior was gutted and rebuilt, so that Richard Lovell Edgeworth and Maria would hardly recognize it if they could return here now.

*Chapter 13*

# Grey Abbey
## COUNTY DOWN

A BRANCH of the family of the Montgomerys, Earls of Eglinton, came from Scotland to County Down early in the seventeenth century and acquired the lands of Grey Abbey on the Ards Peninsula. A hundred years later, William Montgomery and his wife Elizabeth, who was from Buckinghamshire, were living in a house near the abbey ruins in a fine demesne over-looking the waters of Strangford Lough. Elizabeth, whom he had married in 1725, was William's second wife, his first wife, the mother of his eldest son William, having died in 1723.

From Elizabeth Montgomery's notebook it would appear that she and her family and their guests enjoyed potted lobsters, which would 'keep good two months', and that they drank what was called 'lemon wine', made from steeping the rind of sixteen lemons in four quarts of brandy. One hopes that over-indulgence in this potent brew did not give anybody convulsions, for which Elizabeth had her own rather alarming remedy: 'Take the brains of a man that has been put to death or come to some untimely end, you must take care that he has been free from any ill dis-temper, and after he has been buried three or four months, take it out of the grave, take out all the brains and wash them, roll them in betony, rue, lavender and rose-mary . . . put all into an earthen pot and set it in a warm oven after bread till it grows so dry as to make it a fine powder.' This powder was to be mixed with a 'syrup' made by boiling up the skull.[1]

Elizabeth's stepson, the younger William Montgomery, who became a Member of Parliament, was living here in 1769 when James Boswell came with a Mr Boyd, with whom he was staying, and another gentleman, to look at the ruined abbey. Boswell had crossed over from Scotland to Donaghadee and was on his way to Dublin to pay court to the sixteen-year-old Mary Ann Montgomery, who came of a different branch of the family. While he and his two companions were admiring a window of the abbey church, which he described in a letter as 'exceedingly Gothic and covered with a thicker ivy than I ever saw, which greatly adds to its appearance',[2] a young gentleman who was 'walking about with dogs and his gun' came up to them. He was William Montgomery's eldest son, an officer in the Army named

Grey Abbey. The entrance front.

William like his father and his grandfather; he knew Mr Boyd and Boswell's other companion and invited the three of them up to the house, which at that period was known as Rosemount.

'We went with him,' wrote Boswell, 'and found it to be an excellent house of Mr Montgomery's own planning and not yet finished. He was not at home but his lady and two daughters were very obliging, gave us bread and wine and begged we would stay dinner.' They were expected back to dinner with Mrs Boyd so declined this invitation; though before they left they had time to walk about the place and admire the views over Strangford Lough. 'There is also a good deal planted,' Boswell observed. 'I saw here a singular thing, at least to me; a goldfinch's nest in a young pine. I believe birds never build in pines till they are well grown up, and then only large birds such as crows.'[3]

The 'excellent house of Mr Montgomery's own planning' was a handsome three-storey block with two-storey wings ending in curved bows. It stood on the site of an earlier house that in turn had replaced an earlier house elsewhere in the demesne, both previous houses having been destroyed by fire. The new house took several years to build; when Boswell came here, the family were living with the builders on top of them.

In 1782 William Montgomery's clergyman son Hugh – who was now the son and heir, his military brother William having been killed in America in the previous year – married Emilia Ward, a daughter of the first Viscount Bangor. It was

Grey Abbey. The garden front, showing the Gothic windows in the bottom storey of the bow.

Grey Abbey. The Gothic ceiling of the octagonal drawing room.

Grey Abbey. One of Hugh Montgomery's gardeners working on the lawn near the Abbey ruins in the nineteenth century.

probably through Emilia's influence that the three-sided bow in the centre of the garden front of the house was given Gothic windows in its bottom storey, this rather unusual appearance of Gothic in the garden front of an otherwise Classical eigh-teenth-century house being reminiscent of Castleward, her own family home at the opposite corner of Strangford Lough. The octagonal drawing-room inside the bow was decorated in Georgian Gothic, like the saloon at Castleward. Another unusual feature that the house acquired over the years was a new entrance by way of a Doric porch in front of one of its wings, the porch being balanced by a similar projection at the opposite end of the façade.

Hugh and Emilia Montgomery had seven sons and two daughters. The house seems to have been pretty lively when the young people were grown up and still unmarried; William, the eldest son, writing to his sister Emily from London in 1815, mentions that an aunt of theirs was proposing to spend only one night with them on her way to Castleward: 'You are all too gay for her at Grey Abbey.'[4] Tragedy, however, struck the family in that year – Hugh, the second son, a captain in the Guards, was severely wounded at Waterloo and never recovered; he was to die two years later. While he was serving in France in 1814, he wrote to his mother telling her that, if they reached Bordeaux, he would send a case of the best claret to his brother Arthur 'for his own particular use'.[5]

The claret-loving Arthur and his brother William married two sisters, Lady Amelia and Lady Matilda Parker, daughters of the fifth Earl of Macclesfield. William and Amelia spent some time in Florence after their marriage, so that when they returned to Grey Abbey in 1828 their seven-year-old son Hugh and his nurse were objects of some curiosity, as they could speak only Italian. The Italian nurse married the Scottish gardener and young Hugh was taught writing by the clerk in the estate office and given other lessons by the local clergyman and also by his aunt Matilda; she and his uncle Arthur were then living at Grey Abbey before buying a place of their own in the vicinity. At the age of nine, Hugh was sent to school in England. When he came home for his first holidays he found his mother in weeds and all the household in mourning; for his father had died in Dublin from a chill caught at the Curragh Races.

Hugh married Lady Charlotte Herbert, a daughter of the second Earl of Powis and a great-granddaughter of Clive of India. She was an accomplished water-colour artist and would invite other ladies to come and sketch with her in the park at Grey Abbey; there was a man whose job it was to arrange the cattle so that the ladies got the particular beast they wanted in front. As chatelaine of Grey Abbey and as a mother, Lady Charlotte was rather frightening; her nine children were terrified of her and would sometimes hide from her and from their father by climbing up the nursery chimney.

Meals in the nursery were scanty. The children, always hungry, would stand on the stone stairs going down to the kitchen and waylay the footmen as they went to and from the dining-room, struggling with them in dead silence in order to grab some food. This was not easy, for the footmen held their trays high; but there was an occasion when George, the youngest of the boys, managed to get a whole kidney. For George, who had a distinguished career in the Chinese Customs and became a Mandarin, this triumph was unforgettable. The children fared better with regard to ponies than they did in the way of food; each had a pony tied to a tree in readiness. They all rode well, particularly the eldest girl Lucy; the fence that she used to jump became known as Lucy's Leap.[6]

The eldest of the children, yet another William Montgomery, came of age in July 1868. He returned home from his regiment, the Scots Guards, at short notice; when he arrived by train at Newtownards he was met with a carriage and a hundred of the tenant farmers were there on horseback to greet him. This cavalcade accompanied him to Grey Abbey where the horses were taken out and the carriage was pulled by a crowd of people, headed by the band of the Antrim Rifles playing 'Home Sweet Home'. There were arches of evergreens over the village street, some bearing mottoes such as 'The Hope of Grey Abbey'. Up at the house, a deputation of tenants read an address to which young William and his parents replied; the deputation was then given refreshments in the dining-room. Later that afternoon, the

children from the local school and their teachers, together with the wives and daughters of the men on the place, were given tea in a large tent. The band played for the
rest of the evening and there were 'athletic sports'; then, after dark, the Birthday Boy
was drawn in a carriage through the village to see the illuminations; tar barrels blazed
on the surrounding hills.

On the following day, Lady Charlotte laid the foundation of the new parish
church that was being built in the demesne close to the ruined abbey; then, at five in
the afternoon, the tenants and other friends, 250 in number, were given dinner in a
marquee near the house. At a certain time the family and 'various gentry', including Lady Charlotte's brother Lord Powis and the Montgomerys' clerical cousin
Henry Ward, walked over from the house to the marquee, where the band played
'The Harp that once through Tara's Hall'. A month later the tenants entertained
William Montgomery to dinner in one of the outbuildings; two hundred people sat
down in a large room decorated with banners and evergreens. William, the young
guardee, caused much laughter by quoting in his speech the nursery rhyme:

> Who comes here?
> A grenadier.
> What do you want?
> A pint of beer.
> Where's your money?
> In my pocket.
> Where's your pocket?
> I forgot it.[7]

By the time William married, in 1891, he was a colonel. His bride was Alberta,
daughter of Queen Victoria's private secretary, Sir Henry Ponsonby; the Queen
travelled up to London specially for the wedding. Alberta was one of the Coterie
known as the souls; soon after her marriage her fellow-souls, the future Prime
Minister Arthur Balfour, who was then chief secretary for Ireland, and George
Wyndham, who was then his private secretary and who later became Chief
Secretary himself and brought in the Wyndham Land Act, came to Grey Abbey.
Hugh Montgomery and Lady Charlotte gave a large house party for them and
William and Alberta helped to entertain the guests.

William retired from the Army in 1900 as a major-general and he and Alberta
came to live at Grey Abbey; they had no children and William's bachelor brother
Francis lived with them. He was somewhat eccentric and ate by himself in the
drawing-room, sitting at a low level in the space between two half-moon tables put
together so that his head came just above the table-top which was covered with a
white cloth liberally spattered with tomato ketchup, giving the effect of a severed

A house party at Grey Abbey in 1891. Hugh Montgomery sits on the far right, with his wife Lady Charlotte next to him; the newly-married William and Alberta Montgomery sit together in the middle. The Montgomerys' formidable neighbour Theresa Marchioness of Londonderry sits between Alberta and Lady Charlotte; next to William sits the future Prime Minister Arthur Balfour who was then Chief Secretary for Ireland. The handsome George Wyndham, who was then Balfour's private secretary and who later became Chief Secretary himself and brought in the Wyndham Land Act, sits third from the right at the back.

head. Once, when his brother and sister-in-law and their guests were about to set off on the dignified Sunday walk to the church in the demesne, Francis said he was not feeling well enough to come. But when the others were walking back after the service, they saw him pretending to be a mad monk in the abbey ruins. While in church, William would turn round and count who was there; if anyone was missing, he and Alberta and a footman would arrive in a gig at the person's house bringing calf's feet jelly, on the assumption that anyone who was not in church must be ill.[8]

Alberta took a great interest in the neighbourhood. She taught the children in her Sunday school, she ran young people's clubs, she gave 'informal homely parties' in the house and in the grounds. When she left Grey Abbey in 1927 after William's death, the women and girls presented her with a farewell address. 'You have shown unfailing interest in our lives and homes. Your visits to our houses, your friendly chats by our firesides, your joys in our joys, your sharing of our sorrows, we shall greatly miss. Many a marriage has been blessed by the sunshine of your smile; and often we have felt that our loved ones who have left us rest the more peacefully for your tears . . . The most enduring of your poems is that written in our hearts by the pen of your personal affection.'[9]

William Montgomery, now a retired Major-General, and his wife Alberta, with the tenant farmers of the estate and two of the local clergy in front of the house.

William was succeeded at Grey Abbey by his brother Robert, who was also a major-general, and on Robert's death in 1931 the place passed to the eccentric Francis; fortunately his highly efficient spinster sister Evelyn was able to take charge. During the Second World War, when there were troops quartered in the yard, Evelyn put an 'Officers only' notice on the door of the yard lavatory. Francis died in 1941 and Grey Abbey was inherited by his nephew Major Hugh Montgomery, the son of his brother George, who secured the kidney. Major Montgomery was then serving in the Army, and he and his wife and their two sons did not come to live here until after the end of the war. They found the house empty of furniture, having been occupied by the Electricity Board; they were given £500 which was supposed to cover the cost of redecorating it from end to end. They had to work hard; and to make matters worse, the agent died soon after they arrived. Major Montgomery had to get up at dawn to help with the milking. His wife ran the house with two girls from the South; cooks, butlers and footmen were a thing of the past.[10]

Grey Abbey is now the home of Major Montgomery's son Mr William Montgomery and his wife Daphne, a sister of the present Viscount Bridgeman. In the difficult climate of today, it is among the best maintained of Irish country houses; and it is always full of guests, for Mr and Mrs Montgomery have many interests, particularly to do with the arts. During a recent summer, the Montgomerys and their guests dined alfresco at a long table on the lawn; and when dinner was over, everybody sang under the stars. Such is the hospitality of Grey Abbey under the present dispensation that when a certain gentleman, renowned for his amusing talk, came to tea, he stayed for three months.

*Chapter 14*

# Gurteen Le Poer

## COUNTY WATERFORD

IN 1866 the young Edmond de la Poer, who had recently been made a Papal Count, built Gurteen Le Poer, a Tudor baronial mansion in the Suir Valley among the woods of his ancestral estate at the north-western corner of County Waterford; it was the third successive house here. Designed by Samuel Roberts, it was of grey stone, impressively turreted and battlemented, with a tower on the entrance front facing north across a castellated forecourt to the River Suir and Slievenaman. The garden front, facing south, was more Tudor than baronial with gables and mullioned windows. Inside the house, the galleried top-lit hall, divided by a screen of Gothic arches from the staircase, was given a baronial air by armour

The architect's impression of the house, with the flag flying from the tower.

The hall.

The dining room, with the antlers of St Hubert's Stag, the de la Poer crest, over the chimneypiece. The portrait to the left of the fireplace is of Edmond de la Poer's brother Raymond, who lived in County Kilkenny.

The large drawing room in Victorian days.

A croquet party at Gurteen soon after the present house was built. Edmond de la Poer is standing second from the left near Edith Osborne, with whom he was then in love; but kept silent knowing that her parents would never have allowed her to marry a Catholic. Edith's sister Grace, who afterwards became the Duchess of St Albans, is standing second from the right. The party also includes the girls' mother, Mrs Bernal Osborne from Newtown Anner.

and weapons; the dining-room was also baronial, with a carved oak chimneypiece surmounted by the head of St Hubert's Stag, the family crest, complete with antlers and crucifix. Edmond was the heir-male of the great Norman-Irish family of de la Poer or Power, which was represented in the female line by his kinsman the Marquess of Waterford. Over the centuries, the family name had become Power; but Edmond's mother, who was herself a Power from Kilfane in County Kilkenny, had, after her husband's death, reverted to de la Poer, the original Norman render-ing of the name, and her children had followed her in this respect.

Having been still single when he built his new house, Edmond married, in 1881, Mary Monsell, daughter of the first Lord Emly from Tervoe in County Limerick. She was nearly twenty years younger than him, a Catholic, as he was, and half French, which would have made them all the more compatible, for he had the manner of a Frenchman of the *ancien régime*, while having no French blood himself; he liked reading French memoirs of which he built up a fine collection in his library at Gurteen. They had three sons and three daughters; by the autumn of 1897 Arnold, the youngest of the sons, was old enough to join his brothers Rivallon and young Edmond at the Oratory School near Birmingham. 'The house so dull and lonely without them,' their father wrote in his diary after the three boys had set off on their journey to school by way of Waterford and Milford Haven.[1]

He cannot have found it all that lonely, for the three girls, Elinor, Ermyngarde and Yseult, were still at home, taught by a governess who was soon to be replaced by a German fräulein with the aristocratic-sounding name of von Arday. And apart from his wife and children, there was company almost every day. Neighbours were forever coming to luncheon or tea or just calling in: the Duchess of St Albans and her family from Newtown Anner, members of the Donoughmore family from Knocklofty, members of the Waterford family from Curraghmore, a little further away. Then there were Edmond's two brothers and their wives and three of his sisters – one of them married to General Sir Charles Gough, VC – and their respective families, all of whom lived within easy distance. And there were officers from the barracks in Clonmel. To add variety, neighbours brought people who were staying with them. The Duchess of St Albans brought Lord Basil Blackwood, a brilliant younger son of the Marquess of Dufferin who was to be one of Lord Milner's 'Kindergarten' in South Africa. Edmond's brother Raymond brought Mrs Rennell Rodd, the wife of a future ambassador to Italy. The Countess of Bessborough, who lived in County Kilkenny, brought Princess Marie Louise of Schleswig-Holstein, a granddaughter of Queen Victoria.

There were frequent tennis and croquet parties. At a tennis party in June 1897 there were twenty-eight women but only seven men. During the following summer there was a tennis and croquet party of eighty-four; while in September 1899 130 people were invited to one. In August 1896 there was a tennis party of about seventy on the same day as a grouse shoot. The shooting party included Edmond's nephew Captain Hubert Gough, who when shooting grouse here two years later was suddenly taken ill with fever, presumably malaria contracted when serving abroad; a carriage had to be sent to pick him up.

On the day before the shooting party in August 1896, Hubert's brother Johnnie Gough came to have a shot at the deer on the place; he went out at 3.30 in the morning but got nothing. Of the many officers from the barracks and other sportsmen who 'came to try for a buck', few were lucky. Mr LivingstoneLearmonth, who came to tea one day when there was a house party staying and then went out to look for a buck in the rain, returned wet through a few hours later having not seen one. By that time dinner was over so he was given some cold meat.

The house party that was staying when Mr LivingstoneLearmonth turned up had, by way of entertainment, a tennis and croquet party and a game of *vingtetun* after dinner. Usually the house parties at Gurteen were either for shoots or for local dances. Edmond, in his late fifties, regarded himself as too old to dance; but his wife Mary would set off in the landau with the younger members of the party and not return until the small hours. 'Mary, who wore the diamond tiara, looked very handsome,' Edmond wrote approvingly in his diary after seeing her off to the County Tipperary hunt ball. When Mary, accompanied by Lord Waterford's debutante sister Lady Clodagh Beresford, who was staying in the house, went off to a private dance in February 1898, Edmond had a High Anglican clergyman from Oxfordshire, who was also staying, to keep him company. The two stayed up until after one 'talking of the points of difference between the Catholic and Protestant churches'. Mary and Lady Clodagh did not come back from the dance until five in the morning.

One occasion when Edmond did actually dance was when he partnered Margaret McLoughlan, the upper housemaid, after her wedding in 1898. The whole family, together with Edmond's two Nugent nieces and Major Chichester from the barracks, went to the local Catholic church for the ceremony, which was interrupted by the unexpected arrival of a funeral, the coffin being carried up the aisle preceded by two priests chanting 'a doleful dirge'. This does not appear to have cast any particular gloom over the celebrations and the dance held that evening in the servants' hall at Gurteen was a great success. After an early cold dinner, the family went to join in the fun; Edmond danced with the bride, Mary with the bridegroom, one Patrick Connolly from Clonmel. The fifteenyearold Rivallon, eldest of the three de la Poer boys, proposed the bride's health and 'made a very good little speech'. The family retired at about eleven, having enjoyed 'a capital supper'.[2]

In April 1899 the de la Poers gave a dinner followed by sports for thirtytwo of the people working on the place. The meal was at noon and the family had a cold lunch at two. They then went outside to watch the sports which were somewhat marred by the bad weather; though the obstacle race and the donkey race were a success. As well as providing treats for their servants, the de la Poers looked after them when they were ill. One January at midnight, Edmond and Mary heard Mary's maid Agnes, who occupied the room above them and had flu, coughing very badly. Not wanting to disturb the other servants, they went down to the kitchen and came back with linseed and a saucepan. Mary then went up to Agnes's room, made up the fire and heated the linseed to make a poultice for her. Then at about four in the morning she went up again and found that the fire had gone out; she went down for sticks and coal, lit the fire and made Agnes comfortable. As Edmond commented in his diary, 'a good night's work'. Another winter, when Cleary the gamekeeper was seriously ill with flu, Mary spent the night at his lodge and helped his wife and sister-in-law to nurse him. This time Edmond was unable to help being laid low with flu himself. Cleary seemed better after Mary's nursing; but he had a relapse and died three days later. He died just after the shooting season ended; but a few years later, when the ten-year-old son of Kavanagh the forester died, the shoot was put off.

More alarming than the annual visitation of flu was an epidemic of scarlet fever one Christmas; because of the risk of infection, the family did not go to the local church on Christmas Day but a priest came and said Mass for them in the chapel in the house. He came again to say Mass on New Year's Day and Epiphany, when, just as they were going into the chapel, the hall chimney caught fire. Mary took charge and made the butler, the coachmen and other servants go to the top of the tower carrying cans of water which they poured down on to the blazing chimney, eventually putting the fire out.

On the Sunday following the chimney fire, the priest came as before; but he could not come on the Sunday after that, so because of the scarlet fever the family missed Mass and Mary read prayers in the schoolroom. It was unfortunate that L'Abbé L'Heritier, a French priest who often came over to stay from Tervoe, Mary's old home in County Limerick, and said Mass in the chapel, was not here at that time. L'Abbé L'Heritier was not the only Catholic cleric who stayed at Gurteen during this period. Dr Sheehan, the Catholic Bishop of Waterford, would occasionally stay a night after administering confirmation in the local church. He came to stay when the de la Poers' youngest daughter Yseult was confirmed; on that occasion the parish priest gave a priests' dinner for fourteen and the de la Poers' cook went to help with it. Once, when the Bishop was staying, a Persian priest called at the house, begging for some charity in Persia. The Bishop was able to vouch for him and Edmond gave him a pound and invited him to luncheon. Then, as he had missed his train, Mary, who was driving into Clonmel, took him with her and gave him an extra ten shillings. Not long after the visit of the Persian priest, two Persians came to the house selling embroidered silks. 'Too dear for us,' Edmond remarked in his diary; but they bought a rug.[3]

When L'Abbé L'Heritier was staying, he went bicycling with the family. The bicycle was Edmond's favourite means of locomotion and Mary's too; they and their children and friends bicycled long distances. They were unusual among the Irish gentry of their time in not being particularly horsey. When Edmond, in the summer of 1898, went for a ride with his fourteen-year-old daughter Elinor, it was a rare occurrence; when Mary, during that same summer, tried a new horse, she wore her bicycling dress and was afterwards 'somewhat done up', for she had not ridden for nearly twelve years. To house the family bicycles, which had hitherto been kept in the outer hall, Edmond built what he called the Bicycle Tower. He buried a bottle near it containing a paper stating that it had been put up by him; the document was signed by Mary and the three girls and by Major Chichester and other friends who were there at the time.

Bicycling into Clonmel one day in February 1900, Edmond had an unpleasant experience: a man 'somewhat under the influence of drink' would not let him pass. He had to dismount, whereupon the man seized the front wheel. Eventually Edmond grabbed him by the collar and gave him a shove which brought him to the ground. He got back on to his bicycle and pedalled away while the man shouted that he would kill him.[4]

The man may have been pro-Boer, the de la Poers being very much on the side of Britain in the South African War which had broken out in the previous autumn. Edmond's nephews Hubert and Johnnie Gough and his cousins Sir John and Derrick Power from Kilfane were serving in South Africa. A Union Jack, provided by Major Lysaght at the barracks, would soon be flying from the tower of Gurteen; hitherto no flag seems to have been flown except on St Patrick's Day when they flew a green flag with a harp and crown which Rivallon had painted during his last half at the Oratory. On the day that the Union Jack was hoisted, Edmond sent his sympathy to a daughter of their neighbour the Duchess of St Albans whose fiancé had been killed in South Africa a few days before. The war was to take its toll of Edmond's family: Sir John Power, known as Jack, was mortally wounded and his brother Sir Derrick, who succeeded briefly to his family's baronetcy, died in South Africa of fever. Just before Sir John Power was wounded, Fräulein von Arday heard the banshee at Gurteen. Edmond also heard the banshee wailing outside the terrace door a few months earlier, just before an old friend of the family died.

To bring the war even closer to Gurteen, Malone, the caretaker, went off to South Africa as a Reservist. On the night when the three de la Poer girls and two of the boys were acting *Cinderella* in the servants' hall for the benefit of the servants and some people from outside, their mother was told that Malone's wife was ill. So she went off in the pony-trap to see her and was relieved to find her not as bad as was feared.

Mary de la Poer in the garden at Gurteen in 1900 with her dog Turkey and her second daughter Ermyngarde who was then aged thirteen. Edmond de la Poer can be seen standing behind them, wearing his gardening clothes.

*Cinderella* was not the only theatrical performance of the young de la Poers. Another year they put on *Box and Cox* in the servants' hall; the room was crowded with servants and people from round about. In the words of their proud father, 'all acted their parts capitally'. An earlier performance by the youthful company was *Bluebeard*, which, like Cinderella, was put on at Christmas time. Another Christmas there was no play but they had a fancy dress Christmas dinner. Edmond's sister Annie Nugent and her two girls were staying and also Major Chichester, who came and stayed on many occasions even though he was quartered only a short distance away in Clonmel. When he was staying one July, a bantam cock in a basket was hidden behind the curtains in his bedroom 'by way of a lark'. At about four in the morning the cock started to crow, which woke Chichester, who 'wisely put the bird out of the window'.[5]

The summer of the bantam seems to have been a good one; there was 'a beautiful light night' in September when they all went out after dinner and walked about. They found the servants and some of their friends dancing in the old avenue near the kitchen. During another hot summer they decided to dine alfresco and a table was set for them on the terrace; but just as they had finished their fish course a shower drove them back into the dining-room.

Gurteen had a fine garden and pleasure grounds; although they were not short of

A game of croquet at Gurteen in 1902. Mary de la Poer is sitting on the ground, her daughter Elinor, then aged eighteen, is on the right. Between them stands Edmond de la Poer's nephew Jack Perry, from Woodrooff on the other side of Clonmel. On the left is Bertie Ponsonby, son of the Earl and Countess of Bessborough from County Kilkenny.

labour in those days, Edmond spent a great deal of his time weeding and cutting laurels. People from round about were allowed to walk in the grounds, but a party of women and children who were caught picking the rhododendrons were given a piece of Edmond's mind and forbidden by him ever to come inside the place again. When not cutting laurels, cleaning and rearranging the pictures in the house or bicycling to visit neighbours, Edmond attended meetings of the district council which had been set up by the recent Local Government Act. At the first council election, he had come at the bottom of the poll: 'There is something too absurd in a de la Poer being so defeated,' he had observed sorrowfully.[6] He had, however, been co-opted unanimously when the council first met; and to uphold the family honour, Mary was elected for a neighbouring division. To celebrate her victory, the men on the place had a great bonfire. Mary herself was away at the time, but her youngest son Arnold, just back from school, and all the servants went out to watch it. As the night was cold, Edmond did not venture outside; but he and the girls and Fräulein von Arday watched the bonfire from the room over the billiard room.

Mary de la Poer with her daughters Ermyngarde and Yseult at Gurteen in 1902.

Billiards and billiard fives were played frequently at Gurteen. During a game of billiard fives in August 1905, a ball played by the nineteen-year-old Arnold shot off the table and broke a window. Edmond seemed to have preferred the more sedate 'bumble puppy' bridge, while Mary and her friends played bridge of a more serious sort; when Edmond's sister Mary Perry and the Earl of Donoughmore and his American wife came to luncheon, they and Mary played bridge until teatime.

Shortly before Arnold's accident with the billiard ball, Lord Osborne Beauclerk, the son of their neighbour the Duchess of St Albans, came over to dinner in his motor car. Motors were still a novelty – they did not yet have one at Gurteen – but that evening, Elinor's piano playing after dinner made more of an impression on her father than did 'Obby' Beauclerk's motor; she played well and had a good touch, thanks to Fräulein von Arday's tuition. Obby was a young eligible, but one fears that his mind would have been less on Elinor and her playing and more on the buck that he was hoping to shoot after the dinner party was over. He and Rivallon and Arnold sallied forth with their rifles at 1.30 in the morning, but the wind and the rain were against them and they got nothing.

Elinor was twenty-one that year, but she must have been away for her birthday, which is not mentioned in her father's diary. For her next birthday, her parents gave her fifteen shillings, which does not seem very generous, even considering the value of money in those days. Her sister Ermyngarde only got ten shillings when she was nineteen a month later. Ermyngarde's birthday was celebrated with a tennis party and her uncle Raymond came over from County Kilkenny in his motor car; the cook, the butler, the upper housemaid and Mary's maid – not Agnes but a successor – were taken for a drive in it. Yseult, the youngest of the de la Poer girls, who was seventeen a little earlier that year, was given ten shillings as Ermyngarde was, but a little more notice seems to have been taken of her birthday; her health was drunk at dinner. On Yseult's twelfth birthday, her health was proposed at dinner 'in an amusing way' by Elinor, and the servants were given a couple of bottles of Marsala so that they too could drink her health.

In that same month, May 1906, Edmond and Mary celebrated their silver wedding with a dance for the servants and estate workers and their families and friends, about 150 in all. The dancing was in the servants' hall which was decorated with flowers and evergreens; the supper was in the diningroom and there was wine and light refreshments in the schoolroom, which was reserved for 'some particular women friends of the servants'. When, a little after 9.30, Edmond and Mary made their entry, they were very surprised to see a handsome silver rose bowl standing on the table in the middle of the room; every man and woman working on the place had subscribed towards it. John Kavanagh, the forester, and Patrick Donovan, the butler, presented it to them, each making a charming speech. Edmond and Mary stayed at the dance until four in the morning when they took their leave to 'great cheering'. The dance went on until half past five.[7]

In the following December an English girl who was a friend of Elinor's came to stay; she was called Muriel Best and was a granddaughter of the second Lord Wynford. She and Rivallon, who was two years her senior, did some target shooting and she shot very well; they went in the landau with Elinor and Ermyngarde to visit neighbours; she took photographs of the house and the place. One evening the hall carpet was rolled back and there was dancing. After Muriel had been at Gurteen for little more than a week, she and Rivallon announced their engagement. Next day there were congratulations from all the household and Edmond gave the servants champagne with which to drink the health of the happy couple.

They were married in London in the following July, Muriel having been received into the Catholic Church in March. She took Patricia as her confirmation name and was henceforth always known as Patricia or Patsie. In thanksgiving for her having become a Catholic, Edmond put up a statue of the Virgin Mary in a grotto over one of the terraces.

On the evening in October when Rivallon and Patricia arrived back at Gurteen for the first time after their marriage, the nearby village of Kilsheelan was lit up with candles in all the windows; men pulled their carriage from the railway station to the house preceded by torchbearers and followed by a large crowd. Arches with lamps had been put up on the avenue, the first with an inscription that said 'Welcome to

Edmond and Mary de la Poer with their eldest son Rivallon and his bride Patricia and their daughters Elinor and Yseult on the steps of Gurteen in about 1907. Elinor, who was soon to marry Humphrey Weld, stands on the left next to Patricia; Yseult sits near her mother, holding the dog.

Edmond and Mary de la Poer with their eldest son Rivallon and his bride Patricia and their daughters Elinor and Yseult on the steps of Gurteen in about 1907. Patricia stands behind Rivallon; Yseult sits on the left holding the dog, Elinor, who was soon to marry Humphrey Weld, sits on the right.

the Happy Pair', the third, nearest the house, inscribed with 'Cead Mille Failthe'. When the carriage drew up at the hall door, Rivallon and his father made speeches of thanks and a band played. The bandsmen, sixteen in number, were then given supper in the servants' hall after which they played in the hall while the family had dinner – a cold dinner, so as not to give the cook too much trouble. Next day the ladies of the family helped to cut sandwiches for the dance that was being held that evening in the coach-house for the employees, who were given a dinner in the servants' hall that afternoon. The dance was meant to start at 9.30, but the musicians from Carrick-on-Suir did not turn up. Somebody played an accordion, and the dancing began; later one musician arrived, instead of the three who had been expected. Despite this setback, the dance was a success and went on until six, the family retiring at three. A couple of days later Mary gave a large tea party to introduce Patricia to the neighbours. The guests filled the two drawing-rooms; tea was in the dining-room and there were three bridge tables in the library.

When Rivallon and Patricia arrived back, they were accompanied by Elinor, who had just announced her engagement to Humphrey Weld of the well-known English Catholic family; the celebrations were also meant for her. She and Humphrey Weld were married in the local church by the Bishop of Waterford in December. It was raining on the day, but with the help of the Duchess of St Albans' carriage and Lord Waterford's motor and other vehicles lent by kind friends or hired from Clonmel, the bridal party and everybody else staying in the house were conveyed to and from the church without getting wet. The ceremony was followed by a lunch for about a hundred people.

In that year when Rivallon and Elinor both got married, Yseult, the youngest of the de la Poer children, went to her first public dance, a hunt ball in Clonmel. There were twelve at dinner and the dance was a great success. The gentlemen of the house party arrived back at 5.30 in the morning in a motor car belonging to one of them; the ladies half an hour later in the landau. Motors were now appearing at Gurteen ever more frequently; one day that autumn Lord Basil Blackwood arrived from Newtown Anner on his motor cycle.

Lord Basil, a hero out of the pages of his friend John Buchan, was killed in the Great War. The war also claimed Ermyngarde's brother-in-law Henry Elliott; she had married Fred Elliott in 1908, when Donovan the butler had mounted the skeleton of a stag's head on the wedding cake to make the de la Poer crest. Another victim of the war in the family circle was Johnnie Gough, who died of wounds early in 1915 having become a brigadier-general and chief of staff to Sir Douglas Haig. His brother Hubert, who had been in the news before the war broke out as leader of the so-called 'Curragh Mutiny', had been promoted to the rank of major-general on the field of battle; he was to rise to being General Sir Hubert Gough, commander of the Fifth Army.

Rivallon and young Edmond, who served in the Army and Navy respectively, survived the war, Arnold being unable to fight owing to ill-health. For a year after war was declared, life at Gurteen went on much the same as ever. Mary worked for the local St John's Ambulance. A French lady came to call in December 1914 and told of how her relations were shot by the Germans in the streets of Dinard; a Belgian baron and baroness now living in Cahir came to luncheon in May 1915. Edmond and Mary went to Clonmel in the motor – they now had a motor of their own – and visited some other Belgian refugees who were living there; Edmond planned to send them firewood.

Edmond died in August 1915 during a visit to England. In 1919 Rivallon and Patricia and their six children – who ranged in age from eleven to five months – came to live at Gurteen, having first overhauled the drains, which were giving trouble, put in extra bathrooms and carried out other improvements. Mary, decorated with an OBE for her work for St John's Ambulance during the war, had retired to Glen Poer, another house belonging to the family a short distance away.

Having taken up residence, Rivallon and Patricia lost no time in giving a dinner and a dance for the employees to celebrate the ending of the war. The dance was in the coach-house, with tables for sitting out in the stable yard, for it was July; the stable yard was decorated with flowers from the conservatory. Rivallon and Patricia opened the dance by partnering Mr and Mrs Ellis, the steward and his wife, in a quadrille. At the dinner beforehand, having said a few words, Rivallon proposed the health of the King, which everybody drank even though the Troubles were beginning. Rivallon would have felt bound to propose the loyal toast, for he was the

The house from the garden.

Lieutenant for County Waterford as his father had been before him.

Gurteen was not much affected by the Anglo-Irish conflict. Rivallon was able to devote himself to farming, to improving the water garden and making a rose garden. However, in the Civil War, which followed the setting-up of the Free State in 1922, the peace of the de la Poers' existence was disturbed. Men calling themselves the IRA demanded a levy of £100, and when Rivallon told them he did not have it to give them, drove away fourteen of his cattle. A party of men came in search of arms; seventeen Republicans turned up one night at eleven; they slept in the servants' hall and had breakfast, tea and dinner the next day. Another lot came three weeks later; by Christmas 1922 Rivallon reckoned that he and Patricia had put up over a hundred Republicans for the night, not counting those who just came for food. On Christmas Day they were not even able to go to Mass, the bridge over the Suir being broken and the river too swollen to be safely crossed in a boat. However, they managed to make the day 'as cheery as possible for the children, and they enjoyed themselves'. Just before Christmas the children's old governess braved the Republicans and came over from England to stay at Gurteen in order to take back some things she had left here.

One night in the following April there was a fearful hammering on the hall door. 'This is the end,' Rivallon thought to himself. 'The IRA have come to burn the house.'[8] But this time the nocturnal visitors were Free State soldiers, forty-eight of them; they spent the night, as the Republicans had done, in the servants' hall, and next day they moved into the stables, where they were to remain for some months. By now, the Civil War was virtually over.

In 1922, at the beginning of the Civil War, Rivallon had gone to London to attend the Committee of Privileges of the House of Lords which was considering his claim to the sixteenth-century barony of Le Power and Coroghmore. This peerage had been dormant ever since the senior branch of the family, from which Lord Waterford was descended in the female line, became extinct in the male line at the beginning of the eighteenth century; Rivallon claimed it as the senior heir-male. The committee decided that he had proved his claim but for the outlawry of a Jacobite ancestor, which would need to be reversed by Act of Parliament. Unfortunately, the British Government considered that it would be inappropriate for it to reverse the outlawry now that Ireland was independent; and so there the matter rested. In the hope of becoming an Irish peer Rivallon did not use the papal title of count which he had inherited from his father.

After the Civil War ended, life at Gurteen went back to normal. Some of their neighbours had left as a result of the Troubles, but quite a number remained, notably Obby Beauclerk, who had married the widowed Marchioness of Waterford; so that he and she and the young Beresfords, her children by her first marriage, came often to Gurteen on their way to and fro between Curraghmore and Newtown Anner.

Once Obby turned up just as Rivallon and Patricia were setting out for Waterford, so he was left to have lunch on his own. On another occasion his wife came bringing some American friends, Mr and Mrs Tree from Virginia.

The officers from the barracks now belonged to the past and there were no more big tennis and croquet parties, though the two tennis courts and the croquet lawn at Gurteen were kept in good order and frequently used. Rivallon continued with his improvements to the gardens and grounds and he also made the house a little more up to date. In 1924 he put in what was known as the 'one pipe' central heating system, which made the big hall and the gallery pleasantly warm. 'The mornings now are quite nice to get up in,' he observed, after a frosty night in April. In order to get the hot air from the hall into the former billiard room, now the smoking-room, he made a tunnel of chairs covered with old sheets; he was pleased with the result and thought of getting a collapsible canvas pipe made, but does not seem to have done anything more about it.[9]

While Gurteen was up to date by the standards of Irish country houses in the 1920s and reasonably well maintained, it was not entirely proof against the rigours of the Irish weather. One day in January 1925 it rained so hard and blew such a gale that Patricia abandoned the idea of taking the younger children to a Christmas tree at their Perry cousins near Clonmel. At seven that evening leaks started all over the house. The rain came pouring into the upper tower room; it came down into the lower tower room and then into Patricia's bedroom. Then down it came into the large drawing-room and into the smoking-room. Rivallon had to move the smoking-room carpet and tables. At the same time the rain came into the library through the room above it. Somebody ventured out on to the roof and found that the gutters were choked with dead leaves, which was the cause of the trouble. In the dark and the wind, they tried with great difficulty to clear them, succeeding in doing so by about 8.30. The gutters should, of course, have been cleared of dead leaves in the previous autumn.

The maintenance of the house was likewise at fault with regard to the chapel. In 1926 it was found that damp had been coming in for some time and that much of the woodwork was rotten; the window above the altar needed renewing. While the work of restoration was going on, the local parish priest, who came regularly to say Mass in the chapel on a weekday, had to say Mass in the schoolroom.

Although there had been a wireless at Gurteen since 1925, there was still no electric light; in December 1926 they gratefully accepted the gift of two Aladdin lamps from the Beauclerks who no longer had any use for them having put in electricity at Newtown Anner. The chandelier in the hall still had candles in it, though these were only lit on special occasions. Rivallon hoped to have them lit for the dance that he and Patricia gave in January 1929, but found that, owing to a draught, they guttered. So he had some smaller chandeliers made which were satisfactory. Among other preparations for the dance, a porch covered with tarpaulins was put up over the hall door, while their seventeen-year-old elder son Edmond cut ice from the frozen pond for the hock and the claret cup. A band from Kilkenny arrived on time so that by 9.30 the dance was in full swing. As well as neighbours such as the Beauclerks and the Bagwells of Marlfield, there were guests from further afield such as the Ponsonbys of Kilcooley Abbey. In all, about ninety people came; 'both the hall and library were comfortably full of dancers', Rivallon recorded with satisfaction.[10]

Three days after the dance, young Edmond had a narrow escape when he collided with a bus as he turned into the main road on his bicycle. His head was badly cut and he had to have stitches; fortunately he suffered no worse injury. They were having a party for the Waterford hunt ball that evening; Patricia went off to the dance but Rivallon stayed behind with Edmond who was nursed by the parlourmaid and another woman. When their nineteen-year-old daughter Patricia, known as 'Tish', returned from the dance, instead of going to bed she went and sat with Edmond; she stayed with him until noon when the doctor came.

Tish's elder sister Fanny was the first of the de la Poer children to marry; she married a sailor who was a neighbour, Lieutenant-Commander Geoffrey Mandeville of Anner Castle. The wedding took place in the local church in August 1933; the reception was at Gurteen, Geoffrey and Fanny receiving the guests, 160 in number, in the large drawing-room. Their first child – Rivallon's and Patricia's first grandchild – was born at Gurteen a year later. Geoffrey was away when the happy event occurred; Tish and her younger sister Val had to go into Clonmel to telephone the good news to him, for they did not yet have a telephone at Gurteen. Fanny's next child was born in 1936, but by that time her mother Patricia was dead, a victim of pneumonia which she contracted early that year; had it been a couple of years later she would probably have survived, for there would then have been antibiotics.

Rivallon put up a stained-glass window of the Immaculate Conception in the chapel in Patricia's memory; it was there just in time for the anniversary of her death, when a priest came to say Mass. 'The window looks lovely,' Rivallon wrote, 'and whenever I visit the chapel the memory of my dear one will be brought back to me forever fresh.'[11] On the evening before the stained-glass window was put up, Gurteen had electric light for the first time; the house had just been wired and the diesel engine working the generator had been started.

On the last night of 1937 there was a hunt ball to which everybody went except for Rivallon, who, for the first time in his life, saw in the New Year by himself. He thought sadly of Patricia and took comfort in the knowledge that she at any rate was happy. On the second day of the New Year, things were more cheerful; he gave a tea for fifty people from round about, there was a Christmas tree and they played games. After dinner the house party played charades. His youngest daughter Denise and

The hall at Gurteen, showing the suits of armour which Denise and Rosemary de la Poer managed to get into during a house party early in 1938.

his daughter-in-law Rosemary – his son Edmond's bride – managed to get into two of the suits of armour in the hall. 'They looked very wild standing on the stands and moving their heads and arms.'

The following Christmas, Rivallon once again gave a dance. In order that the hall, where the dancing took place, should not be used as a passageway, the guests were made to enter through the side door, which meant that they had to pass through the chapel. Mary de la Poer, Rivallon's mother, who was now about eighty, came to the dance and stayed until 11.30. Rivallon took the young Marchioness of Waterford, the widowed daughter-in-law of Obby's wife, into supper. At the end of the dance they played the Irish national anthem, 'The Soldiers' Song', followed by 'God Save the King'.

The dance ended at 3.30 in the morning of New Year's Eve. That evening, Rivallon was not on his own; there were nine people staying and they did not go to any hunt ball. But being tired after the previous evening's dance, they all went to bed before midnight. 'I finish my writing for 1938,' Rivallon recorded in his diary. 'A year which has seen war in Spain and China and very nearly a world-wide one. Let us hope that 1939 will not make this "nearly" into a reality.'[12] He was spared the reality, for he died suddenly in March 1939. Gurteen was inherited by his son Edmond, who sold the house some thirty years later, keeping the use of the service wing into which he and his wife Rosemary moved. The estate is still owned by the family.

# Chapter 15

# Kilfane

## COUNTY KILKENNY

JOHN POWER, founder of the Kilkenny Hunt and one of the great hunting men of early nineteenth-century Ireland, lived at Kilfane, a Georgian house in County Kilkenny with a ruined medieval church containing the effigy of a knight known as 'Long Cantwell' at the edge of its demesne. It was in fact his wife's family home; she was Harriette Bushe, a kinswoman of the 'Incorruptible' Chief Justice Charles Kendal Bushe who lived nearby at Kilmurry. The house had a centre of three storeys with a Doric porch and single-storey wings. The principal rooms extended along the front, on either side of a pillared hall; they included a large library with a pillared alcove and a dining-room which, being in one of the wings, had a higher ceiling than the rooms in the centre of the house. In the library hung a life-sized portrait of Napoleon as King of Rome; John Power may have admired Napoleon being a strong Whig. Once, when he was out hunting, hounds ran up Tory Hill in the south of the county; the horses were dead beat so he dismounted and, leading his horse up the hill, exclaimed, 'I wish every Tory was rolled out flat!'[1]

One evening after hunting, John Power is said to have brought a stranger home to Kilfane who turned out to be the Devil; the story is told, with variations, about other country houses, notably Castletown in County Kildare. According to the Kilfane version, Power played cards with his mysterious guest, who kept winning; and, stooping to pick up a card, he noticed that he had cloven hooves instead of feet. As at Castletown, the Protestant parson and the Catholic priest were both summoned and although the Powers were Protestants, it was the Catholic priest who was successful – to be rewarded by Power with the gift of a chandelier. The Devil went out through the skylight over the back stairs, which for ever afterwards tended to give trouble, particularly in the hunting season.

John Power's brother Richard, who had a house in Dublin, spent a great deal of time at Kilfane. He was a good rider and went out with the hunt when he was here; but he was not a particularly keen foxhunter. His ruling passion was acting; he ran a private theatre in Kilkenny. When he was at Kilfane, he rehearsed his plays in the library, using the pillared alcove as a stage.

Kilfane in those days was renowned for its hospitality; John and Harriette Power

Kilfane.

were a charming host and hostess. Apart from the Prince of Darkness, their most distinguished guest was perhaps the Viceroy, the Earl of Mulgrave – soon to made Marquess of Normanby – who came to say in 1836. After he left, he offered Power a baronetcy; as a staunch Whig, Power was at first inclined to refuse the honour, even though it came from a Whig government. His friends, however, persuaded him to accept it.

An earlier guest at Kilfane was the Countess of Desart, who lived at Desart Court on the other side of Kilkenny; she asked the Powers' seven-year-old daughter what her name was and the child answered 'Fanny Pug', explaining that she was called this because of the shape of her nose. Fanny was by far the youngest of the Power children – her mother used to call her 'The Agreeable Surprise'; her eldest brother John was more than twenty years her senior. One of her earliest memories was the death of her uncle Richard; she saw him being put into his coffin. This harrowing experience did not cast any undue gloom over her childhood and youth at Kilfane, which she remembers as having been 'happy as the day was long'. She was 'very wild' and hated her lessons; she had governesses and masters to teach her, but her 'grand object' was to do as little work as possible.[2]

'I had many companions of my own age and with them made expeditions into the mountains, where we had picnics,' Fanny recalls. 'And if my father gave us a couple of bottles of cider our picnic was complete.' They would go rabbit coursing; Fanny's brother John kept greyhounds which they appropriated for this purpose. This made him very angry, for the greyhounds were meant for coursing matches; he retaliated in a rather cruel way by having Fanny's little dog, which she had used for putting up the rabbits, killed. She had been devoted to the dog and never really forgave her brother; from then on they were 'at constant war'.[3]

Though she seems to have been something of a tomboy, Fanny tells us that she was 'a very delicate child' and often ill. She was ill when her parents left her at Kilfane with her nurse, old Kitty Butler, while they went off to Cheltenham. Kitty attributed her illness to a surfeit of raisins, but Fanny told her parents when they returned that the cook had made her ill by giving her meat that was burnt. 'Now that Mamma was come back she would be afraid to do so.'

Fanny maintains that she was simple in her tastes and 'never cared much for fun'. When she was nearly seventeen she went to her first ball, which was in Waterford. 'I thought it most delightful but still was always glad to return home.'[4]

In 1840, just after Fanny had celebrated her twenty-first birthday, an eligible young man came to stay at Kilfane. His name was the same as that of her father and her brother, namely John Power, but he came from a different branch of the great Norman-Irish family of Power or Poer; in fact he was the head of what was now the senior branch. He had a fine estate in County Waterford and was a Member of Parliament. One evening during his visit he came into the drawing-room rather suddenly and found Fanny and some of her girlfriends playing cards. As he entered they seemed confused and he heard a suppressed titter. He enquired as to what stakes they were playing for and they refused to tell him. When the game was over he heard that the stake for which they had played was himself and that Fanny was the winner. He took the hint, obtained her father's consent and they were married soon afterwards.

As the bride was a Protestant and the bridegroom a Catholic, they had two ceremonies. They had a Protestant ceremony in the little parish church in the grounds of Kilfane, not far from the ruined medieval church, conducted by Fanny's brother Ambrose, who was Archdeacon of Lismore. They afterwards had a Catholic ceremony in the library conducted by Dr Kinsella, the Catholic Bishop of Ossory. Fanny had eight bridesmaids; among them there must have been some of the losers in the game of cards. About a hundred people were entertained to 'a grand breakfast'; and after the cake was cut, each guest was presented with a pair of gloves.

The moment came when Fanny was handed into the carriage by her father. 'I felt that on leaving my beloved home I left happiness and affection behind,' she afterwards wrote, though she was certain that her 'dear Johnny' was devoted to her and that 'a kinder or more affectionate husband never lived'. The carriage in which she and Johnny set off on the five-hour drive to Gurteen, their future home, had four horses and postillions. It was much grander than the Kilfane carriages: her father used to say that 'the carriage did not make the gentleman'. In the dicky at the back sat Johnny's servant Tommy Power and Fanny's maid Kitty Murphy, whom her mother used to call the 'Mountain Nymph' because she came from the mountains near Kilfane. As well as being homesick, Fanny did not feel very comfortable in the closed carriage, 'having indulged rather freely in plum cake'.[5]

A local bard sung of Fanny's marriage:

In praise of a lady of honour
Though her perfections I cannot explain
The matchless beauty and virtuous
The lovely Miss Power of Kilfane.

The widows and orphans will miss her
To them she was always a friend;
To the poor and the needy all round her
Her charity flew without end.

Long live this young couple together
To enjoy their family's name.
May all blessings from Heaven attend them
When they parted the green shades of Kilfane.[6]

Alas, the young couple were destined not to live very long together. Faced with financial troubles in 1851, Johnny shot himself. Fanny was at Kilfane, staying with her brother and sister-in-law, when she heard the tragic news.

Fanny's brother John, whose wife was also called Fanny (which must have been confusing), had succeeded their father as the second Baronet in 1844. He continued the tradition of hospitality at Kilfane, giving the house more bedrooms by adding an extra storey to the back of the wings. When there was a race meeting in the locality in 1850, everybody was invited back to Kilfane for dinner and for a 'glorious dance' which went on until four in the morning.

During the 1860s, Kilfane was usually full of young people. The Powers had four sons and a daughter at home, as well as an adopted daughter, and they invited large parties of young people for their benefit. A young man who was invited often was Hamilton Cuffe, afterwards the fifth Earl of Desart; he remembers Kilfane in those days as 'an enchanting pandemonium' and Sir John Power as 'a man of peculiar charm, a very typical Irishman and the most delightful and haphazard of hosts'. When the young men arrived to stay, which was usually in the evening, they were taken to the part of the house where the bachelors' rooms were and met by a 'quaint old servant' who would open all the doors in the passage and say, 'Take your choice.' He flung all their luggage into a heap and each young man seized what belonged to him and tried to get possession of the best room.

Having assembled for dinner, they would have to wait a long time before Sir John appeared. He would enter the room and say to his wife: 'Lady Power, me dear, have you seen the key of the cellar anywhere?' Everybody searched behind the cushions, under the sofas and 'about the room generally'; the key would eventually be found in Sir John's pocket. He would then disappear to the cellar and after a further delay they went into dinner at last. From one end of the table Sir John would announce to his wife, who was at the other end, 'Me dear, I'm sorry to say the cook's not very well.' In fact the cook was drunk, which inevitably happened when there was a party, so that 'the dinner was rather a matter of accident than the pursuance of any regular order'. After dinner there would be dancing in the drawing-room and then the young men and boys got together and 'sang and bear-fought till about three o'clock in the morning'.[7]

In the daytime when the weather was good the young people went off for picnics in a one-horse vehicle which they called a 'shandrydan'; the seats in it were not fixed so that going uphill they frequently slid off into the road, together with their occu-pants. Some of the young men once borrowed a donkey-cart and started out with one donkey and plenty of rope. They borrowed donkeys from every farm they passed and tied them to the cart, which was eventually pulled by about sixteen donkeys.[8]

The hard-drinking cook was succeeded by a chef from England whose culinary skills were such that some of the local women and girls who worked under him in the Kilfane kitchens became notable cooks themselves. The two sisters Bridget and Kathleen Holland went on from Kilfane to cook in London and in Paris, one of them winning a competition in Paris for skinning and cooking a rabbit. Two other sisters made use of the training acquired at Kilfane to run successful boarding houses in New York. Cooks trained at Kilfane were, like the Miss Holland who went to Paris, particularly good at preparing poultry and game; which figured so largely on

The two sisters Bridget and Kathleen Holland,
who having worked in the Kilfane kitchens
went on to cook in London and Paris.

Sir John Power, the 4th baronet,
who was mortally wounded in the
South African War.

the menu here that two women were constantly employed plucking birds for the table.

To join the indoor or outdoor staff at Kilfane was the ambition of many a boy and girl living round about in the later years of the nineteenth century. The staff was mostly recruited from among the tenantry, or from families already employed in the Big House or on the estate. The work was hard but it offered security and – in the case of those fortunate enough to have been trained by the chef – good opportunities. The tenants and employees also had a social life of their own. There was the tenants' ball, the harvest home supper, the children's sports. At Christmas, the children had a party in the hall and they were given toys and crackers, just as the grownups were given Christmas hampers. The Powers provided medical care as well as entertainment and Christmas cheer, sponsoring beds in Dublin hospitals for the use of their dependants.

The second Sir John Power died in 1873 and his son Sir Richard died at a comparatively early age in 1892. Sir Richard's widow, Florence Lady Power, was living at Kilfane when Edmond, Count de la Poer and his wife Mary came to stay in 1897. Edmond was the eldest son of Fanny Power of Kilfane and of the ill-fated Johnny Power of Gurteen; he had reverted to the original Norman rendering of his name and been made a papal count. While he and his wife were here, there was a meet of the hounds and the Marchioness of Ormonde came over to luncheon from Kilkenny Castle with her two beautiful daughters, Lady Beatrice and Lady Constance Butler; Lady Constance had modern ideas and was interested in medi cine. Another day Mary de la Poer drove with Lady Power to see the ruins of the medieval Jerpoint Abbey. Edmond de la Poer went with them on his bicycle; he also went bicycling with Lady Power's unmarried daughter May.

Also at Kilfane when the de la Poers were here was Lady Power's elder son Jack, now the fourth Baronet, who like May was unmarried. In the summer of 1899, Jack and his brother Derrick went with their mother to watch the great military manoeu vres that were being held on the borders of County Kilkenny and Queen's County. Lady Power introduced her sons to Lord Roberts, telling him that they were both just about to go into the Army. He was pleased to hear this but said, 'I'm afraid they will not see much fighting unless they go out to India.'[9] Two months later the South African War broke out. Both Jack and Derrick went to the war; Jack was mortally wounded and Derrick died in South Africa of fever.

Jack and Derrick were succeeded at Kilfane by their sister May, the baronetcy going to an uncle. Miss May Power, who never married, lived alone at Kilfane after her mother and her younger sister Vera had moved into Kilfane Cottage, a smaller

Derrick Power, who succeeded his brother
Jack as the 5th baronet, but died soon afterwards
in South Africa of fever.

Miss May Power at the dedication ceremony in 1929 of the handball court which she had built at Kilfane for the local people.

house nearby. For a number of years things went on the same as ever. The children's sports were held each summer; the children and their mothers were given tea on the lawn while Miss Power sat at a table loaded with prizes. In 1929 she built a hand-ball court for the local people near the little Protestant church and a ceremony was held for its dedication.

Then things became more difficult; the house and grounds ceased to be well maintained, the number of servants and men on the place steadily diminished. Miss Power took on a man named Mick and gave him one of the lodges on the under-standing that he would get married. He failed to do so and one day she reproached him for this, speaking to him through a manhole, for he happened to be working in a drain. 'Miss Power,' he said, looking up at her, 'I'll get married when you do.'

She was looked after by her old butler, O'Keefe, who had been with her for many years. Her sister Vera, who had married, still lived at Kilfane Cottage, but she was not on good terms with her. She became increasingly eccentric, keeping a shotgun on the table in the hall which she fired into the air to scare away trespassers. When Count de la Poer, grandson of Edmond de la Poer, who went bicycling with her in 1897, called with his wife and reminded her that they were cousins she said, 'I'll have to think about that!' One day in 1954 she appeared unexpectedly at Kilmurry, the neighbouring country house, and said to Mrs Archer Houblon who lived there: 'Doreen, do you know what O'Keefe has done to me? He's died, that's what he's done, and he knew how much I needed him!'[10] By now she was nearly eighty and Kilfane was very run-down; soon afterwards she abandoned the house and went to spend her remaining years in a house in the yard.

# Chapter 16

# Lismore Castle
## COUNTY WATERFORD

LISMORE CASTLE is familiar to everyone who has crossed the bridge over the Blackwater to the north of the town of Lismore, its fawn-grey towers rising high from a cliff covered with trees that seem to float on the surface of the river. Now predominantly of the seventeenth and nineteenth centuries, it incorporates some of the towers of the medieval castle of the Bishops of Lismore which itself took the place of a castle built by King John. Earlier still there was a famous monastery here, founded by St Carthagh, and a university to which students came from all over western Christendom. Lismore is still the see of a bishop; the spire of its cathedral rises from behind the wood on the far side of the bridge to the castle.

The first Protestant bishop, the notorious Myler McGrath, granted the castle and its lands to Sir Walter Raleigh, who sold it to Richard Boyle, one of the most remarkable of the Elizabethan adventurers. Having come to Ireland from England as a young man with only £27 3s, a diamond ring and bracelet and his clothes, he ended as Earl of Cork and one of the richest and most powerful noblemen in the kingdom; three of his four younger sons were also given peerages. He was a land speculator on a grand scale; he built towns, developed industries, introduced settlers.

From about 1610 onwards, Boyle – who became Earl of Cork in 1620 – rebuilt Lismore Castle, which was in a state of ruin when he acquired it. He surrounded the castle courtyard with gabled ranges joining the old corner towers, and on the side farthest from the river he built a gatehouse tower, incorporating an old Celtic-Romanesque arch which must have survived from Lismore's monastic days; above it he put his motto 'God's Providence is my Inheritance', which was his way of proclaiming that he was self-made.

His principal living-rooms were on the side of the castle above the Blackwater; the dining-chamber projected outwards to the very edge of the precipice, with a 'compass window' or oriel from which there was a sheer drop to the river far below. Also on this side of the castle was a chapel, probably dating from the Bishop's time. Lord Cork, as he now was, enriched it with panelling, stained glass and a pulpit. In 1627 his youngest son Robert Boyle, who was to become famous as the father of modern chemistry, was baptized there.

Fishermen below Lismore Castle in about 1890.

Lismore Castle. The entrance to the courtyard. Over the gateway are the arms of the Great Earl of Cork with his motto 'God's Providence is my Inheritance'.

The principal rooms of the castle in the time of the 'Great Earl' were richly furnished by the standards of seventeenth-century Ireland. The dining-chamber was hung with tapestry and had a Turkish carpet; there were chairs and stools of crimson velvet fringed with silver, gilt bedsteads with quilts of Indian embroidery. There was a profusion of silver plate; Lady Cork is recorded as having cut her knee badly on a silver dish when she fell getting down from her gilded bed one morning – perhaps it was a silver chamber pot.

Lady Cork had 'gentlewomen' in attendance on her, some of whom were relations or connections by marriage like Letitia Hopwood who, when she came over from England to enter the Lismore household, brought twelve cheeses from Warrington which made her particularly welcome. Lord Cork arranged marriages for some of the young women in his household; when Mary Evesham, another of his wife's attendants, married John Ward of Dublin, the ceremony took place in the castle nursery and was performed by Lord Cork's chaplain, Robert Naylor, who was also his cousin. During the ceremony, the Great Earl presented the bride with £100 in gold – the equivalent of several thousand pounds today – which she handed over to her husband.

The humbler members of the household included old Davy Gibbons, a footman or messenger who was rewarded for thirty years' service by the lease of lands in Waterford rent free; and William Chettle, who was given £20 and a bond for £195 as well as presents of clothes. One New Year's Day, Lord Cork gave him one his own cloaks which he had never worn, 'of London Russet lined throughout with black velvet'. The Lismore servants tended to wear the Great Earl's cast-offs instead of livery.

Although the Great Earl was leader of the Protestant English settler faction in Munster, he had Irish servants as well as English – one of them gave trouble by speaking 'treasonable words'. In the same way his guests at Lismore included old Irish and Norman-Irish Catholics such as the MacCarthys, the Keatings and Lord Roche, as well as members of the leading Protestant settler families such as the Bechers, the Hydes and the Daunts. There were also frequent visitors from England, for whom a trip to Lismore would have been rather like a journey to Kenya early this century. Sir Henry Lee of Ditchley, immortalized in Scott's *Woodstock*, came to see after some investments; various young bloods came, hoping to marry Munster heiresses. The English visitors included many relations. There were poor relations like the grocer Roger Boyle, whom Lord Cork settled on a farm in the Galtee Mountains, which was not a success as he knew nothing about farming. There were fashionable relations such as the Great Earl's son-in-law George, Lord Goring, the future Royalist general, who having stayed six or seven weeks at Lismore disappeared without saying goodbye, leaving his wife and servants behind him but taking the 'choice grey gelding' that Lord Cork had given him.[1]

The inhabitants of the castle also included Lord Cork's wolfhounds, which he bred; he sent one of them to Charles I's sister Elizabeth, the Winter Queen. When his guests were not out hunting, they played cards or dice, or were entertained by wandering theatrical companies. On one occasion the children put on a masque, for which they were given five pounds.

Food for the castle came mostly from Lord Cork's own farms and gardens and from the deer park which he had enclosed. Smoked fish and barrelled cockles came from his fisheries at Ardmore and Crookhaven; freshwater fish from his fishponds. Like the Ascendancy of a later age, he did much of his shopping in London; it was done for him by an amiable friend, Sir John Leeke, who travelled backwards and forwards between a castle near Lismore and Claydon in Buckinghamshire, the seat of his wife's cousins, the Verneys.

The Irish Rebellion of 1641 and the wars that followed put an end to the Great Earl's pleasant life at Lismore. The silver plate had to be melted down to pay for soldiers; the castle was strengthened with iron gratings and chains made at Lord Cork's ironworks. In 1642 the Confederates under General Purcell besieged the castle; but they were repulsed after eight days, leaving 201 dead whereas only one of the castle's defenders was killed. Lord Cork, who was away at the time, rewarded Captain Brodrip, the commander of the garrison, with five pounds and another of his own cloaks. The castle was again attacked by the Confederates in 1645, two years after the Great Earl's death; this time it was captured and sacked. The attackers were commanded by the Earl of Castlehaven, a guest of the Great Earl in happier days, who during the siege rode off to Kilkenny, declaring that he was 'not willing to be present at the destruction of a house where I formerly had received many civilities'.[2]

Lord Castlehaven exaggerated when he wrote of the 'destruction' of the castle, though it was left in a ruinous state. The Great Earl's eldest son and successor, who became Earl of Burlington in the English peerage, made it habitable again some time before 1689 when James II came to Lismore on his way from Cork to Dublin. James dined and spent a night at the castle; having approached from the south, he had no idea that it was on such a height until he looked out of the window of the dining-chamber after dinner, when he almost fainted at the sight of the great drop to the river.

The Great Earl's eldest son acquired large estates in England through his marriage to the heiress of the Cliffords, Earls of Cumberland; and his immediate successors took little interest in Lismore. In the middle of the eighteenth century, the castle was once again in a state of ruin, probably dismantled to save the cost of maintenance. It continued to be neglected after it had passed to the Dukes of Devonshire through the marriage of the only daughter of the fourth Earl of Cork — better known as the amateur architect and patron of the arts Lord Burlington — to the fourth Duke of Devonshire in 1748. The fifth Duke and his Duchess, the beautiful

Lady Georgiana Spencer, hardly seem to have been aware of their Irish castle; but their son fell in love with it and began restoring it after he succeeded as the sixth Duke in 1811, employing an architect named William Atkinson.

Some rooms in the north range were habitable by September 1812 when the young Duke came to stay, bringing his aunt, the Countess of Bessborough, sister of Georgiana Duchess, her daughter Lady Caroline Lamb and her son-in-law William Lamb, the future Prime Minister Lord Melbourne. It was a rather fraught visit, for Caroline had been brought to Ireland by her husband and her mother in the hope of curing her infatuation for Byron; she was already an advanced neurotic and was determined to be as tiresome as she could to her cousin 'Hart', as the Duke was known to his family, having been Marquess of Hartington in his father's life-time. 'Caroline would entertain you with her account of Lismore, which makes Hart furious,' Lady Bessborough wrote to a relation in England. 'She says that when she saw this ruined castle at a distance, she had prepared in her mind for every sort of difficulty and adventure – ghosts, knights in armour – that she expected to wind through extensive, though deserted, parks up to the portcullis on the outside and wander about vast apartments full of tattered furniture and gloom within. Instead of which . . . Hart handed her into, not a Gothic hall, but two small dapper par-lours neatly furnished, in the newest Inn fashion, much like a Cit's villa at Highgate.'

Caroline also insisted that the castle was very damp and argued incessantly with Hart on this point. One night, as her mother reported, 'she suddenly opened the door very wide, saying "pray walk in, Sir. I have no doubt that you are the rightful possessor, and my cousin only an interloper, usurping your usual habitation". For a long time nothing came, when at last with great solemnity and many pauses in hopped a *frog*, Caroline following with two candles to treat the master of the Castle with proper respect, she said.' Like so many neurotics, Caroline, while driving her family to distraction with bouts of melancholy or hysteria, was charming to strangers. When Hart gave a party, she was the life and soul, dancing Irish jigs and flirting with the local men.[3]

Hart, who never married and is consequently remembered as the Bachelor Duke, a scholar, connoisseur and horticulturalist, paid regular visits to Lismore for the next ten years, entertaining many of the neighbours to dinners and balls. His restoration of the castle continued during these years. The principal rooms, about which Caroline Lamb was so unkind, were made mildly Gothic; the old dining-chamber became the drawing-room, keeping its oriel window with the spectacular view.

It was during this period that Lismore appeared in fiction, as 'Dunore' in Lady Morgan's novel *Florence McCarthy*, published in 1816.

The splendid cavalcade at last arrived before the turreted gates of the castle of

Dunore; and as the carriages rolled over the pavement of the gloomy court, and the tenants of the old rookery in the rear of the castle screamed their disapproba, tion of the unusual intrusion, Lady Dunore's susceptible spirits again sank from their high-wound pitch.

'God send us safe out of this wild country!' said her ladyship, with a deep sigh.

'Amen' said young Crawley, most emphatically.

'Amen,' repeated Lord Frederick, most theatrically; adding

> 'The raven himself is hoarse
> That croaks the fatal entrance of Duncan
> Under my battlements.'

'Good heavens!' exclaimed Lady Dunore. 'How can you, Lord Frederick? . . .'

The carriages stopped before the last gate, and the lights flashed full upon — 'God's providence is my inheritance'.

The fact that the Great Earl of Cork's motto appears above the gateway of the fictional Dunore, just as it does at Lismore, leaves one in little doubt as to the castle's identity. But the whole picture suggests Lismore as it was before it was fully restored; it is certainly what Caroline Lamb had imagined it would be like. There is an echo of Caroline's visit to Lismore in more recent literature; the narrator in Anthony Powell's novel *The Valley of Bones* is stationed, during the Second World War, at 'Castlemallock', said to be modelled on Gosford Castle in County Armagh, and his wife tells him of a quotation from a letter from Byron to Caroline Lamb when she was in Ireland: 'The diversions of Castlemallock may exceed those of Lismore.'

When the Bachelor Duke left Lismore after his visit in 1822 he wrote: 'Goodbye, beautiful place and country.' Yet it was eighteen years before he came again. There must have been some special reason for this, for when he eventually did decide to come again in 1840, it was, as he admits in his diary, 'after great struggle'. On this visit he was accompanied by Joseph Paxton, his gardener, architect, factotum and friend, who fell in love with Lismore as the Duke himself had done and made many suggestions for improvements. But the Duke only came once or twice during the next ten years, and in 1844, when he was short of money, he actually thought of selling Lismore; but having come over to make arrangements for the sale, he was once again struck by the beauty of the place and determined to keep it.

From 1849 until his death in 1858 he came to Lismore almost every autumn and stayed a month or two; while Paxton, who became Sir Joseph in 1851 after design, ing the Crystal Palace, completed the restoration of the castle. The ruined chapel in the north range was reroofed in 1850 and became the Banqueting Hall or ballroom, with a baronial interior in glowing colours designed by Pugin. This was the castle's only grand room; the other rooms in the north range which the Bachelor Duke

The banqueting hall at Lismore Castle in about 1890. A gentleman about to go shooting reads a note handed to him on a salver by one of the footmen.

restored before 1822 were of more liveable proportions. Paxton enlarged the castle and gave it more battlements and towers; but the rooms in the south and west ranges were for use, rather than for show, while the east range was a self-contained house for the agent. The agent had lived in this part of the castle as far back as 1690; it now became quite a grand house in itself, as befitted the status of the Duke's agent in the county.

When the Bachelor Duke came to Lismore during the 1850s, he was greeted on his arrival with bonfires and triumphal arches, flags and fireworks. The Lismore Philharmonic Society played in his honour, which was not the only music he heard when he was here, for he brought his own band with him – as well as his own doctor, an army of servants and a houseful of guests. The dinners and balls he had given on his earlier visits were repeated on a grander scale; and as well as entertaining the surrounding gentry, he gave no less lavish dinners and balls for the townspeople of Lismore and for his tenants.

The most memorable of the Bachelor Duke's entertainments at Lismore was the ball that he gave for his niece the Duchess of Sutherland and her daughter Lady Constance Leveson-Gower, who came in November 1851 and stayed until the New Year. The music was provided by Messrs Richardson and Son's 'powerful and brilliant Rock, Bell and Steel Band', which sounds rather out of period. Charles

Coote, the Duke's pianist, accompanied by his son on the violin, played a galop that he had composed and dedicated to Lady Constance. The presence of the Duchess of Sutherland at the castle caused a sensation locally, for she was Mistress of the Robes to Queen Victoria; there were rumours that the Queen herself was coming to stay. These rumours proved to be unfounded, though the Queen's representative, in the form of the Duke's nephew Lord Carlisle, then Lord-Lieutenant of Ireland, stayed in 1855 and 1856. Another distinguished guest in 1856 was Lord Cardigan of the Light Brigade.

The Bachelor Duke became very much attached to Lismore. He liked the Irish because of their natural gaiety; he would walk about the streets of the town, greeting friends. Even when the castle chimneys were smoking and other domestic arrangements had broken down, he wrote: 'With the drawback of inhabiting a splendid *pigsty* I enjoy being here more than anywhere else.'

In the time of the Bachelor Duke's cousin and successor, the widower seventh Duke, life at Lismore was quieter. When the Duke's second son Lord Frederick Cavendish brought his bride, the former Lucy Lyttelton, here in April 1865, the only other people staying apart from the Duke were his daughter Lady Louisa Cavendish and his youngest son Lord Edward.

Instead of the Bachelor Duke's lavish entertainments, there were just a few neighbours to dinner, including the elderly Catholic parish priest who, as Lucy noticed with some distaste, 'spat on the carpet'. Lucy was not anti-Catholic; she and her sister-in-law Lady Louisa went to visit the convent in Lismore where she described the nuns as being 'very merry' and 'brisk'. And while the manners of the Catholic priest may not have pleased her, she thought the sermon that a local Protestant clergyman preached in Lismore Cathedral on her first night there was 'dreadful'. She herself was a devout High Anglican and spent some of her time at Lismore reading *Thoughts for Holy Week* with her husband.

Apart from devotions, entertaining the neighbours and visiting nuns, life at the castle when Lucy was here centred on the river. She and her sister-in-law and two gentlemen went boating; the gentlemen rowed upstream, the ladies down. And the salmon fishing for which the Blackwater is famous loomed as large then as it has done ever since. 'Lou and I fished or rather toddled up the river,' Lucy wrote soon after her arrival, 'throwing lines with no result, encouraged by a dear, enthusiastic Paddy and enjoying the delightful day.' When Lucy was here in 1868, her eldest brother-in-law, the Marquess of Hartington – the bearded Victorian statesman who was to dominate the Liberal Party for many years and nearly became Prime Minister – fared not much better. He hooked a fine fish but it got off after half an hour's playing. He took it philosophically, but his father the Duke who was with him 'came home very much aggravated' and kept exclaiming 'that scoundrel of a fish!'[4]

When Lord Hartington had become the eighth Duke, he and his German-born

King Edward VII plants a tree at Lismore in 1904. On the right is his host, the 8th Duke of Devonshire.

Duchess – known as the 'Double Duchess' as she had been the widow of the Duke of Manchester when her married her – came to Lismore for about three weeks each year and had many people to stay, including King Edward VII and Queen Alexandra, who came in 1904. The Duchess could be rather alarming; the Duke, although amiable, was no longer young and not a very tidy eater; he would tip his plate towards him when he wished to spoon up the juice and upset it all down his front. At dinner parties, a neighbour, Lady Clodagh Anson, who lived across the river from the castle, was usually put next to him; and she would start dabbing him with her napkin and scolding him in the same way as she scolded her children when they spilt things at table: 'Now, why don't you look what you're doing?' The Duke would take this very meekly, and seemed grateful for her assistance.

The eighth Duke was childless, but his nephew Victor Cavendish, who succeeded as ninth Duke in 1908, had a large family. The new Duke and Duchess spent three months of the year at Lismore, from January to April, arriving in a special train with children, governesses, nannies, ponies and dogs. For the children, those three months were always a joy, with more time being given to hunting than to lessons. On Sunday afternoon the Duke and Duchess, their children and their guests would go for a long walk through the woods, usually ending up at Ballysaggartmore, the home of the Ansons, who were related to the Duchess as well as being connected to her by marriage. As they approached the Ansons' boundary they would chant in unison, 'We are coming to tea.' Even in those days of servants, Lady Clodagh, on hearing the 'distant chant', had to start cutting up and buttering bread and opening pots of jam in order to be ready to feed them when they arrived.[5]

In January 1937, towards the end of Duke Victor's reign, a new agent came to Lismore; he was Humphrey Eley, son of a Suffolk landowner. Being young and single, he did not occupy the self-contained agent's quarters in the east range, but was given some rooms in the north-west corner of the castle, close to the kitchen, from which his meals were brought to him in his large living-room overlooking the river. 'The cooking is first-rate,' he reported to his parents. This was to be expected, for the kitchen did not just serve the Duke and Duchess on their periodic visits, but had to keep up a constant high standard for their younger son Lord Charles Cavendish and his American wife, the dancer and film star Adele Astaire, who now lived here most of the time. Adele was away when, a couple of weeks after Eley's arrival, a lady came to dinner with Lord Charles and drank so much that she passed out. Eley and the retiring agent, who had not yet left, were called in to assist; they eventually managed to get the lady into a car and Lord Charles drove her home. There was a rather similar crisis a few days later when three local worthies were invited back to the castle after a duck shoot; all three of them became so drunk that they had to stay the night.

Within a month of his arrival, Eley had to organize a farewell party for the retiring agent. The employees of the estate and such wives as had cared to come gathered in the Banqueting Hall and were given 'a tremendous feed and vast quantities of porter'. Lord Charles and Eley had thought it would be nice to have a piper playing; they then decided to get a pipe band from Fermoy, three pipers and three drums. This was to be a surprise, but Eley was as surprised as anybody when three cars drove into the courtyard and out got thirteen bandsmen, 'all in full rig', the Pipe-Major explaining that a band of six would not have fitted the occasion. They played in the Banqueting Hall and many of the assembled company danced jigs; then Paddy, the head gardener, 'delivered a long and impassioned speech'. Lord Charles proposed Eley's health, much to his horror, for this meant he had to reply. 'I rolled off a lot of stuff about "Good old Ireland",' he told his parents, 'which seemed to go down all right, anyway I hadn't the remotest idea what I said as I was far too frightened to remember anything.' Everybody then marched through the town, headed by the band, to watch a cinema show in the local hall. When the cinema was over, the guests departed; but the band returned to the castle and, having been given supper, started playing again, marching round and round the courtyard. The maids all came out and there was dancing until three in the morning, when the bandsmen, rather against their will, were bundled into their cars and sent home. One of the cars crashed a couple of miles from Lismore, but no one was badly hurt.[6]

Young Eley, surprisingly, does not appear to have fallen for the glamorous Adele Astaire, who returned about this time. While others remember her as having 'sparkled like a fairy'[7] in the rooms of the castle, he wrote rather ungallantly of her:

'Adele is still here and caused more trouble than all the seventy employees put together, which is saying a good deal. Her one ideal is to spend money and she is always demanding "tiled dairies" and "new lorries" or some such extravagance. It makes it very difficult for me as I am responsible for showing "a profit" at the end of the year. Cavendish, however, backs me up nobly and so far I have managed to defeat her fairly successfully, but at the same time, I don't feel that I am in her "good books"!' He was sufficiently in her good books for her to send for him one evening to play peggoty with her. Annoyed at being interrupted in his letter-writing, he was in no way flattered by the invitation as most young men would have been, but took a malign pleasure in winning sixpence off her, having 'defeated her soundly'.

In April the Duke came on a visit that kept everybody, as Eley put it, 'on the hop'. He attended Sunday service in the cathedral and, like his aunt Lucy, did not approve of the sermon; but whereas she had kept her disapproval to herself, he 'kept up a running commentary of "Rot, Rubbish, Nonsense, etc" and by the end had the poor Dean completely demoralised'. The Duke was now nearly seventy and very infirm, having not fully recovered from a stroke that he had suffered twelve years earlier; he reminded Eley of 'an overnourished Pekinese'. But though he could hardly walk, he insisted on reading the lessons and 'tottered to the lectern'.

One afternoon, Eley had to take him round the castle farms in a car; when they were crossing a field the car stuck in the mud and two horses had to be sent for to pull it out. However, the Duke 'took it with very good grace'. To add to Eley's troubles, Admiral the Earl of Cork and Orrery, the male heir of the Great Earl of Cork, was on a visit to Ireland and arrived to look round the castle. Word had somehow leaked out that he was coming and 'the whole place was paved with photographers'.

The next excitement was the advent of the telephone; it had been coming for the past eight months and trenches had been dug through the garden and across the courtyard for the wires, 'making a pretty good mess'. Eley was horrified when he saw the instruments being put in. 'They are of the type which were discarded in England before the War,' he wrote. 'They look as if they have been brought direct from the British Museum. Adele nearly had a fit when she saw them.' And while the castle was at last on the telephone, its inhabitants were unable to make calls after seven in the evening, when the local exchange closed down for the night.

Soon after the telephone was installed, Adele's dachshund produced eight puppies. She burst into tears when Eley told her he was going to have half of them drowned, eight being, in his opinion, far too many for a young dog to rear properly. However, he seems to have relented and all but one of the puppies were reprieved.

In July Eley had not only Adele to cope with, but also her mother, Mrs Astaire, who had a permanent suite of rooms in the castle and came to stay for the rest of the summer. When she arrived, Eley was up to his eyes with a church fête in the castle grounds, and he did not even have the moral support of Lord Charles, who had gone to Dublin to see one of his horses run. At the end of the month Adele left for England to make a new film, but her departure was followed by the arrival of the Duchess, of whom Eley had heard alarming reports. He found her 'a very charming and interesting person', though she clearly stood no nonsense. 'I showed her round everywhere,' he wrote, after she had left, and she put her nose into everything and was, I think, fairly satisfied. However, it had been a somewhat nerveracking few days and my staff showed amazing speed at disappearing whenever she was around!'

When the Duchess had gone, Eley was able to settle down to a quieter life and do a little fishing and shooting; at any rate until Adele returned from her filmmaking. And he had to 'dash off' at the end of August to interview a kitchen maid. In October he noticed that the leaves were beginning to turn; he looked forward to enjoying the autumn colours from his window. Every prospect pleased – and Adele and her mother were about to leave for Paris. 'I shall be deserted,' he told his parents, 'it will really be quite a welcome change.'[8]

Lord Charles Cavendish, who died in 1944, was the present Duke's uncle. Since 1947 the present Duke and Duchess of Devonshire have paid regular visits to Lismore, which now belongs to their son, the Marquess of Hartington. Their guests here have included distinguished members of their family such as the Duchess's eldest sister Nancy Mitford and the Duke's uncle by marriage Harold Macmillan, as well as his sisterinlaw Kathleen Marchioness of Hartington – a sister of President John F. Kennedy – and his aunt Adele's brother Fred Astaire. Nancy Mitford was here in 1960 for the whole of May, spending most of her time with her great friend Edward SackvilleWest – the original of Uncle Davey in her novels – who had a house on the other side of the mountain in County Tipperary. 'I'm stunned by the beauty, emptiness and *pure* prenewworld atmosphere of Ireland – can't imagine why you don't live here,' she wrote from Lismore to another great friend, Evelyn Waugh. 'Some v. nice neighbours, too. Marvellous butchers, one had forgotten what meat can taste like.'[9]

Harold Macmillan was brought here by his wife, who was Lady Dorothy Cavendish, the Duke's aunt. She had memories of her childhood visits to Lismore and loved coming back; he, too, always seemed content here, fishing in the daytime and joining with enthusiasm in the acting games that the Duke and Duchess and their guests used to play after dinner. In these games, Macmillan was always the star, no matter what part he took, whether it was bookmaker, toff, miner or Labour politician.

On one of his visits, when he was Prime Minister, he decided to walk all the way back to Lismore after fishing at Careysville, near Fermoy, where the Duke owned another fine stretch of the Blackwater. Growing rather tired and bored, as it seemed

Harold Macmillan walking with his host the present Duke of Devonshire while staying at Lismore when he was Prime Minister.

Lady Dorothy Macmillan with Miss Elizabeth Winn in the lower garden at Lismore.

further than he had bargained for, he stopped to talk to a donkey who was standing by the hedge. 'Ass,' he enquired portentously, 'how many miles to Lismore?' To his intense embarrassment a man poked his head up from behind the hedge, having heard the Prime Minister of Great Britain asking a serious question of a donkey.[10]

Another guest at Lismore was John Betjeman. He was here one day in the 1960s, wearing a velvet smoking-jacket and carpet slippers, when an elderly gentleman from County Cork came to lunch, bringing his dog', a fierce Jack Russell. After lunch the dog made a mess in the drawing-room. 'Not my dog, wrong bore,' said the County Cork gentleman, as though casting aspersions on the Devonshires' Labrador. A footman came to clean up the mess and the Jack Russell followed him back to the kitchen; soon afterwards the County Cork gentleman was sent for and requested to take his dog away, for it was attacking the cook.

The French are said to have an affinity with Ireland, and indeed, many friends of the Duke and Duchess from France have been regular visitors to Lismore. One April, the great couturier Hubert de Givenchy came to stay, accompanied by another eminent couturier, his friend Philippe Venet. During their visit the octogenarian Clodagh Anson, Lady Clodagh's daughter, came to lunch. She was put

Harold Macmillan, when he was Prime Minister, sitting between Miss Elizabeth Winn and the Duke of Rutland in the lower garden at Lismore.

next to Givenchy and charmed him as she charmed everyone she talked to, for she was wonderful company, though she had never heard of him until she met him that day. Having gathered what he did for a living she said to him: 'Now you're a dress-maker and you should be able to tell me if, this year, my cotton frocks should be taken up or let down.' She wished to know because she was going to be staying with her brother in Rome. Givenchy turned to her and said in his courtly way: 'Madame, I can't advise you about that but I should be very happy to make you some dresses.'

He and Venet accordingly went to Clodagh's house with tape measures and mea-sured her, the Duchess lending a hand. In due course, two large cardboard boxes arrived, containing seven different garments by Givenchy, with his compliments. Clodagh was touched and grateful. She no longer had to worry about what to wear in Rome, though she never realised that these clothes, which she had been given for nothing, were worth at least £20,000.[11]

# Chapter 17

# Lissadell

## COUNTY SLIGO

'THE light of evening, Lissadell, great windows open to the south.' So Yeats evoked the grey stone house, home of the Gore-Booth family, among its woods and glades, facing across the pale waters of Sligo Bay to the no less liquid blue of Knocknarea and the Ox Mountains, or eastwards to Ben Bulben. The present house was built in the early 1830s by Sir Robert Gore-Booth, a young baronet of artistic tastes who was descended from the Elizabethan soldier and settler Sir Paul Gore, ancestor of the Earls of Arran. Sir Robert's forebears had been established at Lissadell for several generations, living first in a castle and then in a house close to the shore; it was the rather damp situation of the latter which made him decide to build the present house.

As the architect of his new house, Sir Robert chose Francis Goodwin of London. For its style, he chose an austere form of Grecian, with very little exterior ornament except for a projecting *porte-cochère* on the entrance front, some very simple pilasters and a bow on the front overlooking Sligo Bay. That Sir Robert was influenced by the Neo-Classical idea of Thomas Hope is all the more apparent inside the house. The lofty hall with its square columns and double staircase of Kilkenny marble, the even more impressive gallery beyond, lit by a clerestory and with square pillars along one side and Ionic columns along the other, are typical of this particular taste. The monumental sequence of hall and gallery leads to the lighter and more intimate bow room, with its 'great windows open to the south'.

Sir Robert's father-in-law Thomas Goold, a judge who lived in Dublin, stayed here in 1833 before the house was finished. 'I spent three weeks at Lissadell and find myself (thank God) greatly benefitted by it,' he wrote to the Earl of Dunraven, whose son was to marry another of Goold's daughters. 'The air balmy to a degree and a more gay and joyous party could not be. Sir Robert's house is really beautiful, the demesne has all the great features of sea, mountain and every varying form of ground.'[1]

During the Famine, Sir Robert mortgaged his estate so as to be able to feed everyone for miles around. The hall at Lissadell, no doubt visualized by the architect as the background to a select company of dilettanti, became full of hungry people, for

Lissadell. The 'great windows open to the south' of which Yeats sang are in the bow.

it was here that Sir Robert gave out rations. It could be that the Neo-Classicism grew less cold after that time.

The number of people fed at Lissadell was by all accounts large enough when things were normal and there was no famine. To support the family and their guests, as well as the servants, grooms and other dependants, a sheep was killed every day and a bullock every two weeks; flocks of turkeys, geese, ducks and chickens were raised by the wife of the house steward assisted by another woman and a man; there was a large supply of home-cured bacon while all the game shot on the place was eaten in the house except for what was given away as presents. Sir Robert was a Member of Parliament, so he and his family spent a certain amount of time in London; but when they were at home the house was generally full of guests, often so full that some of the bachelors could not be accommodated in the house itself, but were given rooms in the stables. These rooms were as good as many of the bedrooms in the house and the gentlemen, if they had no valets, were looked after by the footmen who also had their rooms here. The outbuildings at Lissadell also included a riding school.

In the 1830s, the servants who waited in the dining-room when the house was full or when there was a large dinner party included Mr Ball, the house steward, who was the equivalent of the butler, the groom of the chambers, the under-butler and three footmen. There were also two other men: John Kirins, who looked after Sir

Robert's house in the town of Sligo but came to wait at Lissadell when required, and Thomas Kilgallon, the servant of Sir Robert's son Henry. All but Kilgallon wore a livery consisting of a dark blue coat, a red waistcoat, red plush breeches, white stockings and buckled shoes. The footmen also wore white cotton gloves. Kilgallon did valet to Henry Gore-Booth and fetched his hot water as well as waiting at table. His wages were eight pounds a year with his keep and a suit of clothes. When he first came he was illiterate; but the family taught him to read and write.

The kitchen staff was headed by a French chef named Friburg who was fond of whiskey; once or twice a week he would engage a horse and cart to take him into Sligo town where he and the owner of the cart would sit in a public house until it was time for him to return and see to the dinner. Under him came a pastry cook, a kitchen maid and a scullery maid, with extra help when needed. Then there were the two stillroom maids, Mrs Mackay, who was Scottish, and Mary Anne Payne, who was a local; they baked the bread, the 'fancy breads' for the dining-room as well as the 'household bread' for the servants' hall;[2] they also assisted the housekeeper, Mrs Brown, in the jam-making and bottling. The stillroom maids washed up the china, whereas the copper pots and pans were cleaned by the kitchen boys who lit the kitchen fires and raked out the ashes, looked after the boilers that produced hot water for baths and for washing up, and pumped the water from the well up to the tanks on the roof.

There were three housemaids with other women to help them; they had to be up at four in the morning. They carried the cans of hot and cold water upstairs and emptied the baths. They also had to keep the fires going in the reception rooms and in the bedrooms and they acted as lady's maid to ladies who had no maids of their own. Although Sir Robert had been a widower since 1855, his household must have included at least one lady's maid for he had two unmarried daughters, Augusta and Stella Gore-Booth; while his daughter Emily, who was married to Captain Charley Wynne, scion of another leading family of the County Sligo gentry, spent a great deal of time here.

The house parties at Lissadell were mainly for the hunting and the shooting. Sir Robert kept two packs of hounds, a dog pack and a bitch pack; the ladies rode as well as the gentlemen. When the meet was on the other side of the town of Sligo, they went there in a coach driven by Sir Robert, their horses having been sent on ahead of them; and on the way back they would stop at Sir Robert's house in the town to change their clothes and be given tea by the admirable Mrs Kirins. On shooting days, gentlemen who did not shoot went riding with the ladies or else they played croquet, which must have been a little chilly at that time of the year.

In the evening at Lissadell, there was always music. Sir Robert was musical and played the violin and the double bass; his daughter Emily Wynne would accompany him on the piano. There would also be charades, tableaux and amateur theatricals, usually got up by Charley Wynne's brother Edward. When a play was put on, neighbours were invited to dinner to see it. During the winter months, there would be several balls.

After meeting the celebrated medium D. D. Home in London, the Gore-Booths had a craze for spiritualism; the gentlemen would sit up late in a darkened room holding a seance or, as the servants called it, 'turning the tables'.[3] Home himself came to stay and presided over the seances. Sir Robert hoped that the spirits would tell him who had fired the shot that had killed a cousin of his in a riot in Sligo after an election; having failed to obtain a satisfactory answer to his question he rather lost interest and the seances gradually ceased.

An even more remarkable guest than Home was Arthur MacMorrough Kavanagh of Borris in County Carlow, a descendant of the ancient Kings of Leinster who was born without arms or legs yet led an active and indeed adventurous life. When meals were announced, his servant carried him to the dining-room; sitting at table, with his jacket and collar and tie and his heavy skirt, he did not appear to have anything the matter with him. His servant would cut up his meat which he ate with a fork held between his shoulders; he could also hold a glass. He had brought his pony with him, which he rode about the grounds; it had a saddle like an armchair, the reins and whip being strapped to his stumps.

Sir Robert objected strongly to people smoking in the house. He would not even allow it in the billiard room and there was no smoking-room. 'He would say that smoking was only fit for servants and grooms and that if any gentleman chose to indulge in it at Lissadell they might go to the kitchen, where they would find congenial company.'[4] His son-in-law Charley Wynne took him at his word and founded the Pig and Whistle Club, of which the members were any gentlemen staying in the house who wished to smoke before going to bed. When the ladies had retired, the members of the club – of which Charley was 'perpetual Grand Master' – went to the kitchen, which the servants had by now vacated, and where there was a whiskey tray in readiness for them. New members were solemnly initiated and required to carve their names on the vast kitchen table, which in time became covered with names, many of them distinguished. As well as smoking, drinking and chatting, the members of the Pig and Whistle Club amused themselves by killing some of the rats that infested the house, decapitating them with a huge kitchen knife as they popped up through a hole. Each gentleman was allowed five minutes with the knife; each staked a coin and whoever killed the most rats took the jackpot.[5]

In the snowy winter of 1868 the gentlemen at Lissadell had more exciting things to occupy them. A Fenian rising was expected; Sir Robert put the house in a state of defence. Iron plates were fixed to the shutters, windows were sandbagged, guns were mounted on the roof. Trees near the house were cut down. Henry's servant Kilgallon was 'kept busy making bullets in the gun room'.[6]

Each night one of the gentlemen of the family and one of the male guests would ride out on patrol and co-operate with the police. When Charley Wynne was on patrol, which he often was, he and Captain Wood-Martin, the guest who accompanied him, co-operated with the police by playing cards and drinking whiskey punch with Mr Waters, the Sub-Inspector. Next day at Lissadell the ladies would sympathize with Charley and Wood-Martin on the hardships they had endured: 'Out all night on horseback in such weather.'[7]

The threatened rising came to nothing, but while the scare was still on a spoof Fenian attack was staged by Henry Gore-Booth, Charley Wynne, Wood-Martin and Waters — who should, perhaps, have known better — as a practical joke. One night, when the ladies had retired to the drawing-room after dinner, Henry and his fellow-conspirators, who were the only gentlemen in the dining-room — Sir Robert not being present, though he was at home — went upstairs and disguised themselves in old clothes. Kilgallon, who was in on the secret, let them out of the house and locked the hall door after them. Soon the bell began to ring furiously, and there was hammering with heavy sticks on the door. The servants rushed into the hall, the women crying, all certain that the Fenians had arrived. The men outside shouted that they wanted 'Ould Sir Robert' and that they would break down the door if it were not opened. Sir Robert and the ladies followed the servants into the hall; Stella Gore-Booth ran to her father's room for his revolver and gave it to him. The hammering and the shouting for Ould Sir Robert continued; at last Emily Wynne, who unlike her sister Stella was in on the secret, told the house steward to open the door. In rushed the men, through the hall and into the gallery, shouting for Ould Sir Robert. Then Paddy McGlown, the blind piper, who they had brought with them, struck up a jig and the 'Fenians' started to dance. Sir Robert, when he realized that it was a joke, was not amused.[8]

Sir Robert died in 1876 and Henry succeeded to the baronetcy and to Lissadell. Three years later the potato crop once again failed; there were fears of another famine, but fortunately the situation was dealt with in time. Sir Henry, as he now was, did his best to help the people on his estate, speaking to as many of them as he could to find out their circumstances. 'Oh, the poor people have no potatoes! They will have no food, God help them,' he exclaimed on returning to the house after speaking to some of them. He reduced his rents and made a provision store in the house; and he and his family did what Sir Robert had done in the Great Famine and gave out food to the needy 'with their own hands from morning till night'.[9]

Sir Henry Gore-Booth and his wife Georgina, who came from Yorkshire, had five children. Their daughter Constance, the eldest, was a forceful personality and like her sister Eva she grew up to be beautiful. She was very much a law unto herself;

Constance and Eva Gore-Booth as young girls, a painting by Sarah Purser.

The window pane in the ante-room at Lissadell on which Constance scratched her name with a diamond.

she kept a pet monkey and a pet snake, which she would sometimes wear round her neck; she also kept a pet seal. She was allowed to use the anteroom between the drawing-room and the dining-room as her private den; here she would paint and read and entertain her friends. She scratched her name with a diamond on one of the window panes and no doubt made the room pretty untidy, for it came to be known as the Glory Hole. She liked to dress up as a beggar girl; she came once to the back door of Lissadell thus disguised and the servants, not recognizing her, sent her away.

When young men came to stay, she would take them for a drive along the sand-banks in her tandem, which had a loose seat so that she had the fun of watching her unfortunate passenger pitch forward on to his head when the wheel struck a rabbit hole. Most of the young men who came to Lissadell were in love with Constance and some of the older men were too. Once, when her parents were having a large dinner party, a middle-aged admirer sitting next to her put his hand on her knee under the table. She took it and held it up for everyone to see, saying: 'Just look what I have found in my lap!'[10]

She responded favourably to the attentions of one young man. He was Wilfrid Ashley, the tall and handsome grandson of Lord Shaftesbury the philanthropist, whose father had inherited an estate in County Sligo from Lord Palmerston. Their friendship died during a dance that the Gore-Booths had after an amateur performance of a play called *Pilot Rosalie*. Wilfrid was engaged to dance with Constance and for some reason he threw her over; she gave him such a talking-to that he was mortally offended and went off to the billiard room with her brother Josslyn. Wilfrid Ashley was to be the father of one of the most forceful women of her generation, namely Edwina Countess Mountbatten; it is hard to imagine what a tigress he would have fathered had he married Constance.

Life at Lissadell in those days took on an added dimension when Sir Henry's ocean-going yacht *Kara* was anchored in Sligo Bay. Sir Henry loved the sea; he had sailed to the Arctic in *Kara* to rescue his explorer friend Leigh Smith. The faithful Kilgallon had accompanied him on the voyage and had saved his life by shooting a menacing bear which now stood stuffed and grinning in the hall. In May 1892 Sir Henry arrived back in *Kara* from Greenland after an unsuccessful whaling trip; the Lissadell house party was given an excellent dinner on board which started with Tortue Franz Josef Land and ended with Rare Bit au Whales.[11]

Some of the ship's company on the deck of *Kara*. Sir Henry Gore-Booth stands in the centre, holding a harpoon; standing on the far left is his cousin and fellow-yachtsman the 4th Earl of Dunraven.

A group at Lissadell in about 1894, including Georgina, wife of Sir Henry Gore-Booth and her daughters Constance and Eva. Georgina sits in the centre, with her husband's cousin the 4th Earl of Dunraven standing behind her.

A neighbour of the Gore-Booths on the other side of Sligo Bay was George Pollexfen, whose nephew, the young poet William Butler Yeats, spent the winter of 1894–5 with him. While he was here, Yeats paid two visits to Lissadell; he described the Gore-Booths as 'a very pleasant, kindly, inflammable family ever ready to take up new ideas and new things'. Josslyn, the elder son, was 'theoretically a Home Ruler and practically some kind of humanitarian, much troubled by the responsibility of his wealth and almost painfully conscientious'; while Constance and Eva were 'two beautiful figures among the great trees'.[12] Yeats made particular friends with Eva, who was herself a poet, confiding in her about 'his unhappy love for Maud Gonne'.[13] There is a story of how, when Yeats stayed here for the first time, he appeared in the middle of the night to say that he had seen a ghost that he had not seen for twenty years.

Constance found what seemed like love in 1900, the year of her father's death, when she married the Polish portrait painter Count Casimir Markievicz. During the stormy years of their marriage, Constance and Casimir found a haven at Lissadell; they saw more of each other here, as far from her world of the Gaelic League and the Abbey Theatre as from his favourite Dublin pubs. One Christmas they put on a series of plays in Sligo town. Casimir also occupied himself by painting full-length mural portraits in the Lissadell dining-room of members of the family together with the gamekeeper, the forester and Kilgallon, who was now the butler. He dressed these life-sized figures in the tweeds and dark suits of the 1900s, but gave them the timeless faces of Russian ikons. By now, Constance's pretty sister-in-law Mary had taken over from old Lady Gore-Booth as mistress of the house, Sir Josslyn, as he now was, having married in 1907. When he and his bride returned from their honeymoon a party was given in the riding school at Lissadell for the employees of the estate; more than three hundred people were present. Three years after his marriage Sir Josslyn acquired a motor car, a 20 hp Wolseley-Siddeley, and he allowed Constance to drive it. Yeats also drove the car on one of his visits.

Kilgallon now wore a grey beard and like many good old servants he had his 'little ways'. In 1913 the young Irish Guards subaltern Edward Stafford-King-

Constance, a portrait by her
husband Casimir Markievicz.

CEAD MILE FAILTE

The party given in the riding school at Lissadell to celebrate the return of Sir Josslyn and Lady Gore-Booth from their honeymoon.

Harman from Rockingham in County Roscommon and his brother Cecil came to stay for a ball. They had not met Sir Josslyn before, though their two families had intermarried in the past, and when he greeted them on their arrival, Edward unfortunately mistook him for the butler; he was already rather cross with them for being late. But while fearing that their host might not have been best pleased with them, the two young men did not expect to be treated as they were next morning. They had barely gone to sleep, having been dancing until well into the small hours, when Kilgallon woke them and said gruffly: 'You must get up, you've got to go.'

'Go?' the two brothers asked in sleepy astonishment, noticing that it was only just after six. 'We've been asked to stay three days.'

'You've got to go, those are my orders.'

There was nothing for it but to get up and get dressed. At seven, without any breakfast or even a cup of tea, the two unfortunate young men were bundled into the carriage and driven into Sligo town to catch the eight o'clock train. They felt very offended with the Gore-Booths, only to learn through a neighbour that the Gore-Booths were very offended with *them*. Eventually the mystery was cleared up: the Gore-Booths had indeed expected them to stay for three days, but the wretched

Sir Josslyn and Lady Gore-Booth in later life.

The children of Sir Josslyn and Lady Gore-Booth outside the bow window of Lissadell in the nineteen-twenties. From left to right, Michael, Hugh, Bridget, Brian, Rosaleen, Aideen, Gabrielle and Angus. Michael succeeded his father as 7th baronet, Hugh and Brian were both killed in action in World War II; Angus eventually became the 8th baronet.

Angus Gore-Booth with the elderly Kilgallon.

Hugh Gore-Booth with a seal washed up from Sligo Bay. The seal appears to have been less fortunate than the one which his Aunt Constance kept as a pet many years earlier.

Kilgallon had taken it into his head to get rid of them after barely a night.[14]

During the Great War, when the sons of so many Irish country houses were in khaki at the front, Constance Markievicz, now parted from Casimir, was to be seen marching through the streets of Dublin in a dark green uniform as one of James Connolly's principal lieutenants in the Irish Citizen Army. She fought with the insurgents in 1916, was condemned to death, then reprieved and sent to prison in England. In the general election of December 1918 she was among the victorious Sinn Fein candidates, thereby achieving the distinction of being the first woman MP; but like her colleagues she refused to take her seat at Westminster and sat in Dublin as a member of the first Dail. In 1920 there was a strike of farm workers at Lissadell and Sir Josslyn had to milk his own cows until his hands bled. In the circumstances, it was not very kind of Constance to write to him as she did, reminding him that he came of a family of 'tyrants and usurpers'.[15]

Having fought with the Irregulars during the Civil War, Constance worked for the Dublin poor until she died in 1927. It was after Constance's death that Yeats wrote his celebrated lament for her and for her sister Eva Gore-Booth, the poet, who had never married and who had died a year earlier:

Lady Gore-Booth in the bow room at Lissadell.

> The light of evening, Lissadell,
> Great windows open to the south,
> Two girls in silk kimonos, both
> Beautiful, one a gazelle.
> But a raving autumn shears
> Blossom from the summer's wreath;
> The older is condemned to death,
> Pardoned, drags out lonely years . . .

These lines are well known; yet the poet whose spirit continues to inhabit Lissadell is not Yeats but Eva Gore-Booth. One thinks of her here as a girl, with Constance; one thinks of her later in life, working among the poor of Manchester, but dreaming of mountains, woods, a big grey house and the sea:

> My heart was very far away
> I saw Ben Bulben's rose and fire
> Shining afar o'er Sligo Bay.

*Chapter 18*

# Mitchelstown Castle
## COUNTY CORK

GOING through the Galtees into County Cork is like crossing a frontier. Even so down-to-earth a person as the agriculturalist Arthur Young had this feeling. The mountains seemed to him like 'the boundaries of two conflicting empires', giving Mitchelstown, immediately to their south, 'a situation worthy of the proudest capital'. Mitchelstown still looks like the capital of a principality, if not of an empire, with wide avenues and Georgian squares.

One thing is missing – the castle of its ruler. That was there until 1922, the spectacular Gothic Revival successor to the stronghold of a branch of the Geraldines holding the romantic title of White Knight. Three sons of a thirteenth-century Lord of Decies and Desmond were knighted and the knighthoods became hereditary. The White Knights, who sprang from the eldest, became extinct in 1608 – cursed, it is said, because one of them betrayed his kinsman, the Earl of Desmond. Their estate in Cork, Tipperary and Limerick – so large that it was called White Knight's Country – and perhaps the curse as well, passed by marriage to the family of King, descended from Sir John King, an Elizabethan settler who had obtained grants of land in Roscommon and Sligo and whose son Edward, drowned in the Irish Sea, inspired Milton's *Lycidas*.

The Kings grew in importance during the seventeenth and eighteenth centuries; by the time Arthur Young came to Mitchelstown they had risen to being Earls of Kingston. Young, who worked as an agent to the first Earl's son and heir Lord Kingsborough, found him a most admirable and improving landlord. He enlarged the Mitchelstown demesne, enclosing it with a wall more than six miles long, and in 1776 he added a third storey and wings to the early eighteenth-century house which incorporated part of the White Knights' castle.

It was to this house that the writer and feminist Mary Wollstonecraft came in 1786 as governess to the Kingsboroughs' three daughters. Though everybody tried hard to be nice to her and to appreciate her conversation and wit, she did not like the life here. She complained of the 'solemn stupidity' of the older members of the family and of being 'almost tormented to death by dogs'. Of Lady Kingsborough she wrote: 'She rouges and in short is a fine lady without fancy or sensibility.' She also

found her 'very proud and ready to take fire on the slightest occasion' while admit-
ting that she was 'very civil, nay kind'.

Of the other women of the Mitchelstown house party, Mary wrote: 'We move in
so different a sphere, I feel grateful for their attention, but not amused. I am treated
like a gentlewoman – but I cannot easily forget my inferior station.' As well as her
three charges there were three Fitzgerald girls living in the house, half-sisters of Lady
Kingsborough, who was herself only thirty-two. Mary called them 'a set of silly
females'.[1]

For all of Lady Kingsborough's airs and Lord Kingsborough's 'unrefined fun',
Mary may have sensed an atmosphere of uneasiness. The Kingsboroughs' marriage
was going wrong; a few years after Mary left, they parted. Lady Kingsborough
retired to a cottage at Windsor, though Mitchelstown was actually hers, since she
was the heiress of a senior branch of the Kings. Lord Kingsborough lived on at
Mitchelstown with a mistress, who bore him two children.

The break-up of the Kingsboroughs' marriage was the prelude to an event in
1797 which seemed to change the whole character of the Kings, making them
Gothic in the sense of a Gothic novel. The Kingsboroughs' daughter Mary King
eloped with her cousin Henry Fitzgerald, a married man. She was duly brought
back by her parents. But Fitzgerald was foolish enough to follow Mary over to
Ireland, and her father shot him dead at an inn a few miles from Mitchelstown. Lord
Kingsborough, who by then had become the second Earl of Kingston, was tried by
his peers for murder. He was acquitted, but died within a few months.

Mary was not the only one of the second Earl's children to have a stormy passage.
Her sister Margaret, having been taught revolutionary ideas by Mary Wollstonecraft,
left her husband Lord Mount Cashell, a County Cork neighbour, and settled in
Italy with a lover, becoming a friend of Shelley whose second wife was Mary
Wollstonecraft's daughter Mary Godwin. Shelley wrote of Margaret as 'The Lady'
in *The Sensitive Plant*. The second Earl's son and heir, a larger-than-life character
known as 'Big George', started his career by running away to the West Indies with
an Irish society girl whom he did not marry. Having had three children by her, he
was persuaded to return to Ireland and marry Lord Mount Cashell's sister Lady
Helena Moore. In the 1798 rebellion, when he commanded the militia at the age of
twenty-seven, he was taken prisoner by the rebels and just escaped being killed by an
angry mob. He is said to have behaved harshly during the rebellion. Yet he was kind
to his tenants and liked by the people as a whole. He was, in fact, a great medieval
lord out of his time: tall, strongly built, with a large nose and an imperious temper,
despotic, as the White Knights had been, but open-handed and devout.

In 1823 Big George, who was now the third Earl of Kingston, swept away the
eighteenth-century house at Mitchelstown together with the relics of the old castle
of the White Knights, and commissioned the fashionable architects, the brothers

'Big George', 3rd Earl of
Kingston, as a young man.

James and George Richard Pain, to build him a castle bigger than any other house
in Ireland. He specified that it should have a tower called the White Knight's Tower
and another tower called the Royal Tower, containing a bedroom for King George
IV who had promised to come and stay with him as soon as the castle was ready.

Quickly the new walls rose up, of a pale grey local limestone that must have
looked wonderful in the ever-changing mountain light. And then, according to the
poet Aubrey de Vere, an industrialist started a factory in Mitchelstown; a huge
chimney rose up at the same time as the White Knight's Tower. Big George drove
into town. 'I am come to wish you goodbye, boys,' he told everyone. 'This place is
but a small place, and there is not room in it for me and that man . . . I go to England
tomorrow.'[2] That night, the 'boys' visited the industrialist, with the result that it was
he and not Big George who went.

Within two years, at a cost of over £100,000, the castle was finished. While it
did not quite manage to be larger than any other house in Ireland, it was one of the
largest and most successful of the earlier Gothic Revival castles. It stood on a high
plateau that jutted into a valley like a bastion. The buildings formed three sides of a
court, the open side consisting of a number of towers linked by a terrace facing the
mountains. From the north, the castle appeared as a romantic group of towers on

Mitchelstown Castle. A romantic group of towers on top of a cliff, facing the Galtee
Mountains

Mitchelstown Castle. The White Knight's Tower.

top of a cliff. The White Knight's Tower on the east front resembled a tall Tudor
gate-tower and was the main entrance. The hall led to a gallery ninety-three feet long
with a ceiling of plaster vaulting, at the far end of which was the grand staircase.
Opening off the gallery in the south front were the drawing-room, anteroom,
dining-room and library.

In the end, George IV never came, but Big George entertained as though he had
a royal house party the whole time. Even complete strangers were received with hospitality at the castle, which had sixty bedrooms, not counting the servants' rooms;

Mitchelstown Castle, the south front.

there were sometimes as many as a hundred people staying. All were dazzled by the splendour, by the display of plate and the army of servants. One of the under-cooks was a young man named Claridge, who later founded Claridge's Hotel.

Rich as he was, Big George began to suffer from money worries. Then, in 1830, there was a by-election in Limerick. Big George expected his tenants to vote for the candidate of his choice. Instead, they all voted the other way. Big George's absolutism was broken and, breaking, it broke him. The day after the election, all his tenants were summoned to the castle. They crowded into the gallery and Big George faced them from a dais at the far end. Suddenly he shouted: 'They are come to tear me to pieces!' He had gone mad and was taken to London, where he died in 1839.

Because of his madness, Big George's creditors attacked his son Edward, Lord Kingsborough, a scholar of distinction who had himself spent £32,000 in producing his monumental work, the *Antiquities of Mexico*. In 1837 Lord Kingsborough was imprisoned for debt and died of gaol fever. Big George's second son, the bachelor Robert Henry, who became the fourth Earl, continued to keep open house at Mitchelstown. A lady who stayed here in his time compared it to 'the residences of the German princes'. The day after she arrived, fourteen of the party set out to visit the stalactite caves some five miles away to the north. 'Wild-looking peasant girls' held candles, and directions were shouted in Irish. The writer was absorbed in 'strange and indescribable feelings' and she lost no time in remarking: 'No wonder the peasants who come her should be superstitious.' Lord Kingston's guests who visited the caves were entertained at Mountain Lodge, his shooting-box nearby, which had nine bedrooms and an attractive garden.

In 1842, a young couple, Robert and Helena Perceval-Maxwell from County

The gallery where Big George confronted his tenants.

Down, came to stay. Helena was a cousin of Big George's nephew Lord Mount Cashell, with whom they had been staying at Moore Park, a few miles away, before coming on to Mitchelstown. Lord Kingston had invited a large party to meet them. There were thirty-two at dinner, all of whom were sleeping in the castle. The party included a County Down neighbour of the Perceval-Maxwells, the young Archibald Rowan-Hamilton of Killyleagh Castle, a grandson of the United Irish leader Hamilton Rowan. Catherine, his bride of four months, was with him; they were stationed in Cork, for he was soldiering. 'She has never seen Killyleagh Castle, but talked a great deal about it,' Robert Perceval-Maxwell observed. 'I hope she does not expect anything like Mitchelstown.' His admiration of Mitchelstown knew no bounds: 'The castle is the most beautiful thing of the kind I should think in England or Ireland.' And yet he found the rooms 'not uncomfortably large', though lofty. He was no less impressed by the garden, which he describes as 'princely', noting that the glass houses were 488 feet in length and the conservatory, which was being roofed with plate glass, 100 feet by 40. He was told that the garden cost Lord Kingston nearly £1,000 a year to maintain; though the labour force he mentions, a gardener and ten apprentices, does not sound anything unusual for those days.[3]

In 1844 came the crash, and the bailiffs arrived at Mitchelstown. Lord Kingston and his house party decided to close the doors against them. So the castle, less than twenty years old, withstood a siege. It lasted a fortnight, after which the garrison surrendered. Creditors took possession of the castle and the land in Tipperary and Limerick was sold by the Encumbered Estates Court. Lord Kingston retired to London where in 1848 he was charged with sodomy, but failed to appear to stand trial and forfeited his bail. Eventually, like his father, he went mad.

The young Anthony Trollope, who was then a post office official, spent some time in Cork and in Clonmel in 1844, the year of the Mitchelstown 'siege'. He would have heard many stories about the castle and passed it more than once; he certainly had it in mind when he wrote about 'Desmond Court' in his novel *Castle Richmond*, published in 1860, though his portrait of Big George – and indeed of the 'Celtic tale-bearers' – is hardly fair.

> All the world must have heard of Desmond Court. It is the largest inhabited residence known in that part of the world, where rumours are afloat of how it covers ten acres of ground; how in hewing the stones for it a whole mountain was cut away; how it should have cost hundreds of thousands of pounds, only that the money was never paid by the rapacious, wicked, bloodthirsty old earl who caused it to be erected; and how the cement was thickened with human blood. So goes rumour with the more romantic of the Celtic tale-bearers. It is a huge place – huge, ungainly and uselessly extensive; built at a time when, at any rate in Ireland, men considered neither beauty, aptitude, nor economy.

On the death of the fourth Earl in 1867 Mitchelstown passed to his younger brother James who became the fifth Earl. He and his wife Anna, who was very much younger than him, received a tremendous welcome when they came to live at the castle. He set about putting the reduced estate to rights, but by then he was approaching seventy and died only two years after inheriting. Having no children, he left Mitchelstown to his widow instead of to the cousin who succeeded to the earldom. In 1873 she married as her second husband William Downes Webber, continuing, as was then customary, to call herself Anna Countess of Kingston after her remarriage. Willie Webber, a landowner in County Sligo and in what was then known as the Queen's County, took charge of the Mitchelstown estate, which carried a crippling mortgage of £236,000; it should have brought in nearly £18,000 a year, but after the mortgage interest had been paid, there was only about £8,000 a year left for the upkeep of the castle and demesne as well as for living expenses.

For the next ten years, economy reigned at the castle. The scarcity of fruit in Lady Kingston's barmbracks – those spiced currant loaves which, sliced and buttered, are a familiar feature of the Irish tea table – became a byword with her neighbours. Once, when Robert Cole Bowen of Bowen's Court was having tea with her at Mitchelstown, another gentleman, who happened to get a slice of barmbrack with

a currant in it, held it up for him to see, at which he remarked, in his best County
Cork French, '*Vous avez raisong.*'[4]

To make things even more difficult for Lady Kingston and her husband, they
were involved in the agrarian troubles of the 1880s known as the Land War. In
December 1880 some 1600 of the Mitchelstown tenants – with whom they had hitherto been on the best of terms – came to the castle demanding a rent reduction on
account of a fall in the price of butter. Owing to the mortgage interest, Lady
Kingston was unwilling to grant this reduction, thereby causing a dispute that
dragged on into the following summer. The tenants refused to pay their rent and held
a great demonstration, processing by torchlight through the square outside the castle
gates accompanied by the local band playing Nationalist airs. Lady Kingston took
up the challenge and served eviction notices on a number of tenants; and while this
made some of them pay their rent, others resisted and there was an ugly riot in which
policemen were stoned and people injured by charging dragoons. By the end of June
a small army of 700 soldiers and 300 police were encamped around the castle to
protect its occupants. But by September, the tenants had capitulated, more interested
in saving the harvest than in continuing their campaign. There was a similar dispute
in 1887 which led to a protest meeting outside the castle gates when a large crowd
confronted the police, who having retreated into their barracks under a barrage of
stones and blackthorn sticks, fired two volleys, killing two and seriously wounding
twenty. This so-called 'Mitchelstown Massacre' prolonged Lady Kingston's troubles by several months as well as embarrassing the Conservative Government.

Things were more peaceful – and more prosperous – at Mitchelstown in the early
years of the present century. People who came here remembered Lady Kingston as
a quiet, intelligent old lady with a feeling for beauty; she would say of Nanking
porcelain: 'The white must be white of a young eye.'[5] Willie Webber had flowing
white hair down to his shoulders and always wore what was known as a 'German
cape coat'.[6] He was a Jaeger addict and thought it immoral to sleep in anything but
woollen sheets. He made a ritual of his habits; after dinner the butler would bring
in a silver salver on which rested a finely chased spirit lamp, some straw spills in a
stand, a snuff-box containing tobacco and a small and elegant pipe. Having slowly
filled the pipe, he lit a spill and then lit the pipe with it. He then took three puffs and
put the pipe down on the salver, which the butler immediately removed. The butler
at Mitchelstown in those days was a German, as was the housekeeper, the rest of the
indoor staff being mostly Scottish.

The after-dinner pipe-smoking ritual was followed by classical trios in the anteroom. An elderly cousin played the violin; Willie himself played the cello, his feet
encased in massive Jaeger house-boots, and any guest who was able to play it played
the piano. Guests who obliged by playing the piano in these trios included George
Bernard Shaw. He and his wife Charlotte, who was one of the County Cork

The drawing room at Mitchelstown Castle in the days of Anna Countess of Kingston.

Townshends, stayed at Mitchelstown every year during this period; Charlotte Shaw and Lady Kingston were great friends and would sit talking happily together while their menfolk made music. There was no country house at which Shaw was more welcome than he was at Mitchelstown, despite the political differences between him and the conservative Lady Kingston. Nothing was too good for him and Charlotte; they were always given the King's Bedroom in the Royal Tower which Big George had made for George IV, a room so large that it was said to be difficult to see across it on a misty night. Shaw's carroty beard, protruding from the sheets in the vast state bed, clashed with the crimson canopy. There was a great stir in the household on one occasion when a telegram came stating that the 'celebrated author' had left behind his pyjamas.

Lady Kingston died in 1909. Willie Webber lived on at Mitchelstown with an elderly companion, Miss Minnie Fairholme, who acted as hostess at the annual garden party, when the local band would play, charging five pounds for doing so. The last of these garden parties took place on, of all days, 5 August 1914. It was rather windy, so Willie and Miss Fairholme preferred to stay indoors and greeted their guests at the far end of the gallery, where, nearly a century earlier, Big George had confronted his tenants. Having shaken hands, the guests were expected to go outside. One of them was the fifteen-year-old Elizabeth Bowen, who had driven over from Bowen's Court with her father in a pony-trap. As she afterwards recalled: 'Wind raced round the Castle terraces, naked under the Galtees; grit blew into the ices; the band clung with some trouble to its exposed place. The tremendous news certainly made that party, which might have been rather flat. Almost everyone said they wondered if they really ought to have come, but they *had* come – rightly: this was a time to gather . . . For miles around, each isolated big house had disgorged its talker, this first day of the war. The tension of months, of years – outlying tension of Europe, inner tension of Ireland – broke in a spate of words.'[7] The war made no difference to the position of the German housekeeper at the castle. Somehow she managed to stay on, whereas the German butler had left a few years before.

In June 1922, during the Civil War, the castle was occupied by the Republicans. Poor Willie Webber, now nearly ninety, had to take refuge in a house outside the castle gates. The Republicans stayed until the middle of August; then, as the Free State forces were approaching, they evacuated the castle, burning it as they moved out. On Willie's death in 1924 the property reverted to one of the King family, Colonel Alec King-Harman, who claimed £150,000 compensation for the burning of the castle but eventually received no more than £27,500. This, of course, would have been totally inadequate had he wished to rebuild, which he did not, having already inherited another great house of his family, Newcastle in County Longford. So most of what remained of the Mitchelstown estate was sold and the ruin of the castle was demolished, the ashlar having been bought by the monks of Mount Melleray for their new church. That garden party of August 1914, after a little more than ten years, seemed to Elizabeth Bowen 'like a dream'; and the castle itself was 'a few bleached stumps on the plateau'.[8]

# Chapter 19

# Mount Stewart
## COUNTY DOWN

I N 1737 Alexander Stewart, whose family had been small gentry in County Donegal since the reign of James I, married Mary Cowan, the sister and heiress of an East Indian nabob. A few years later his wife's trustees bought her an estate in County Down, including a fine demesne overlooking Strangford Lough which was renamed Mount Stewart. Here, from 1771 onwards, their son Robert, who eventually became the first Marquess of Londonderry, built himself a house. Though it was on a comparatively modest scale – two-storeyed, with a hall flanked by a library and a dining-room – it was not completed until 1783; while the work was going on, the family and their guests had to make do with a temporary house and a series of cottages, or 'cabins', along the shore. 'My apartment is a snug cabin upon the shore of a vast arm of the sea,' Robert's second father-in-law, the Lord Chancellor Earl Camden, wrote on one of his many visits.[1]

As well as building the house, Robert Stewart built the Temple of the Winds, an octagonal banqueting house on a hill above the lough designed by his namesake, the painter, architect and antiquary 'Athenian' Stuart, who based it on the Tower of the Winds in Athens. Here the family and their guests would go after dinner to drink port or claret brought up from the cellar below. The eminent Belfast physician and politician Dr Alexander Haliday, when called away from one of these convivial gatherings to attend on a patient, said with some feeling: 'I could have stayed.'[2] Soon after it was built, the Temple of the Winds may well have saved the lives of Robert Stewart's son and heir, the seventeen-year-old Robert, and a companion, who were sailing on the lough when their boat capsized. They were rescued thanks to having been seen by young Robert's tutor and the estate agent, who happened to be looking out over the lough from the temple. Young Robert's half-brother Charles Stewart was also nearly drowned in the treacherous waters of the lough when he was a boy. The two half-brothers were devoted to one another and had a wonderful time together at Mount Stewart, with its woods and its rocky coves.

In 1790, at the age of twenty-one, young Robert entered the Irish House of Commons. His election cost more than £30,000, which seriously depleted the family finances, based though they were on an East Indian fortune; there were to be

Mount Stewart, the Temple of the Winds.

no more building works at Mount Stewart for more than a decade. However, from the point of view of young Robert's career, it was money well spent, for he rose rapidly in politics, particularly after the second Earl Camden, the brother of his stepmother, became Lord Lieutenant of Ireland in 1795. It also helped his father's advancement; having been raised to the peerage as Lord Londonderry in 1789, the elder Robert was made a viscount in 1795 and in 1796 he became Earl of Londonderry, giving the younger Robert the courtesy title of Viscount Castlereagh by which he is known to history.

At about the time when the elder Robert was made an earl, the French traveller De Latocnaye came to Mount Stewart. He was gratified by the way in which Lord and Lady Londonderry received him. 'She lives here a very retired life in the bosom of her amiable family,' he wrote of his hostess, 'to the education of which she devotes the whole of her time.'[3] De Latocnaye was here when Lords Londonderry and Castlereagh were administering the oath of allegiance to volunteers for the Yeomanry Corps they were raising, Ireland being then in a state of unrest with rumours of a French invasion. Writing to his wife from Mount Stewart in November 1796, Castlereagh reported that three or four hundred had taken the oath on the previous day. 'We had a very jolly dinner; Cleland quite drunk, Sinclair considerably so, my father not a little, others lying heads and points, the whole very happy and "God Save the King" and "Rule Britannia" declared permanent.'[4]

A few years later, when he was at the height of the Irish phase of his career — having acted as Chief Secretary during the rising of 1798 and helped to bring about the Union — Castlereagh wrote to his wife from Mount Stewart on homelier matters. 'Last night we had a ball in the nursery at which Elliot danced a fandango with Jenny Bowman . . . The gardens here are in great beauty. The steam apparatus is admirably adjusted.' He also observed of a friend and fellow-MP who was staying: 'The Knight of Kerry is so much more interesting when he gets up early and does not drink.'[5]

Mention of the 'steam apparatus', which presumably served the hothouses, would suggest that Lord Londonderry carried out improvements to the garden of Mount Stewart before he set about enlarging and remodelling the house, which he did from 1804 to 1806. Castlereagh obtained designs from the fashionable London architect George Dance, though the work was actually carried out by John Ferguson, a Belfast man. A new entrance was made; the original entrance hall became a music room with double doors opening into the rooms on either side. A new staircase hall was added, with an imperial staircase leading up to the bedrooms, which Lord Londonderry insisted should be higher than Dance had proposed, even if this made the house 'less pleasing' from the outside. 'I like airy sleeping rooms, which are particularly eligible in case of illness,' he told the architect.[6]

While Lord Londonderry was remodelling Mount Stewart, his son Castlereagh was in the British Cabinet, facing the might of Napoleon as Secretary for War. Later, as Foreign Secretary, he played a decisive part in Napoleon's downfall; and at the Congress of Vienna and afterwards helped to settle the future of Europe. Such was his prestige on the Continent that he corresponded direct with the Tsar of Russia, Alexander I, on affairs of state. In August 1818 the Tsar's brother, the Grand Duke Michael, visited Mount Stewart, where he was entertained by Lord and Lady Londonderry, Castlereagh himself being away in London. He crossed from Scotland to the nearby port of Donaghadee in a British warship; a faster 'advice boat' was sent on ahead to tell the Londonderrys when to expect him, giving them time to invite a large company to meet him and to 'regulate the operations nec-essary in the kitchen', as Lord Londonderry put it in a letter to Castlereagh. So when the Grand Duke arrived, at four in the afternoon, twenty-nine people sat down to a magnificent dinner. The Grand Duke sat between two marchionesses: his hostess, whose husband had been made a marquess two years earlier, and the Marchioness of Donegall. 'As she is very flippant in French and talking nonsense, she was of some use in helping to keep up the conversation,' Lord Londonderry wrote of the latter. At the end of dinner the ladies did not leave the table, for the Grand Duke was known to drink very little wine.

More guests arrived at eight that evening and the house became quite full; 'Such was the curiosity to get a peep at the Russian prince' that all the neighbourhood wanted to be of the party. At eleven, a 'splendid, elegant supper' was laid out, but the Grand Duke did not avail himself of it and retired. Lord Londonderry heard from the servants that an altar was set up in his bedroom 'with a picture of the Virgin Mary' and that he had spent an hour in prayer as was 'his usual custom'. The Londonderrys were only able to offer beds to a few of their Irish guests, for the Grand Duke was accompanied by the Russian Ambassador to the Court of St James and his personal physician as well as seven attendants. Most of the company had, at a late hour, to get into their carriages and drive away.

The Grand Duke, who was not in the habit of appearing at breakfast, did not come down next morning until just before the carriages were ready for his departure on the first stage of his journey to Dublin. Before he left, Lord Londonderry took him on the jaunting car to the Temple of the Winds and 'told him it was venerated as a most sacred building', having been instrumental in saving Castlereagh's life. There was also time for him to admire the gardens; he was particularly impressed by the grapes and peaches which were growing in profusion.[7]

Castlereagh, who became the second Marquess of Londonderry in 1821 and was driven to suicide by overwork in the following year, was succeeded as the third Marquess by his half-brother Charles, a distinguished soldier and diplomatist. The third Marquess married as his second wife the wealthy Frances Anne Vane-Tempest, heiress to estates and coal mines in the north of England. With the help of Frances Anne's money and with William Vitruvius Morrison as architect, Mount Stewart was greatly enlarged; the original house became one end of a long, two-storeyed Classical block with an Ionic *porte-cochère* and a vast central hall lit from above.

Having been enlarged, Mount Stewart was neglected in favour of Wynyard,

Mount Stewart.

Frances Anne's family seat in County Durham. When the fourth Marquess inherited it in 1854, it had become very run-down and he had to spend a considerable
amount of money to make it habitable. The fourth Marquess was the third
Marquess's son by his first marriage, so that Frances Anne's fortune went not to him,
but to his half-brother. However, he was childless so that his half-brother eventually
became the fifth Marquess and inherited Mount Stewart as well as Wynyard and the
rest of Frances Anne's great patrimony.

The fifth Marquess died in 1884 and was succeeded by his son Charles, one of
the leaders of the Ulster Unionist movement. Or perhaps the real leader was
Charles's wife, the proud and handsome Theresa Lady Londonderry, who is said
to have found in political intrigue an escape from domestic unhappiness; though the
celebrated story of how her husband never spoke to her except in public after learn-
ing from another lady, whose lover she had stolen, that she had been unfaithful to
him is not true; they may have been estranged for a while but they were reconciled.
Staunchly wedded though she was to Ulster Unionism, Theresa included among
her friends the fascinating Daisy Countess of Fingall who was a Nationalist as well
as a Catholic. When Daisy Fingall stayed at Mount Stewart, the Londonderrys
used to send her and her maid to Mass at the Catholic church in Newtownards,
which had been built by the Catholic wife of the fourth Marquess.

On one of her first visits to Mount Stewart, Daisy was sitting in the hall with her
hostess who told her that among the other guests there would be 'a clever young
lawyer from Dublin who may be useful'. Presently the door at the end of the room
opened and a face appeared. 'Oh, my dear, what an awful face!' Daisy exclaimed
under her breath to Theresa, who went to the door to greet the new arrival. She
brought him back to introduce him. 'Mr Carson . . . Lady Fingall says you have an
awful face.'

Carson became a frequent guest at Mount Stewart, together with other leading
Unionist politicians, such as Arthur Balfour and Bonar Law; but the
Londonderrys' guests also included people from outside the political world, such as
the literary critic Edmund Gosse and the aristocratic Hungarian couple, Count and
Countess Apponyi. 'The immediate assimilation of the Apponyi was a triumph,'
Sir Horace Plunkett, a fellow-guest, wrote afterwards to Theresa. 'I verily believe if
Sir Anthony McDonnell had romped in with the D.....d Rosaleen on his arm you
would have made them feel at home.' Sir Anthony McDonnell was Under-
Secretary for Ireland, known for his flirtations with Dark Rosaleen, in other words
Nationalist sympathies. Plunkett himself, though no Nationalist, had schemes for
Ireland of which Theresa disapproved; yet they were still great friends. 'I hardly
knew how I had enjoyed my visit till I got to work,' he told her in the same letter.
'The hospitality was ideal.'[8]

Theresa was a good hostess; she would go around her guests' rooms before they

Group at Mount Stewart during the visit of King Edward VII and Queen Alexandra in 1903. The King and Queen stand together; their host, the 6th Marquess of Londonderry, stands on the left of the Queen with the Viceroy of Ireland, the Earl of Dudley, standing between them and a little back; Theresa Lady Londonderry stands on the right of the King. Princess Victoria stands in front of the pillar to the left of Lord Londonderry with the Londonderrys' daughter Lady Helen Stavordale standing behind her. To the left of Princess Victoria is Theresa's brother the Earl of Shrewsbury who drove the King and Queen in his motor; to the left again is the Londonderrys' son-in-law Lord Stavordale. Second from the right is Lord Londonderry's brother Lord Bertie Vane-Tempest who was almost his double; when Lord Londonderry was Viceroy of Ireland in the eighteen-eighties Lord Bertie used to station himself in a strategic position in the Throne Room of Dublin Castle so that the debutantes, mistaking him for the Viceroy, would offer him their cheeks to kiss.

arrived, choosing books that she thought would interest them, making sure that the writing tables were adequately supplied with paper and envelopes. When King Edward VII and Queen Alexandra were coming to stay in 1903, she felt that Mount Stewart had to be 'tidied up for the great occasion'; for while the house was, in her opinion, 'one of the most delightful and comfortable in the world', it 'looked extraordinarily shabby'. There was only one bath with running water, and that was in the Londonderrys' own rooms on the ground floor; so they planned to give their rooms to the King, the Queen being relegated to rooms on the first floor which had a fine view of the lough. The billiard room, in the centre of the south front, was made into what Theresa called 'a comfortable living hall with chairs, writing tables and flower baskets'. The drawing-room, which was furnished in the Victorian manner with screens and palms and groups of chairs, was left as it was, except that it was given new cushions and chair-tops of embroidery worked by local women.

A fortnight before the King and Queen were due to arrive, the Londonderrys' daughter-in-law Edith Castlereagh nearly died of pneumonia. However, she got over the crisis and the royal visit went on as planned. The King and Queen and their daughter Princess Victoria arrived on a Saturday in July in time for tea in the newly-arranged 'living hall', after which Theresa took them through the other reception rooms and showed them the chairs from the Congress of Vienna. It seemed to her that they imagined she was 'drawing the long bow'; however, when she showed them a print of the Congress in which the chairs were clearly recognizable, they believed her and were very much impressed'.

Next day, the Archbishop of Armagh, Primate Alexander, took a service in the domestic chapel. The day was brilliantly sunny, so later in the morning the Queen and Theresa went for a walk along the shore of the lough; the tide was high, the distant Mountains of Mourne were looking particularly beautiful; there was, as Theresa afterwards recalled, 'a strong smell of seaweed and sweet briar' and 'masses of birds circling and crying, terns, brown and white gulls, cormorants and sand snipe'.[9] The Queen was without a hat, which rather surprised the people who saw her from the road.

They walked back to the house for luncheon, during which the band of the Royal Irish Constabulary played. Afterwards they motored over to Clandeboye to visit the former Vicereine of India, the widowed Marchioness of Dufferin and Ava. The King and Queen and Theresa were driven by Theresa's brother, the Earl of Shrewsbury. The Queen was terrified that he would run over a dog and every dog they met did its best to be run over; however, he managed to avoid them all. Next morning, the King and Queen left, having posed for 'the inevitable photograph' and each planted a copper beech. In the visitors' book, the Queen wrote, a little ungrate-fully: 'Beautiful place, but very damp.'

The Londonderrys usually spent most of their time at Wynyard and at their London residence, Londonderry House, coming back to Mount Stewart only for short visits. But they spent more time here in 1913 and 1914 when Lord Londonderry was involved in the Ulster Unionists' resistance to Home Rule. This enabled Theresa to do plenty of sailing. She was an intrepid yachtswoman and sailed her little boat *Red Rose* without mishap on the dangerous waters of Strangford Lough, which had nearly cut short the life of the great Castlereagh and in which a number of the Mount Stewart servants were drowned on an ill-fated boating trip. Unlike her husband, she was a good sailor and would sail on happily in rough weather while her passengers were seasick.

In 1913 she was sailing as early as March, but in April of the following year she noted with regret that her sailing had been curtailed 'owing to gales and Ulster Volunteers'. One weekend that April, she and her husband entertained a house party at Mount Stewart which included Carson, now leader of the Ulster Unionists, and his principal lieutenant, Captain James Craig. Theresa 'had a strong impression that something was going to happen'. She went for a walk with

Carson and told him she felt there 'was something in the air', but 'he, in his usual impenetrable style', said nothing to her whatever. She went out later with Craig, who likewise said nothing. However, on the following Tuesday, Lord Londonderry told her that something was indeed going to happen and that he was off to England, feeling that, as Lieutenant for County Down, it would be wiser for him to be out of the way. He asked Theresa if she would like to come with him, but she 'had the most extraordinary feeling of it being impossible to go'.

So Theresa was left alone in the house with her thirteen-year-old granddaughter Maureen. On Friday she heard that their motor cars had been ordered to go to Donaghadee, a few miles away on the coast. They were to bring back some of the shipload of rifles and ammunition that was being illegally landed that night at Larne, for use by the Ulster Volunteers in case they had to fight to resist Home Rule; some of the arms were put on to another vessel and taken from Larne to Donaghadee.

After dinner that night, Theresa took Maureen up to bed, promising her that if she heard any more news she would come up and tell her, for the girl was very interested in what was going on. Theresa then sat alone in the drawing-room until Miss MacDonald, the gamekeeper's daughter – who was the only person apart from herself who knew anything, since her father had gone to help unload the arms – came to tell her that two companies of Ulster Volunteers had gone to Donaghadee, which indicated that things were moving. She then went to bed, no doubt having first passed this information on to her excited granddaughter. Next morning Miss MacDonald came to her bedroom at 7.30 to tell her that the 'compliment' was in. Theresa got up and dressed and walked out to where the arms were stowed. 'I thought them the most beautifully packed bundles I had ever seen,' she wrote. 'Each bundle containing five rifles, bayonets and ammunition, and were all German Mausers.'[10]

While 'German Mausers' would soon be opening fire in Flanders and elsewhere, those that Theresa admired and the rest of that shipload were not, in the event, fired in anger; not, at any rate, in Ulster. The Ulster Unionists managed to bring Northern Ireland into being without having to use force. By that time, Theresa and her husband were both dead; but their son, who became the seventh Marquess of Londonderry, was a member of the Northern Ireland Government from 1921 to 1926. This meant that he and his wife Edith spent more time at Mount Stewart than his parents had done. The house, which had been used as a convalescent home for soldiers, sailors and airmen during the Great War, was modernized and redecorated; central heating was put in, and the drawing-room ceased to be Victorian, rather to the regret of Daisy Fingall. 'All the screens and little cosy nooks had disappeared,' she wrote, after seeing the room as it now was. 'There could be no opportunity of conversation in such a room that everyone could not hear.'[11]

The 7th Marquess of Londonderry and his wife
Edith outside the garden front of Mount Stewart,
she holding her Kerry Blue Terrier.

The surroundings of the house, which had been rather hemmed in with trees, were opened up and Edith Londonderry laid out elaborate gardens, providing plenty of work for demobilized servicemen after the end of the war. Below the south front of the house, facing towards the lough, she made a terrace which she decorated with stone animals carved by local craftsmen. These represented the select club of friends that she had formed called 'The Ark', each member being given the name of a bird or beast or mythical creature. Edith herself was 'Circe the Sorceress'.

A prominent member of the Ark was Ramsay MacDonald, who was given the name of Hamish the Hart. Edith had taken the Labour leader under her wing, just as Bonar Law, likewise a stranger to the fashionable world, had been taken under the wing of Theresa. When Ramsay MacDonald came to stay at Mount Stewart, he was given Elinor Glyn's novel *Did She?* as bedside reading. Next morning at breakfast, Edith asked him how much he had read of the novel and he replied: 'Oh, about fifteen pages. In fact, until she did!'[12]

The people who stayed at Mount Stewart during the years between the wars ranged from the Duke and Duchess of York, the future King George VI and Queen Elizabeth, to the left-wing Irish playwright Sean O'Casey. Others included Yeats, the painter Sir John Lavery and his beautiful Irish-American wife Hazel, and the writer and wit Oliver St John Gogarty. There was a special bond between Lord

Ramsay MacDonald at Mount Stewart, standing between the 7th Marquess of Londonderry and the 1st Viscount Hailsham, a Lord Chancellor who was the father of a subsequent Lord Chancellor.

The 7th Marquess of Londonderry in flying kit. A painting by Cuthbert Orde.

Londonderry and Gogarty in that they could both fly. Lord Londonderry was an intrepid pilot, landing an autogyro at Mount Stewart the very first time he flew one. In 1931 he became Secretary of State for Air in the National Government. When he and Edith arrived at Aldergrove, the Royal Air Force station near Belfast, after his appointment, they were besieged by journalists. One reporter climbed over the Mount Stewart wall, but was repulsed by the housekeeper, a redoubtable Yorkshirewoman. Lord Londonderry gave some of his land near Newtownards for Northern Ireland's first civil airfield; henceforth, he and his flying friends, such as Gogarty, were able to land their planes almost at the gates of Mount Stewart. When Daisy Fingall was here, the Marquis of Clydesdale, the future Duke of Hamilton, appeared at tea in his flying suit and goggles, having just landed; next day the whole party, except for Daisy, flew off to Germany.

Lord Londonderry would go for a flight in the same way as other people would go for a drive in their cars. Gogarty recalls being taken flying by his host when staying here. They circled twice over the house, where the Red Hand of Ulster, picked out in crimson begonias in one of Edith's gardens, could be seen clearly from the air, and 'swung out over the bright sea'.[13] As well as flying over Lough Strangford, Lord

Lord and Lady Londonderry racing their yacht on Strangford Lough.

Edith Lady Londonderry flying.

Londonderry followed his mother's example and went sailing on it; Edith would go with him. And she, too, learnt to fly; though owing to her other commitments she did not have enough lessons to enable her to fly solo.

Mount Stewart in the 1930s, according to Gogarty, was 'a house so hospitable that after a few days you wouldn't know which of you owned the place'. He was one of the house party when the young Jack Leslie, son of writer Shane Leslie, came to

Group outside the garden front of Mount Stewart at the christening of Jane Stewart, grand-daughter of Lord and Lady Londonderry and daughter of their son and daughter-in-law Lord and Lady Castlereagh, in 1932. The Londonderrys sit in the middle, Edith Londonderry holding the baby. The Castlereaghs are on the right, with the Londonderrys' youngest daughter Lady Mairi Stewart standing next to her brother. Dr Charles Frederick D'Arcy, Church of Ireland Archbishop of Armagh and Primate of All Ireland, sits on the left with Lord Londonderry's chaplain Canon Whatham standing behind.

stay. The guests were woken in the morning by a piper walking round the house; the piper, still wearing the kilt, then helped the footmen to take water up to the bed-rooms, where there were china basins but no running water. The piper also played at dinner, where four footmen waited. Little cards in silver frames on the dinner table told the guests what tunes the piper would play; a favourite was the beautiful and haunting 'Lough Catrine'.

Edith Londonderry, who had Scottish blood – her mother was a daughter of the third Duke of Sutherland – kept up a Scottish atmosphere at Mount Stewart by having as a permanent member of the house party a kilted Scot from the Outer Isles named Duncan Morrison who sang Scottish songs at the piano and taught his fellow-guests reels and jigs. He was not the only permanent or semi-permanent guest; there was Mr May, the resident clergyman, who took services in the rather grand domestic chapel, and there was old Mrs Blakiston-Houston who stayed for months on end, helping Edith with her needlework and with the potpourri which was made on trays in a room under the staircase, filling the house with its scent.

The house party when Jack Leslie was here included the Londonderrys' daugh-

The Londonderrys' youngest daughter, now Lady Mairi Bury, in the smoking room at Mount Stewart with her cockatoo on her shoulder. A painting by Julian Barrow. Edith Londonderry's portrait by de László hangs over the chimneypiece next to a Lawrence of the great Castlereagh.

ter Maureen and her husband Oliver Stanley, who was a member of the British Government. Another member of the government who was staying was Leslie Hore-Belisha. By way of contrast, there was a Spanish infanta and there was Sir Hedworth Williamson, one of those Edwardian figures who lived by staying at country houses and dining out in London. And, of course, there was Gogarty, who never stopped talking. 'Irish piffle!' Edith Londonderry would exclaim as he talked away.

As a change from Scottish songs and reels, the house party acted a play in the central hall. They had composed it themselves and it was topical; Jack Leslie played the part of a character whose name was thinly disguised as Pusholini. It must have been hard for a tall and slender young man, as he was, to impersonate Il Duce; but he did his best, wearing a black shirt and giving the Fascist salute.

One evening young Leslie was late for dinner; he came in after the rest of the party, about eighteen in number, had sat down. His host and hostess took it very well, but his grandparents, when they heard about it, wrote him a very cross letter. 'The old Londonderrys would never have invited you again,' they told him.[14]

Lord Londonderry died in 1949. During his last illness, the grand piano was carried upstairs and put in the corridor outside his bedroom so that Duncan Morrison could play to him. After her husband's death, Edith carried on much the same as before at Mount Stewart. There were still thirty-five servants in the house, though some of them may not have been quite up to pre-war standards; thus there was a butler, a forthright Ulsterman, who when passing the cream said confidentially: 'Don't take too much, it's running out.' The kilted Duncan Morrison still entertained the house party with his Scottish songs, as well as playing at the annual New Year's dance for the staff. There was also a gentleman from London who told people's fortunes with a crystal ball; he was supposed to be able to tell young men about their future girlfriends. Edith herself provided further entertainment by racing her dachshunds along the dining-room table two at a time.

Edith Londonderry died at Mount Stewart in 1959 in her eightieth year. Until the end of her life she worked hard in the gardens which she had created and which had now come to maturity. Once, when she was gardening, dressed in trousers and with only her behind protruding from the foliage, some visitors came and asked for Lady Londonderry. 'If you wait, I'll tell her,' she said. And she went into the house, put on a smart dress and some of the Londonderry jewels and came out to greet the visitors who did not realize she was the person they had just been talking to.

Mount Stewart passed to the Londonderrys' youngest daughter Lady Mairi Bury. In 1976 she gave the house to the National Trust, the gardens having been made over to the Trust some twenty years earlier. Lady Mairi continues to live in the house; in 1995 Julian Barrow painted her in the smoking-room, sitting beneath portraits of her mother and the great Castlereagh, her cockatoo perched on her shoulder.

# Chapter 20

# Newtown Anner
## COUNTY TIPPERARY

IN MAY 1816 the fifty-nine-year-old baronet Sir Thomas Osborne brought his young English bride back to Newtown Anner, his home near Clonmel in County Tipperary, a many-windowed house facing south across the Suir valley towards the Comeragh Mountains. Sir Thomas had himself given the house its principal front, which had a hall door with a large fanlight and an extra storey at each end. The door beneath the fanlight led into a pillared hall, beyond which were other spacious rooms.

To the new Lady Osborne, who was Catherine, daughter of Major Robert Smith of the Royal Marines, the house seemed 'immensely large'. She reckoned that one could 'dance thirty couple both in the drawing room and dining room'. She was no less impressed by the demesne and the surrounding country. 'I have seen no chain of mountains half so beautiful as those which bound the lovely prospect from every window in front of the house,' she wrote.

The moment they arrived, which was early in the morning, Catherine was taken by her husband to look at the kitchen garden. 'Welcome to your home, my Lady', said Mr Quin, the head gardener, 'with all the Irish warmth of manner', taking off his hat. But Catherine was displeased with him a day or two later when Sir Thomas showed him a large piece of ground full of pretty shrubs which she wanted to make into a garden and he insisted that it was too late in the year.

Catherine had never seen such a well-run house as Newtown Anner. 'Everything goes by clockwork' she observed. Being English herself, she was inclined to attribute this to the fact that the butler was an Englishman. This dignitary came at the head of a household of about thirty, including four footmen. Unlike in some houses, where the upper servants dined separately, the servants at Newtown all sat down together in the servants' hall; except for the kitchenmaids, the groom and the whipper-in to Sir Thomas's pack of hounds, who waited on the others and dined afterwards.

Sir Thomas delegated all authority over the male part of the establishment to the butler and insisted that Catherine should do the same with regard to the women, giving orders only to the housekeeper and to her lady's maid; 'she should never give

Newtown Anner.

orders to the inferior servants, because that would create confusion'. So when she wanted some more coal to be put on the fire in her dressing-room, she told Johnstone, her lady's maid, who rang for the housemaid. The housemaid, when she answered the bell, always brought a duster with her 'to remove every spot of dust from the room'; for as Catherine noticed with approval, the house was always kept spotlessly clean. Another of Sir Thomas's maxims was that the lady of the house ought never to show herself in the kitchen, his mother having never set foot in hers.

When her husband was out or away, Catherine may have regretted not being able to pay the odd visit to the kitchen to see a bit of life. 'I never saw a house so still and solitary as this,' she wrote. 'It is so very much apart from the servants; no door of communication upstairs with their apartments. My maid and I walk along the long corridor from room to room without more fear of interruption from a single being than if we were in the deserts of Arabia.' She would make Johnstone sit with her in her dressing-room 'that I may sometimes see a female face – hear a human voice'. When she was alone she did not use the drawing-room or the dining-room. 'I should feel quite lost in those great rooms where no sound is to be heard but the cawing of rooks and the echo of my own footsteps.'[1]

Both Catherine and her husband liked the noise of the rooks; on the other hand Sir Thomas gave permission, as his father had done before him, for soldiers from the barracks in Clonmel to come and take rooks' nests to make pies of the young birds. To Catherine, the redcoats climbing the trees outside the house in search of the nests were 'a cheerful sight'. The soldiers did not appear to constitute any appreciable threat to the rook population; had they done so, Sir Thomas intended to stop them coming.

Just as Catherine was beginning to settle down, the housekeeper died, which was rather a blow. Sir Thomas wrote to Dublin for a replacement; they hoped she would arrive before his brother Charles the judge and his family came to stay for Christmas. The Christmas guests were preceded by a piano, ordered from a famous Dublin instrument maker; 'I confess I only wish for its arrival as an ornament to the drawing room,' wrote Catherine, who cannot have been very musical.

In the following year Catherine gave birth to a son, whom they called William. She was soon pregnant again and suffering from morning sickness; sometimes she could not face dinner so had an early snack upstairs and then came down to the dining-room where 'by great exertion' she managed 'to sit out the ceremony of dishes and knives and forks'. As well as being put off by the sight of food, she had an 'inveterate aversion to the dining room' which she attributed to its 'desolate appearance and want of paint'.

Even after 'little William' had been joined by a sister named after her, Catherine was inclined to be lonely. 'On this day week I am to lose my cheerful party, when it will be almost worse than if they had never come,' she lamented on one occasion, when there were guests staying. 'Think of the doleful change the week after next will bring forth, imagine me at solitary meals and solitary occupations.' Her occupations included tending her favourite plants and reading, as well as decorating the grotto in the grounds with shells, 'deep in cement and trowel in hand'. This last occupation was hardly solitary, for she had Johnstone and another woman working with her, as well as two girls.

Her gardening suffered a setback when eleven of her best hyacinths were cut down during the night; they were grown from Dutch bulbs for which she had paid very dear. She thought she knew who had done it and that it had been done to prevent Quin, the head gardener, from winning a medal at the local horticultural show two days later. She was foolish enough to tell Sir Thomas, who made her stay away from the show altogether and exhibit nothing. This did poor Quin out of the other medal that he almost certainly would have won for his cucumbers.

A happier episode in Catherine's married life at Newtown was the expedition that she and her husband and a party of friends made to the top of one of the Comeraghs. They went 'in common labourers' carts' together with five or six menservants and about thirty tenants who chose to accompany them. On approach-ing a wood near the old castle where Sir Thomas's ancestors had lived, they were greeted by a large bonfire 'as a symptom of cordial goodwill'; a beautiful sight, for it was now evening.

Sir Thomas died in 1821 and poor little William, having succeeded to the baronetcy, followed him to the grave three years later, carried away by 'a cruel cough'; he was only seven. The baronetcy passed to an uncle, but Newtown was inherited by William's sister, 'poor little solitary Catherine', and her mother was left in charge.

As well as running the place for her daughter, the elder Catherine studied Greek and took up oil painting. 'I scarcely ever stir from home, having grown quite negligent in my visits to the poor,' she wrote in about 1827. She did, however, attend to the needs of the poor Protestants of the locality, who would assemble in her private chapel; and she instructed the Protestant servants in their religion.

She was becoming increasingly religious, Mr Woodward, the clergyman, being now her chief friend in the neighbourhood. She held Bible Society and Church Missionary Society meetings; some of the local Catholics may have suspected her of proselytizing, for when she was driving into Clonmel to attend a 'Reformation meeting' stones were thrown at her carriage. One of the stones broke the tortoise-shell comb in her hair, which she reckoned may have saved her life.

Catherine's religion seems to have been of rather a puritanical sort. When the Cox family, who lived at Castletown, a beautiful country house a few miles away to the east, gave a great fancy dress ball, she had a house party for it but did not go herself. 'I am happy in escaping a bustle so uncongenial with my feelings,' she wrote. 'The country has been quite wild about this ball – nothing but dress talked of. I must think and feel more that these vain amusements are quite inconsistent with serious views of religion . . . as Mr Woodward justly observes, it is not the scene in which we should desire to meet our blessed Redeemer.'[2]

Nevertheless, she was not wholly averse to worldly pleasures. She went on trips to Paris and to Italy as well as to England, bringing back a 'flower table' for the drawing-room and a round table for the garden temple. She put in a shower bath and admitted that her 'animal spirits' were 'much improved' by this modern luxury. She must have had a particular liking for the feel of water trickling down her face. 'I stood out in the rain till called in to my beefsteak,' she reported one April. 'It was really a great grief to me to come in.'

When her daughter Catherine grew up, she let her go to a ball in Clonmel without her, much to the disapproval of the eminent judge Richard Pennefather, Chief Baron of the Exchequer, who was a neighbour. A year later, in 1839, there was a 'fête' at Newtown to celebrate Catherine's coming-of-age. It started early in the morning and went on all day; twenty or thirty thousand people came, 'peasant girls and lads dressed in white, with green ribbon and flowers in their hair', danced on the lawn. 'The behaviour of the people was admirable,' the elder Catherine noted approvingly. 'Not a drunken person to be seen.'

This was the carefree Irish peasantry before the Famine. After the Famine had struck, the elder Catherine's whole time from breakfast until she went out to visit the poor was 'taken up in talking to beggars at the window'. She was tempted to sit in the new library in the morning because it overlooked the garden into which the beggars did not venture; but her conscience would not let her rest while they were at the windows of the drawing-room.

The drawing room at Newtown Anner in Catherine Bernal
Osborne's day. Her mother's gilt wallpaper can be clearly seen.

The drawing-room had been redecorated with a beautiful gilt wallpaper, which
was rather a waste since she had 'given up society'. Young Catherine was now away
for much of the time, married to Ralph Bernal, a radical politician and wit of
Jewish blood who was a rival of Disraeli. 'What a provoking thing is your devotion
to London,' her mother wrote to her sorrowfully. 'I begin to wonder if you seriously
think of selling Newtown . . . you don't seem to have the least idea of coming
home.'[3]

Catherine Bernal Osborne, as she now was, her husband having taken her
surname in addition to his own, did not sell Newtown; and after her mother's death
in 1856 she and her husband and their two daughters spent a considerable amount
of time here. When the two girls, Edith and Grace, grew up, they were much
admired; they both had beautiful hands and attractive voices, both of them were
clever and fascinating. In the words of a neighbour, Mrs Richard Bagwell of
Marlfield, they were 'a remarkable pair to find in an Irish country house'.[4] Mrs
Bagwell subscribed to the popular myth that Edith got her wonderful dark eyes from
her grandmother on her father's side who was a Spanish gypsy; in fact, while her

The beautiful Edith Osborne.

Edith and Grace Osborne by the garden temple at Newtown Anner in about 1870.

Three of the children of the 10th Duke of St Albans,
who married Grace Osborne in 1874, outside the hall
door of Newtown Anner.

Jewish forebears did originally come from Spain, her paternal grandmother was the daughter of a Mr White of London.

Though Grace was the younger of the two sisters, it was she who inherited Newtown, having married the tenth Duke of St Albans, whom her parents had regarded as a more suitable son-in-law than Edith's husband Henry Blake, at the time of the marriage an impecunious police officer. By 1898 the relative situation of the two sisters was somewhat reversed; Grace was a duchess and the owner of Newtown but she was now a widow, the Duke having died a few months earlier after a long illness, whereas Edith was Lady Blake and enjoying many years of glory as a governor's wife. Her husband had been such a success in the Royal Irish Constabulary that he had gone on to a brilliant proconsular career; she was just about to leave for Hong Kong where he had been appointed Governor having been successively Governor of the Bahamas and of Jamaica.

The Duchess gave a small farewell party for her sister at Newtown; the guests included Count and Countess de la Poer, who lived nearby at Gurteen le Poer. Count de la Poer was said to have been in love with Edith as a young man, but had kept silent, knowing that her parents would never have allowed her to marry him because he was a Catholic. He was now happily married to a wife of his own persuasion.

The de la Poers and their children came frequently to Newtown, usually on bicycles, though their son Edmond arrived in a pony-cart when he came to say goodbye
before going back to school in September 1898. While he was here, he played chess
with the Duchess's unmarried stepdaughter, Lady Sybil Beauclerk – the Duke
having been a widower when she married him – and also with the Duchess herself,
who tipped him ten shillings. A few days later Edmond's mother played chess with
Lady Sybil, when she and her husband bicycled over to tea at Newtown bringing
an English Benedictine monk who was staying with them. The Beauclerks do not
appear to have shared their neighbours' enthusiasm for bicycling; they preferred
horses; while the Duchess's married daughter Lady Catherine Somerset and her
husband appeared earlier that summer in what Count de la Poer described as a
'Moto Car'.[5]

As an alternative to horses and motors, there was the River Suir. In May 1899,
when the Marquess of Dufferin's brilliant younger son Lord Basil Blackwood was
staying, the house party went down the river in a boat as far as Carrick, returning
by road. Also staying at this time was the Duchess's other married daughter, Lady
Moyra Cavendish, and her husband Richard, a brother of the Duke of
Devonshire's heir. The Duchess's youngest daughter, Lady Alex Beauclerk,
became engaged to Charles Cavendish, a distant cousin of Richard, but he was
killed in the South African War. When news of his death reached Newtown, the
Duchess was 'broken-hearted' while Lady Alex was 'wonderfully calm'.[6] She
wished she could have remained here when her family left to spend some months in
England.

By 1905 the Duchess's elder son, Lord Osborne Beauclerk, known as 'Obby' –
the new Duke was her stepson – possessed a motor car. He drove over to Gurteen in
it to have dinner with the de la Poers, whose grown-up sons and daughters were, like
him, unmarried, though younger. The Duchess claimed that she could always recognize two of them, Elinor and Arnold, no matter how they disguised themselves.

Later that year, Elinor and Arnold decided to put her claim to the test. They disguised themselves as two female strolling players, 'Mrs Gallagher the Proprietress'
and 'Josephine O'Riorden', and, armed with posters advertising their show, which
they had had specially printed in Clonmel, they came up to Newtown, rang the hall
doorbell and asked for the Duchess. While they were talking to the footman, the
Duchess happened to come downstairs into the hall and they went towards her. She
thought they looked so terrible that she would not speak to them but hurriedly retired
into the drawing-room. They sent the footman after her with one of their posters and
a request to see her, but she retreated into the library. They then went round the
outside of the house and saw the Duchess through a window, but she ran out of the
room and took refuge upstairs. The two unwanted visitors proceeded to make such
a noise that the Duchess, imagining them to be either mad or drunk, sent for the

police. Eventually Bennet the butler, who was in on the secret, told her that the visitors were really the two young de la Poers. She found this hard to believe but was at last convinced and great was the merriment'.[7]

In 1906 Princess Marie Louise of Schleswig-Holstein, a granddaughter of Queen Victoria, came to stay at Newtown and the Duchess gave a dinner party for her. She had been staying with the Earl and Countess of Bessborough at Bessborough in County Kilkenny. Soon after this royal visit, tragedy struck the Newtown household; the young second footman was found shot near the pond close to the house. He was thought to have committed suicide, though the inquest gave a verdict of accidental death. A rather similar tragedy occurred in 1923 when Wallace, the Duchess's old coachman, was drowned in the river.

By then, the Duchess was living in London; she had left Newtown in 1920, finding life here almost impossible owing to the Troubles. The house survived and her son Obby Beauclerk settled down here with his wife Beatrix whom he had married in 1918. She had three sons and three daughters by her late husband, the sixth Marquess of Waterford, so there were usually some young people at Newtown. There was a great deal of coming and going between Newtown and Curraghmore, the Waterford family seat some fifteen miles to the south-east, where the young Marquess lived with his brothers and sisters.

In 1924 what was known as the 'one pipe' central heating system was installed at Newtown and by the end of 1926 the house was lit by electricity. The Aladdin lamps were given away as presents to neighbours such as the de la Poers, who were still without electric light. It was perhaps appropriate that the electricity should have come to Newtown at about the same time as rich Americans came to stay – Mrs and Mrs Tree from Virginia, he thinking of taking over the mastership of the Tipperary Hunt.

Among the people who came to stay in 1927 was Lady Osborne Beauclerk's eighty-two-year-old father, the Marquess of Lansdowne, a former Viceroy of India and Foreign Secretary. He felt unwell the day after he arrived and he died that night. Lord Lansdowne was connected in more ways than one with the Beauclerks, for his daughter Evelyn was married to the Duke of Devonshire, whose brother Lord Richard Cavendish was the husband of Obby's sister Lady Moyra.

In 1934 Obby succeeded his half-brother as the twelfth Duke of St Albans. He did not inherit any ducal seat with the title, so he and his Duchess continued to live at Newtown. The Duchess's sister, the Duchess of Devonshire, who became a widow in 1938, used to come and stay. On Sundays the two sisters would attend the little Church of Ireland church outside the Newtown Anner demesne; the Duke did not always go with them and the church was usually fairly empty. People said that the congregation consisted of two duchesses and a chauffeur.

## Chapter 21

# Rockingham

## COUNTY ROSCOMMON

THE ELIZABETHAN settler Sir John King obtained a lease of the Abbey of Boyle in County Roscommon as well as large grants of land in Roscommon and Sligo. His descendants originally lived in the town of Boyle, first in a seventeenth-century house, then in a fine early eighteenth-century house built by Sir Henry King; but Sir Henry's son, who became Earl of Kingston, preferred to live in a house outside the town. It was called Kingston and stood in the splendid demesne of Rockingham on the shores of Lough Key.

Here Lord and Lady Kingston lived a fairly quiet life. 'Went to church, dined at home' is a fairly frequent entry in the diary that their daughter Lady Eleanor King kept in 1774 when she was about eighteen. They 'rode out in the morning' or 'went out in the cabriole'; they frequently 'went onto the Lake to fish'. Mrs and Mrs French came over from French Park to dine; Richard Lovell Edgeworth came over from

Rockingham. The original Regency house with its dome.

The central hall at Rockingham.

Rockingham. The imperial staircase.

Edgeworthstown in County Longford and stayed three nights. When Lady Kingston was away in Dublin, Lord Kingston and some other gentlemen dined alfresco on one of the islands in Lough Key; poor Eleanor 'dined at home alone'.[1]

Eleanor's brother the second Earl of Kingston married the heiress of another branch of the family, which brought him vast estates in Cork, Tipperary and Limerick. These eventually passed to his eldest son, the third Earl, known as 'Big George', whereas the estates in Roscommon and Sligo were inherited by his second son, General Robert King, who became the first Viscount Lorton. In 1810 Lord Lorton built himself a new house in the Rockingham demesne, an elegant Regency mansion with a dome and a semicircular Ionic colonnade. His architect was John Nash, whose pupils James and George Pain were later to design Mitchelstown Castle in County Cork for his brother Big George. The interior of Rockingham, as the new house was called, was spacious and very much of its period; there was a top-lit central hall with a screen of Corinthian columns dividing it from a very grand imperial staircase, and a round drawing-room. The house was unusual in having no 'back'; the offices were all underground and entered by a tunnel three hundred yards long. Lord Lorton did not want any prospect of his house to be spoilt by the sight of servants or tradesmen. Better still than any prospect of the house were the views from it; particularly the view over Lough Key with its wooded peninsulas and islands. On one island was a ruined castle of the MacDermots, to which Lord Lorton added a folly castle. Another piece of early nineteenth-century Gothic at Rockingham was the gatehouse over the long beech avenue leading from the town of Boyle to the house.

In 1822 Lord Lorton added a third storey to the house to provide more bedrooms. The dome was sacrificed and the house became rather ungainly. Further alterations

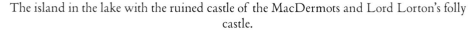

The island in the lake with the ruined castle of the MacDermots and Lord Lorton's folly castle.

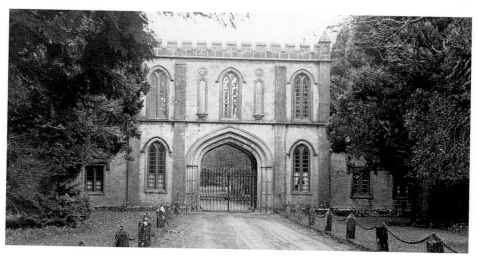

The Gothic gatehouse over the beech avenue.

Rockingham. The house after the addition of the third storey.

were carried out in 1863 after a serious fire; nevertheless, the house still kept its Regency character.

Lord Lorton died in 1854. Since his eldest son, the second Viscount, was now the eventual heir to the earldom of Kingston, Rockingham was settled on his younger son Laurence, who had taken the additional surname of Harman, having inherited Newcastle, the estate of the Harmans in County Longford. According to the settlement, the second Viscount Lorton's elder son, Robert King, had the right to reside at Rockingham; and one April he decided to come here, bringing his mother and his younger brother Henry. He did this to annoy his father, his father and mother being estranged. Laurence King-Harman was then at Newcastle, but the Rockingham agent, Mr Robertson, was staunchly on Lord Lorton's side and having been warned of the impending 'invasion' told Reilly the butler and Dickie the land steward that on no account was Lady Lorton to be admitted. And he wrote an indignant letter to Lord Lorton in London telling him the news.

Lady Lorton, Robert and Henry arrived by train at Carrick-on-Shannon and drove to Rockingham in two post-cars. While Dickie the land steward galloped into Boyle to alert Robertson, the invaders approached the house by way of the tunnel. They had made friends with a man named Peyton, who came along the tunnel with them and rang the bell of the basement door. The door was opened by Reilly the butler who asked Peyton what he wanted; while they were talking, Robert, who had been standing on one side, rushed in and claimed possession of the house. Lady Lorton and Henry now entered and tried to persuade Reilly to give them the hall door key, which he had in his pocket. Eventually Robert pinioned Reilly against the wall and Henry went through his pockets and took the key. They ordered him out of the house; but two of the other servants, a man and a maid, agreed to work for them.

The house having fallen to the invaders without, so to speak, a shot being fired, Robertson wrote to Laurence King-Harman assuring him that at any rate the family silver was safe in Boyle, as well as the late Lord Lorton's desk with the papers in it. The invaders had been particularly keen to lay their hands on this, presumably in the hope that it contained some document that would give Robert a stronger position at Rockingham. Robertson's morale was boosted by a letter from Lord Lorton ordering that his wife and sons should be ejected, if necessary by force. He tried to starve them out, threatening anyone who took produce from the place into the house with instant dismissal. The gates of the demesne were shut and the lodge-keepers were forbidden to let anyone in without a pass from Robertson, who planned to bring over a force of Laurence King-Harman's men from Newcastle. The loyalty of the Newcastle men could be counted on; whereas the Rockingham employees, believing that Robert would eventually get his way and come and live here, would have been reluctant to antagonize him.

Some of them did in fact turn quisling and work for the besieged party, whose reinforcements included a clergyman named Ward, 'that most consummate villain', as Robertson called him. To add fuel to the flames, Robert wrote an insulting letter to his father, inviting him to join the house party; while Lady Lorton, accompanied by the Reverend Ward, sallied forth into Boyle on a jaunting car and got the town crier to collect a gang of ragamuffins who were made to 'shout for Her Ladyship'.

One hopes they were also given the wherewithal to drink her health.

April became May and still the invaders held out. Robert tried to get control of the demesne, though his rights were limited to the house only. Life was getting uncomfortable for the beleaguered Lady Lorton and her sons; and to make matters worse for them, none of the neighbouring gentry came to call. By the middle of June Mr Noakes, the family solicitor, reported that the invaders were losing heart. Robert offered peace terms, but Lord Lorton demanded unconditional surrender. As a last desperate move, Robert took possession of the boathouse on Lough Key and put an armed guard of seven men on it; but the guard was routed by the forces of Robertson, who removed the boats. The so-called Siege of Rockingham came to an end. The invaders beat a retreat, though not without plunder; for Lady Lorton made off with the family jewels.[2]

Laurence King-Harman was succeeded at Rockingham by his son Colonel Edward King-Harman, a tall and impressive figure known as 'The King'; he mixed freely with all classes and once nearly lost his life when he was stabbed during a drunken brawl in Sligo. He was a Member of Parliament, sitting as a Home Ruler in the 1870s when half the Home Rule party at Westminster were of the

A young lady stands in the conservatory at Rockingham in mid-Victorian times.

Rockingham. Rowing on the lake at about the turn of the century.

Ascendancy. Among those who came to shoot with him at Rockingham was Sir Henry Gore-Booth of Lissadell in County Sligo, a nephew of Lady Lorton of the 'Siege', who was herself a Gore-Booth. Sir Henry's valet Thomas Kilgallon acted as his loader. The loaders had to be out in very good time so Kilgallon came down early to breakfast in the housekeeper's room and found the housekeeper, Mrs Clew, who was 'old-fashioned and prim', sitting by herself and eating nothing, though the bacon and eggs and everything else was there on the table. He bade her good morning and asked if he could help her to anything, but she replied: 'Please do not touch them dishes till my husband comes in.' Kilgallon imagined that her husband was the butler; but Mr Clew turned out to be the gardener, 'an elderly worklike man' who sat down at the head of the table where he would have expected the butler to sit.[3] Rockingham was famous for a woodcock shoot when the beaters landed on one of the islands from a boat and drove the birds out while the guns waited in two or three other boats, not knowing which way they would fly.

Frances King-Harman, the only surviving child and heiress of 'The King', married Dr Thomas Stafford, who had attended her father in his last illness. Dr Stafford was a Catholic, but he agreed to the children of the marriage being brought up as Protestants. Though his wife was now the owner of Rockingham, he continued with his career; his work in medicine and local government eventually brought him a baronetcy. Around the turn of the century, Rockingham was let to various people, notably to that fashionable viceregal pair, the Earl and Countess of Dudley. Thanks to these illustrious tenants, the house was well done up and in advance of its time in having plenty of bathrooms and a telephone.

It is possible that the great Rosa Lewis of the Cavendish Hotel in London came to Rockingham to cook for the Dudleys. In later years at the Cavendish, if Ireland were mentioned, Rosa would say that she had been there once. When asked where in Ireland she had been, she would reply cryptically: 'Rockingham.'

The Staffords were back at Rockingham when their elder son Edward Stafford-King-Harman — who had assumed the two additional surnames as a schoolboy — came of age in April 1912. It was just at the time of Asquith's Home Rule Bill; politics loomed large, as can be seen in the letter that one of the house party, who was an Ulster Unionist, wrote to the even more staunchly Unionist Theresa Marchioness of Londonderry. 'We are having great celebrations here. The Nationalist Boards of Guardians and Councils are presenting addresses which is a good sign in these troublesome times and tomorrow about 5,000 of the people around these parts gather for sports, tea and fireworks. It is a most lovely place and the young King-Harman is starting well. Crowds of Fenians are now arriving for lunch and the devil in me urges me to propound some good Ulster doctrines and watch the results.'[4]

There were more celebrations at Rockingham before Edward's wedding to Olive Pakenham-Mahon, the heiress to Strokestown, another great estate in County Roscommon, which took place in London in July 1914. The marriage would unite the two principal families of the county; had it not been for the Wyndham Act, the land purchase act of 1903, the couple would between them have stood to own something like 70,000 acres. Although the tenanted lands of Rockingham had nearly all been sold under the Wyndham Act, the former tenants were invited to the celebrations and entertained in a huge marquee outside the house; there was a tug o' war between the men from the plains and the men from the Curlew Mountains. Such was the betting on this event that even more drink was consumed than was provided by the generous young host. The celebrations lasted a week; some of the guests are said to have been in so permanent a state of inebriation that they remained for nearly the whole week at Rockingham.[5]

The fact that Ireland then seemed close to civil war, with the Ulster Unionists and the Nationalists arming, cast no damper on the celebrations. Still less were the festivities marred by the news of the murder of an Austrian archduke. But the European war which resulted from that murder was to claim Edward's life; before the end of 1914, he was killed in action.

Edward's younger brother Cecil also fought in the Great War; but he survived to inherit Rockingham and his father's baronetcy. He and his wife and their three children came to live here in 1929. The house had passed unscathed through the Troubles — during which de Valera himself lived for a while in dug-outs in a bog near Lough Key — and things continued to be done in the pre-war manner. A butler and two footmen waited at table; there was a cook and there were four maids. Annie the housemaid was a terrifying figure, all the more so for being tiny. Sir Cecil once overheard her saying to herself, as she polished the brass stair-rods, 'It's not the gentlemen I mind, it's these damned women.'[6] Very different was Hannah the basement

A shoot at Rockingham in about 1930. Cecil Stafford-King-Harman is at the far left, the Earl of Granard at the far right. In the centre is Cecil's father Sir Thomas Stafford, with the Marquess of Headfort holding his arm. On Sir Thomas's other side is the Earl of Kingston, whose father Henry took part in the nineteenth century 'invasion' of Rockingham, together with his grandmother Lady Lorton and his uncle Robert. Next to Lord Kingston and without a hat is Dermot MacDermot, a half-brother of The MacDermot, Prince of Coolavin, whose ancestors owned the lands of Rockingham until the seventeenth century.

maid, who appeared to spend her whole time underground and never see the light of day. She looked after the menservants as well as the floating population of valets, chauffeurs and loaders brought here by guests.

When there was a shoot, the six guns sometimes had as many as thirteen menservants between them. The Marquess of Headfort, when he came to shoot, brought a chauffeur, a loader and a valet, though for some reason he never brought his wife, the former gaiety girl Rosie Boote. Other shooting guests included the elderly General Sir Bernard Hickie, known as Barny, and the Earl of Granard. Lord and Lady Granard sometimes arrived in their yacht, having travelled by water to Lough Key from Lough Forbes, on which Castle Forbes, their home in County Longford, was situated. In summer, Lady Granard would come over to luncheon, bringing some of her rather fashionable house party with her.

For the Stafford-King-Harmans' son Thomas and their daughters Joan and Anne, who were teenagers during the 1930s, a great excitement was the donkey polo which was played on the lawn in front of the house. The donkeys lived in different places — one was tethered in the nursery garden, there was a black donkey which brought in the fruit and vegetables, and others about the place. For the polo matches,

Joan and Anne Stafford-King-Harman on their ponies in 1930,
preparing for various shows, with Rockingham in the background.

the donkeys were properly groomed. The grown-ups played as well as the children, including ladies such as their aunt Bridget Acland, their mother's sister-in-law; their neighbours the Kirkwoods would come over from Woodbrook to join in the matches. There was a rule that one was not allowed to hit the ball if one's feet were on the ground. The donkeys made the game more difficult by always cantering in the direction in which they lived.

A less energetic pastime for the young people was dressing up in the uniforms and old-fashioned clothes that had accumulated in the house over the years. Then there would be boating on Lough Key, expeditions to MacDermot's Castle on the island. The folly adjoining the old castle served as a summer-house until shortly before the Second World War when it was gutted by fire. The sight of the blazing castle reflected in the waters of the lough was spectacular.

The girls would accompany their mother when she visited people on the place who were sick. When Lady Stafford-King-Harman and Joan went to visit Jim Flanagan the shepherd, who had pneumonia, they found he had no oxygen and was dying. His wife said, 'It's no good, it's the will of God'; but Lady Stafford-King-Harman sent the chauffeur into the town of Sligo to bring back more oxygen and he recovered. The Stafford-King-Harmans paid their family doctor to look after the people on the place, for whom Sir Cecil felt a great responsibility. The people showed their gratitude when Joan got married, presenting her with a silver coffee-pot engraved with their signatures.

A few months before Joan married, Thomas came of age. It was 1942 and he was on active service as a subaltern in the Irish Guards, which had been his uncle Edward's regiment and was also the regiment of Joan's husband; he had recently

A shoot at Rockingham in 1937. Anne
Stafford-King-Harman, who with her sister
Joan did great work picking up fallen birds,
standing by the game cart with Lord
Headfort.

been wounded and the celebrations were held at the end of his convalescence. Two hundred people, most of whom worked on the place or had worked here, came to the party and drank Black Velvet out of an immense loving-cup. Old Michael Cartie, who had been at Rockingham for ninety years and could remember Laurence-King-Harman whom he spoke of as 'Honourable Laurence', said it was the best party yet. He still worked here, coming up every Saturday morning with a colleague, both of them in bowler hats, to scratch the gravel on the sweep.[7]

Less than two years after he came of age, Thomas was killed in action. 'Poor Master Thomas, the flower of the flock,' Annie the housemaid said when she heard the news.[8] And she put a little black bow on her white uniform. She could remember when Thomas's uncle Edward was killed. The death of two sons of the house in two successive wars made people believe that Rockingham was unlucky; it was also said to have ghosts, though the family was not much troubled by them.

Though they had lost their only son, the Stafford-King-Harmans continued to live in some considerable style at Rockingham after the end of the Second World War. They employed the English architect Philip Tilden to make the house more

Rockingham after the fire of 1957.

manageable; the basement and the top floor were sealed off and the kitchen was brought upstairs. During the 1950s, Sir Cecil was a prominent figure in the Irish racing world; he also served on the President of Ireland's Council of State. When de Valera became President and received Sir Cecil at Áras an Uachtaráin, the former Viceregal Lodge, he shook him by the hand and said, remembering the dug-outs in the bog near Rockingham, 'Times have changed!'

By then, however, Rockingham itself was but a memory. In the autumn of 1957, when the King-Harmans were away for the Doncaster sales, the house was burnt to the ground. Once again a blaze was reflected in the waters of the lough; this time, it was a holocaust. Sir Cecil considered rebuilding the house as it was before the third storey was added, putting back the dome, but finding that this would be too expensive, he sold the estate to the Forestry Department.

*Chapter 22*

# Springhill

## COUNTY DERRY

Low, whitewashed, high-roofed house with a sense of great age and peace, Springhill in County Derry grew over a period of nearly two hundred years. The two-storeyed centre with its symmetrical entrance front was built in about 1680 by 'Good Will' Conyngham, a gentleman of Scottish settler stock who was to play a leading part in the defence of Derry during the Siege. As befitted those uncertain times, the house was surrounded by a defensive enclosure or bawn; this was taken down early in the eighteenth century and two detached office wings of stone with Dutch gables were built flanking the entrance front, making a deep forecourt. The house was enlarged in about 1765 by Colonel William Conyngham, MP who added a single-storey wing at each end, one of them containing a large and lofty drawing-room in striking contrast to the low, panelled rooms in the centre. Finally, in about 1850, William Lenox-Conyngham added a large dining-room beyond the drawing-room and in the garden front of the house,

Springhill.

Springhill. The Gun Room.

Springhill. The Beech Walk in about 1900. Sir William
Lenox-Conyngham's daughter Charlotte stands under a tree on the left.

which is irregular, going in and out, and faces along an old beech avenue to a ruined tower.

The three daughters of William Lenox-Conyngham, Harriett, known as Hazzie, Jane and Charlotte, ran a sewing class for girls from the cottages; it was held every day in an upper room of one of the office wings. As well as being skilled at needlework, Hazzie and her sisters made jams and cordials. Once after making blackcurrant whiskey they fed the squeezed currants to the hens, who became drunk and reeled about the yard.

In 1854 Hazzie married Marcus Gage, the son of a county neighbour; he had proposed to her standing by the black marble chimneypiece in the library. The drawing-room curtains were dyed olive green for the wedding and there was a family party including the Marchioness of Ormonde, who was an aunt of the bride on her mother's side. Two years later Hazzie's brother William married Laura Arbuthnot, whose sister Eleanor narrowly escaped being abducted by that notorious Tipperary character 'Woodcock' Carden. The newly married couple came to live at Springhill with William's father, his mother being dead; when they arrived at Dungannon after their honeymoon they were met by a mounted escort of tenants who rode behind their carriage as far as the village of Moneymore, where the horses were taken out and a cheering crowd pulled them up to the house, which Laura had not yet seen. The Blue Room had been made ready for them, with new chintz hangings on the four-poster.

Laura fell in love with the house immediately and settled down happily here. She collected beetles, and would look for them when she went for her daily stroll with her father-in-law, up the beech walk and back along the road through the wood. She did, however, find the long dinners every night rather trying. When she left the table at the end of dinner she would go up to bed and have a sleep while her father-in-law and the other gentlemen were enjoying their port, telling her maid to wake her the moment they came out of the dining-room so that she could come down again and join them.

Many people came to stay, bringing their own menservants and grooms, who slept in a dormitory in one of the office wings. As well as the comings and goings of family, guests, staff and hangers-on, there were frequent visits from pedlars, with brooches of coloured glass and other trinkets in their packs; and from beggars, some of whom made memorable remarks. One old man, on being given silver instead of copper, said: 'May Your Honour never die but that every hair of your head may turn into a candle to light you to glory!'[1]

Springhill also had a ghostly visitor, a lady whose apparitions were associated with the death of George Lenox-Conyngham, father of the elder William, who shot himself in one of the bedrooms in 1816, though he lingered a couple of days and died penitent. Two of George's great-grandsons as small boys were in the four-

Sir William Lenox-Conyngham, looking rather like
a ghost, in the Gun Room at Springhill.

poster in what was thought to be the haunted room and they saw a strange lady standing by the fireplace. In the 1880s a female friend who was staying, having taken something to the Lenox-Conynghams' eldest daughter Milly after she had gone up to bed, saw the tall figure of a lady at the head of the oak staircase in the moonlight. The figure moved to the door of a bedroom, probably the room in which George shot himself, threw up her hands as if in despair and then vanished.

Milly's father was now Sir William, having been knighted in 1881. He and Laura had eleven children, the eldest of whom, by the 1880s, were already grown up. Each Christmas they would put on a play, the cast being augmented with friends from outside. The young Mina Lowry from Rockdale in County Tyrone, who came here for the first time one Christmas as a shy girl not long out of the schoolroom, found the drawing-room full of people in eighteenth-century dress; they were rehearsing Sheridan's *Rivals*. Mina was herself given a small part and the in following year she had a part in Goldsmith's *She Stoops to Conquer*, wearing one of the many dresses from other days which were to be found in the chests and cupboards of Springhill. This was the first time she stayed in the house and the first time she met the Lenox-Conynghams' eldest son, yet another William. He was just back from India and was, as she recalled, 'handsome, haughty and aloof'.[2] He refused to act in the play but deigned to officiate as prompter. The play was a success and it was followed by a dance, it being New Year's Eve. Having well and truly seen the New

Sir William Lenox-Conyngham in his donkey chair with some of his family outside
Springhill in about 1904. His wife Laura stands behind him; his daughter-in-law Mina
Lenox-Conyngham sits on a step in the middle holding her infant son William.
Charlotte Lenox-Conyngham stands in the doorway, wearing a boater.

Year in, Mina and the other young guests went up to bed, each being given a candle
in a silver candlestick at the foot of the oak staircase. Mina was in the Blue Room;
she noticed the scent of lavender in the four-poster.

William may have seemed 'haughty and aloof' when she first met him, but she
eventually married him. They came to live at Springhill in 1907, Sir William having
died towards the end of the previous year. During Sir William's illness and the years
of agricultural depression and agrarian unrest, the house had fallen into disrepair;
now, when money was available from the sale of the tenanted land under the
Wyndham Act, they were able to renovate it and put in bathrooms. Mina rearranged
the furniture and made other changes, which she feared might have distressed her
mother-in-law when she visited the house for the first time after leaving it. When
Lady Lenox-Conyngham, as Laura now was, looked around and said: 'Ah! I see
you have made that alteration,' Mina's heart stood still. But to her great relief, her
mother-in-law said, with a smile and a bow, 'It is what I always *longed* to do, and
now *you* have accomplished it.'[3] Lady Lenox-Conyngham was more tolerant of
change than the old man of ninety living in one of the cottages, who said when he
saw the bicycle on which Mina had come to visit him, 'Sir William's mother never
went out except in a coach with four grey horses.'

The widowed Laura Lady Lenox-Conyngham with her ten surviving children and three daughters-in-law. Her eldest son William and his wife Mina sit on her right; her son Jack, who was killed in the Great War, stands third from the left, between his sisters Milly and Charlotte. Milly, who married a County Derry neighbour, James Clark of Largantogher, was a grandmother of Lord Moyola, formerly Major James Chichester-Clark, Prime Minister of Northern Ireland.

Soon after Mina and her family moved into Springhill, the children's nurse saw a ghost; though female, it does not appear to have been the lady seen on previous occasions. One morning, just before dawn, she saw a figure come into the night nursery, where she slept in a four-poster beside the cots of the three children, and bend over each of the cots. She thought it was Mina and was about to strike a light when the figure hurried out. It happened again a few weeks later. Mina had not been in the night nursery when the nurse thought she saw her; but she did not tell her this so as not to frighten her. In *An Old Ulster House*, the delightful family history that she wrote towards the end of her life, she speculates as to whether it was perhaps the ghost of an ancestress of the children, whose own children were ill with smallpox a century earlier; or whether it was one of those instances where the ghost of a living person is seen and she was herself the ghost.[4]

During the Home Rule crisis, Mina's husband agreed to raise the South Derry Regiment of Ulster Volunteers; though having been a regular soldier, he was never very happy about the raising of an unofficial army in Ulster. The Volunteers drilled

by night in the Motor Yard at Springhill, lit by carbide gas which the English chauffeur organized. Mina joined in these martial activities and signalled messages with
a lamp from a hilltop near the demesne. She also formed a nursing corps helped by
two English ladies who came to stay, Katharine Furse, who later became head of the
English Red Cross, and Rachel Crowdy, who after the Great War worked for the
League of Nations. Both ladies had charm and humour and liked poetry; Miss
Crowdy recited Kipling's 'If', which was then new to Mina and to her twelve-year-
old daughter Diana.

In April 1914, the Ulster Unionist leader, Sir Edward Carson, came to stay. The
house was illuminated and there were flags in the forecourt. Carson's valet arrived
ahead of him and laid out his sleeping draught on his dressing table. The family and
house party were assembled at the hall door to greet him; there was a crowd of spec-
tators on the lawn and the motor car in which he drove up was preceded by a gal-
loping outrider. He was accompanied by Captain James Craig, his lieutenant,
together with Mrs Craig and Sir George Richardson, the Commandant of the
Ulster Volunteers.

The Lenox-Conynghams gave a large dinner party in Carson's honour. Very
appropriately, the damask tablecloth depicted the Siege of Derry. Carson's place at
the table was marked by a laurel wreath while the place-cards of everybody else were
in the form of little cardboard sentries, the idea being that they were guarding a place
for the occupant. Outside the house there were real sentries on guard because Carson
was staying.

Diana, William and Desmond, the three Lenox-Conyngham children, aged
between eleven and eight, were allowed to come down for dessert and sat by their
mother, Desmond wearing the cream satin page's outfit that he had worn at a
cousin's wedding. 'Well! Do you belong to my army?' Carson asked them, and the
children replied solemnly that they did. As though it were his own equivalent of the
King's Shilling, Carson let William have another chocolate, his mother having told
him that he had had enough already.[5]

Various people from round about were invited to join the party after dinner. One
of them, a linen manufacturer from Cookstown known as Big Bill, arrived at about
nine and was surprised to find that dinner was still going on. 'Holy God!' he
exclaimed. 'They're eating yet.'[6]

Soon after Carson's visit came the anxious night when Mina's husband and his
various helpers drove off in motor cars to Larne to bring back rifles from the gun-
running. Men waited in the lower yard at Springhill to unload the weapons when
they arrived. As the night wore on they started celebrating and became 'dangerously
noisy';[7] Mina, in evening dress, had to go outside to tell them to be quiet.

While strolling through the Beech Walk during his visit to Springhill, Carson
had suddenly said: 'I see terrible times ahead – bitter fighting, rivers of blood!'[8]

When he said this, he was thinking about Ireland; but before the Irish Troubles there would be 'bitter fighting' and 'rivers of blood' elsewhere. When the Great War broke out, Mina's husband, though not far off sixty, was recalled to his old regiment. The family went with him; they had two days in which to pack and close up the house. Two of his brothers also served in the war; one of them, Jack, was killed in action at the age of fifty-four.

The war was followed by the Troubles. Mina kept a revolver by her bedside and other arms behind the panelling. For some of those months, she and her family were away in Dublin, where her husband had military duties, but having promised to open a bazaar near Springhill, she came back here on her own for two nights. On returning to the house after the bazaar, she saw about twenty men in the shrubbery. They had come to raid the house but had waited until she got back, probably out of consideration for her. They proceeded to ransack every room but found no weapons except for two old swords which they carried off. They gobbled up a six-pound tin of biscuits which they found in Mina's provision cupboard but did not go near a bottle of whiskey, forbidden by their superiors to take drink. One of the men left the mark of his hobnailed boot on the panelling in the gun room.

After this raid there was a police guard on the house; the family silver was buried and other valuables were sent away for safe keeping. Mina and her husband, when they returned here, kept a Verey pistol near them at night so they could send up warning lights if the house were attacked. But the Troubles ended without any further incident and Springhill regained its sense of peace – if indeed it had ever really lost it.

The house was still lived in by the Lenox-Conynghams when Mina died at the age of ninety-four in 1961, her husband having died in 1938 at the age of eighty. On the death of their son William in 1957, Springhill passed to the National Trust.

# Chapter 23

# Tullynally Castle (formerly Pakenham Hall)
## COUNTY WESTMEATH

ENRY PAKENHAM, a parliamentary captain, was granted the lands of Tullynally by Lough Derravaragh in County Westmeath in the middle of the seventeenth century. By 1740, when his great-grandson Thomas Pakenham married the heiress Elizabeth Cuffe, the family had a large two-storeyed house here known as Pakenham Hall; it stood on the slope of a hill overlooking a formal layout of basins, cascades and canals. Thomas's younger brother George Edward, who came here for a long visit a couple of years before the marriage, records in his journal that the household then consisted of a steward, a butler, ten men in livery and a number of persons employed constantly in the kitchen together with a gardener and several 'helpers' – considering the size of the garden, the solitary gardener must have needed a great many helpers indeed. There were eight or ten hunters in the stables and a fine pack of hounds. George Edward, who was making his career as a merchant in Germany, stayed at Pakenham for several months, enjoying himself hunting and shooting and visiting the neighbouring gentry.

The Pakenhams' neighbours included the Edgeworths of Edgeworthstown, twelve miles away across the bog in County Longford. As a youth in the late 1750s, Richard Lovell Edgeworth stayed often with Thomas and Elizabeth, who were now Lord and Lady Longford, Thomas having been made a peer in 1756. Lady Longford, who was a woman of wit with a knowledge of literature, did nothing to thwart young Richard's passion for field sports; when he was at Pakenham, she allowed him to shoot until he was exhausted. But she gave him the key of the library, where he soon spent whole days 'devouring its contents' so that he was soon won over from the pleasures of the chase by those of the intellect.[1]

When Richard Lovell Edgeworth was staying at Pakenham at the age of fourteen, there was a great entertainment with music, dancing and also gambling; it went on for more than one evening. Lord Longford gave Richard five guineas to try his luck at the faro table, at which the stakes were by no means trifling, and he won a hundred guineas. On the following evening Lord Longford asked him if he would like to risk his winnings and in no time he had only a single guinea left. When Lord Longford offered to lend him something he refused and just looked on and was congratulated by his host for 'being in all probability exempt from the vice of gaming'.[2]

The first Lord Longford died in 1766. His wife survived him and was created Countess of Longford in her own right in 1785, five years after her son, who was an admiral, had enlarged Pakenham to the design of an architect named Graham Myers. It was probably at this time that the third storey was added and what had been a courtyard was roofed over to form the vast hall, forty feet square and thirty feet high, which has ever since been the principal feature of the interior. The house was once again altered between 1801 and 1806, by which time Admiral Lord Longford had been succeeded by his son, who was the second Earl, the Admiral having died before his mother. The second Earl employed the great Irish architect Francis Johnston to make the plain Georgian house gently Gothic, with a battle-mented parapet and round corner turrets; by the time he had finished, the name on the builder's bills had changed from Pakenham Hall House to Pakenham Hall Castle. Johnston also added a tower on the side of the house facing the kitchen court-yard containing water closets. There was 'a luxury single one'[3] on the ground floor and two closets side by side on each of the floors above and in the basement. As well as being thus generously equipped with water closets, the house was given a bath-room, probably supplied by rainwater collected on the roof.

At the time when he carried out these alterations, the second Earl of Longford was about thirty and still single. He lived with his mother, a talented woman like his grandmother, and with those of his four brothers and four sisters who happened to be at home. His brothers included Edward and Hercules Pakenham, who were to achieve fame as Peninsular War generals, Edward afterwards being killed at New Orleans during the American War. His sister Kitty was to marry the great Duke of Wellington.

Richard Lovell Edgeworth's daughter Maria, who was seven years older than Lord Longford and had already made her name as a novelist, stayed at Pakenham in September 1805 when 'Sweet Kitty', as she called her, was here. In the following April, Maria was delighted at the news of Kitty's marriage. 'To make the romance perfect we want two material documents – a description of the person of Sir Arthur and a knowledge of the time when the interview after his return took place,' she wrote.[4] Alas, she did not then realize how much unhappiness was to result from that 'interview', when Wellesley, having returned a hero from India, was more or less pushed into marriage with Kitty, though they were incompatible.

Maria stayed again at Pakenham in 1807, after Lord Longford had finished alter-ing and refurnishing the house. 'The furniture is neither Gothic, nor Chinese, nor gaudy, nor frail, nor so fashionable it will be out of fashion in six months, but sub-stantially handsome and suitable in all its parts,' she reported to her father. She was asked to guess how much the red morocco chairs in the library had cost and said a guinea and a half, whereas in fact they had cost nine guineas.

Her father, who among other accomplishments was an inventor, had done Lord Longford a good turn by designing a central heating system for him, with hot air to supplement the turf fires. As a result, the immense hall, which until then must have been bitterly cold, was, according to Maria, 'so well warmed that his children play in it from morn to night' – the children being the offspring of Lord Longford's two other married sisters, Elizabeth Stewart and Helen Hamilton. In fact, as Maria told her father, perhaps with some exaggeration, the whole house, every bedroom, every passage, was 'so thoroughly warmed that we never felt any reluctance in going upstairs or from one room to another'. Lord Longford 'seemed to take great pleasure in repeating twenty times that he was to thank Mr Edgeworth for this'.

Having 'made such a comfortable nest', Maria felt that Lord Longford should 'certainly get some bird with pretty plumage and sweet voice to fill it'. 'Sweet voice' was essential, for he was a good musician and passionately fond of music. But he had, as Maria gathered, been put off 'by a near view of the domestic lives of some fine ladies'. And perhaps the fine ladies, for their part, if they had come to Pakenham, had disliked his habit of putting the clocks forward so that, in Maria's words, they were 'forced to get up (like the Devil) at break of day'. However, when Maria came this time, she found that he had put his clocks 'upon a footing with other peoples'.[5]

Lord Longford was still single when Maria, together with her father and stepmother and an aunt, came to stay in January 1809 when there was snow on the ground. There was a big party; they sat down thirty-two to dinner and that evening twenty of them went to a grand ball given by their neighbour, Mrs Pollard of Castle Pollard. Maria and her stepmother, who was younger than she was, were among those who went; her father and her aunt stayed behind. Lord Longford 'acted his part as Earl Marshal in the great hall, sending off carriage after carriage in due precedence and with its proper compliment of beaux and belles'. Maria and her stepmother went in a carriage with Lord Longford's brother Harry, the future Dean of St Patrick's. On the way back, their postillion, who had, in Maria's words, 'amused himself at a *club*' in the village of Castlepollard so 'did not know the ditch from the road', ran into a snowdrift and turned the carriage over in the ditch when attempting to pass the carriage of a neighbour, Mr Tuite, having managed to pass the carriage of another neighbour, Mr Dease of Turbotston. Nobody was hurt and they were given a lift home in Mr Tuite's carriage.[6]

Maria and her father were again at Pakenham in November 1811 when the house was filled with 'a whole tribe of merry laughing children, Stewarts and Hamiltons'. Lord Longford's mother showed them a picture of Kitty, who was now Lady Wellington though not yet a duchess. Richard Lovell Edgeworth played cribbage with Lord Longford's sister Elizabeth Stewart; Maria, looking on, could not keep up with them. And, as she admitted, she was worse at 'some genealogies and intermarriages which Lady Elizabeth undertook to explain'. Elizabeth eventually lost patience. 'She threw down her arms on each side and exclaimed "Well! You are the stupidest creature alive!"'[7]

It was not until 1817 that the second Earl finally took the plunge and married. His bride came from Worcestershire; she was Lady Georgiana Lygon, whose father had recently been made Earl Beauchamp. A few years after his marriage Lord Longford once again enlarged the house and made it more Gothic, his architect this time being James Shiel.

Georgiana duly presented her husband with seven sons and three daughters. When he died in 1835, the youngest children were still small, though the eldest son Edward, who became the third Earl, was seventeen. After her husband's death Georgiana divided her time between Pakenham and their London house. At Pakenham, she had her three younger children with her; Edward and the other older sons came home from time to time from the Army or the Navy or from school. 'We are all going on here in a vegetating sort of state,' she wrote in 1838. 'The place and country are quite beautiful, but I must say it is very *triste* to be here for days together without having communication with anyone but the governess and children! It requires strong health and still stronger spirits to bear such perfect solitude for long together.'

She was busy with her garden, which had been let go while she was away. '*All* my choice plants are *gone*,' she lamented; she believed that they had been stolen. 'As for the fruit trees, they have been so completely mismanaged that I doubt their *ever* recovering it! Pines and grapes are out of the question for a long time to come! I con-ceive the greatest part of this injury must have been done on purpose!'[8]

Whatever her own feelings about returning to the depths of County Westmeath, the children were delighted to be back. Edward had given the girls ponies; Georgiana was not entirely happy about this. 'As yet they are *not* equestrians,' she wrote, 'nor am I very anxious they should begin riding too early – it often makes girls very forward, which I confess I do *not* like.' While the children were enjoying themselves, so had the governess 'taken to her country life very agreeably'. She was hard at work on the various points of the children's education, complaining that the Irish air made the six-year-old Frank very idle. 'Poor little fellow' his mother wrote sympathetically, 'he never was very fond of his book!'[9]

Although Georgiana complained of solitude, the neighbours were not neglect-ing her. Maria Edgeworth and her stepmother called. Georgiana thought Maria, who was now over seventy, had changed a great deal. 'It arises much from a new set of teeth, which completely alters the shape of her face and her way of speaking.' Lady Farnham, who lived some thirty miles away in County Cavan, sent her a haunch of doe venison. She planned 'a *reunion* of all the neighbourhood to eat it'.

For all their mother's misgivings, the girls took to their ponies and went riding every afternoon. When the weather was too bad for them to go out, they and their small brother played in the hall. Georgiana was often complaining of the weather. 'The rain has been almost incessant, and this with the remains of the storm gives the entire place a look of sad melancholy,' she wrote on one occasion. And in a wet and windy October she complained that it was already like winter and that her rheumatism confined her almost entirely to the house. The bad weather at Pakenham pursued her to London; once when she was there she received 'a most *plaintive* letter' from her gardener telling her about an 'extraordinary hailstorm' which had been 'most destructive not only to the glass but to almost all the fruit'.[10]

Despite the hailstorm and similar misfortunes, Georgiana had eventually to admit that the garden was 'wonderfully improved'. She commended the forester for bringing 'great order' to the walks and plantations, having previously grumbled about his failure to turn up. But while all was sunny out of doors, she now had the 'great annoyance' of 'settling the new butler, no easy matter in so large a house'.

She never ceased to complain of loneliness. 'After having dined (with two exceptions) tête-à-tête *with myself* for three whole weeks, I am anticipating with no little pleasure the arrival of my four young men,' she wrote in 1839. As well as visits from Edward and her other 'young men', she had occasional house parties. Various inlaws, such as the clergyman Harry Pakenham and the Hamiltons, came to stay; there was a large party for a shoot, which was a success, with plenty of pheasants. But when it was over she wrote, a little perversely: 'I am not sorry now to be left a little quiet, for where all the arrangements of this large house depend on one person, *that* is occupation enough.'[11]

'This neighbourhood is duller than can be imagined,' was one of Georgiana's frequent laments. The only people living nearby whom she really liked were some Pakenham cousins and Mr Smyth of Barbavilla, who since his wife died in 1837 was mostly away. Admittedly, there does not seem to have been very much happening. There was the occasional bazaar – she was 'quite proud' when two cushions of hers were sold at one of them for five pounds – and the all-too-frequent parties given by Mrs Kearney, the wife of the local doctor, which were not much to her taste. 'Mrs Kearney sets herself down as Queen Regnant of Castlepollard and torments the neighbourhood with her hospitality,' Georgiana wrote, a little unkindly, after one of these parties, at which the chief attraction was some 'much-talked-of venison' from County Meath. 'She means very well, but quite forgets that after all she is the wife of the dispensary doctor who (as long as he receives the salary) had better be attending his patients than receiving company.'[12]

The attentions of the worthy Dr Kearney must have been required in the summer of 1840 when two of Georgiana's 'young men' each injured a limb, presumably riding; and again soon afterwards when, as she reported: 'The whole phalanx of maids chose to overload the jaunting car coming from church last Sunday and were

Tullynally Castle, formerly Pakenham Hall.

all accordingly *capsized* in the middle of Castlepollard – plenty of broken bonnets and a few black eyes and bruises without end were the consequence. However, only one, the nurse, was seriously injured and she is better. They must all walk to church in future which will be *all the better for their constitutions.*'

Georgiana felt that a strong arm was necessary to control the servants; she would not go away unless she could hand over to her standby, Mrs Alston, 'the only person I know who I should feel satisfied to leave this large house in charge of in my absence'.[13] While she was complaining about the size of the house – 'this house is altogether so large and requires such incessant care to keep it in order, and *above all* well aired, that it is quite overwhelming, and too much for me, who prefer ease and quiet' – it was actually growing before her eyes. Between 1839 and 1842 young Edward's trustees employed the fashionable architect Sir Richard Morrison to alter and enlarge the house yet again. Morrison added a tall tower and battlemented wings joining the main block to the stable court which was likewise castellated. The house came to look not so much like a castle as a small fortified town, a Camelot of the Gothic Revival; its long, picturesque skyline of towers, turrets, battlements and gate-ways stretching among the trees of its rolling park. The surroundings of the house were now naturalistic; the formal layout of canals and basins, which had been such a feature of the place in the previous century, had long been swept away.

One of the new wings contained a private apartment for the family; Edward, when here, occupied the ground floor of it, his mother the floor above. Each had their own bathroom, supplied with water by a pump. The girls were able to have a shower every morning.

Edward, who was nicknamed 'Fluffy' – though not by his mother – never married and seems to have been a somewhat unsatisfactory character. He did not benefit much from the improvements to the house, coming to Ireland less and less as he grew older; he died in mysterious circumstances at a London hotel in 1860 aged only forty-two. He was succeeded by his brother William, a professional solder who had been Adjutant-General to the Forces in the Crimea and during the Indian Mutiny. On his first visit to Pakenham after inheriting, William wrote in his diary: 'Went to the farmyard and spoke to the servants. May God's blessing be on this house and family. Did it very well.' His diary entry of a few weeks later shows a certain disillusionment: 'Place overgrown with shrubs. Servants fat and lazy.'[14]

Having been a bachelor when he became Earl of Longford, William lost little time in marrying. His bride, Selina, was Welsh, a daughter of Lord Dynevor. 'Dear little wife, I love you,' he wrote to her in the summer of 1863, when he was here on his own. The letter was, however, more about household matters than love. 'Miss Cody has cut up rough and I have given her notice to go, or she has given me notice, I am scarcely sure which.'[15]

William also told Selina that the chimney pots were a success and that there was now no smoke in her room. His military career had given him an eye for detail and a liking for technology; he was gradually modernizing the house. Before he married, he put in a new central heating system which he afterwards extended. He replaced Francis Johnston's lavatory tower with a new addition containing fewer but more up-to-date closets. When Selina was expecting a baby and he was once again on his own at Pakenham, he was worried by reports that the baby's bath leaked. 'I shall see a baby washed in it before I leave,' he told her; and he later assured her that the bath was now all ready for when the baby arrived. In the event, Selina had twins.

'I have ordered a grate for Your Ladyship's state bedroom,' William told Selina in April 1865. He was carrying out improvements not only to the house but also to the grounds; a new avenue was being planted and 'obnoxious trees' removed. Writing to Selina during another of her absences, he referred to the woodmen as 'the red-legged ones'; for, as he explained to her: 'They don't put on shoes and stockings until My Lady comes home.'

Like his mother before him, William found the neighbourhood a little limited in the way of society. There were the Pakenham cousins; there were the Pollards. There were the Deases of Turbotston. When Selina was away in the summer of 1868 and William had one of his brothers to keep him company, they were invited to dinner by the Pakenham cousins and also by the Pollards on the same evening; they chose the Pakenham cousins. The Deases brought some visitors over and Mr Dease talked to William about drainage.

As well as his brother, William had his children with him at this time. 'The babies flourish and give great satisfaction to their parents and to their uncle,' he reported to Selina, also informing her that 'a superhuman stew of oxtails had just been disposed of with the happiest effect'. The stew was more of a success than the chops of 'goaty Castlepollard mutton' that Peter, the male cook, gave them a year later. But Peter's cooking was appreciated at any rate by Mr Field, the local parson. After Mr Field had come to luncheon at Pakenham in June 1868, William observed drily: 'He had a great deal to eat, but not much to say.'[16]

William and Selina eventually had five children and to accommodate them Morrison's family wing was turned into schoolrooms and nurseries. The two bathrooms in the wing were done away with, so that the house was back to having only one bathroom. On the other hand the water closets had increased to no fewer than ten and they were dispersed about the house, served by the more reliable water supply that William had installed in 1875. William's other great innovation was gas lighting; the gas was made in the gas house in the farmyard and stored in the gasometer. It lit only the hall, staircase and corridors; the living rooms were still lit by paraffin lamps, the bedrooms by candles.

The central heating had twice been extended, to the corridors of the main block and then to what was now the schoolroom and nursery wing. But in the living-rooms and bedrooms there were still only the good old-fashioned fires – now of wood and coal, turf having been banished to the 'outer extremities'.[17] And for William, when he arrived back alone in January 1877, it was not the crackling bedroom fire which was most welcome, but an even more basic method of heating: 'Mrs Cooke all ready for me with a lovely country dinner and any number of blankets on my bed.'[18]

William died in 1887 and his son Thomas, the survivor of the twins, became the fifth Earl. The new Lord Longford, who like his father was a professional soldier and rose to be a general, married, in 1899, Lady Mary Child-Villiers, a daughter of the seventh Earl of Jersey; when he brought his bride to Pakenham, where his mother Selina and his unmarried sister Katharine were still living, she did not get a very good first impression. Having come from Osterley, the Jerseys' palatial seat near London, and from Middleton, their other family seat in Oxfordshire, she thought it very provincial. For the next ten years or so she did not have to spend much time here on account of her husband's military career, which made it necessary for them to live in various rented houses in England. In 1909, while they were abroad, their children spent Christmas at Pakenham with their nannies. After Lord Longford retired from the Army in 1910, they divided their time between Pakenham and a house in Oxfordshire.

When they were at Pakenham one year shortly before the outbreak of the Great War, they entertained the Viceroy and Vicereine, the Earl and Countess of

Lady Katharine Pakenham in the drawing room at Pakenham Hall, as it then was, in 1899. Her mother Selina Countess of Longford can be seen writing in the recess.

Aberdeen, Lord Aberdeen having come to open the local agricultural show which was held in the grounds. The Longfords' nine-year-old daughter Pansy noticed that Lady Aberdeen's brooch was coming adrift, but did not like to mention it. She thought that Lady Aberdeen's lady-in-waiting, who wore a yellow tie with her blouse, looked very dashing.

Used as she was to the staff at Osterley and at Middleton, Lady Longford could never understand how with only a butler, two footmen and a pantry boy at Pakenham they could clean the silver. The butler, the two footmen and the pantry boy were in fact part of an indoor staff of twenty. On most afternoons, tea would be served in ten different places. Lord and Lady Longford and their guests had it in the drawing-room. The elder children and their governess had it in the schoolroom; the younger children with the nannies and nursery maids had it in the nursery. The upper servants, together with the visiting ladies' maids, had it in the housekeeper's room. The footmen had it in the servants' hall. The housemaids had it in the house-maids' sitting-room, the kitchenmaids had it in the kitchen and the charwomen had it in the stillroom. The laundry maids had it in the laundry and the grooms had it in the harness room. Once a week a riding master came from Dublin to give the children a lesson and the number of places where tea was served went up to eleven; for while he was too grand to have tea with the servants or the grooms, he was not grand enough to have it with the gentry in the drawing-room, so was given a tray on his own.[19]

There was not much done about modernizing the house in the fifth Earl's time. In 1906 there was some idea of putting in electric light, but it came to nothing, presumably because the estimate of £1,350 was regarded as too much. Lady Longford had a bathroom made for her near her bedroom. It was approached by a special passage so that she would not be seen going to the lavatory.

When the Great War broke out, the fifth Earl went back into the Army and on active service though he was then nearly fifty. A year later, he was reported wounded and missing at Gallipoli, having been last seen waving his walking stick as he led his brigade into action. For his wife, there followed ten months of uncertainty, while she clung to the hope that he might still be alive as a prisoner. She took her children to Pakenham for the Easter holidays of 1916, only to be cut off from the outside world by the Easter Rising. Then in June, when all was peaceful again in Ireland, she was told that it had to be assumed that her husband was dead.

Her elder son Edward, who became the sixth Earl of Longford at the age of thirteen, departed from the military tradition of his family. His interests were literary and artistic; he was a poet and a playwright who became chairman of Dublin's Gate Theatre and formed his own company, the Longford Players. His wife, the former Christine Trew, whom he had married in 1925, was a novelist and worked with him in producing plays. Edward and Christine Longford redecorated Pakenham, giving the rooms a Chinese flavour, bringing colour to the hall with hangings of Chinese vermilion.

The house underwent another change at about this time: electric light was at last introduced. The chauffeur was put in charge of the generator, such duplication being necessary with a reduced staff. But while there were not as many servants as there were in 1914, there was still a butler and footman, a cook, kitchenmaids and housemaids; and there was Mrs Cruikshanks the housekeeper. The butler had been footman to one of Edward's aunts at her castle in Wales.

Unlike her mother-in-law, Christine did not have a lady's maid; but a more notable absence was that of the governess, nannies and nursery maids, for she and Edward had no children. But if the high plaster Gothic vaulting of the hall no longer echoed to childish voices, the rooms were, as often as not, full of the chatter of friends; not only friends of Edward and Christine but friends of Edward's brother, the future Labour Cabinet Minister Frank Pakenham, and of his four sisters.

Alastair Graham, Evelyn Waugh and Miss Elizabeth Harman, now the Countess of Longford, at Pakenham Hall, as it then was.

When Frank Pakenham came to stay in the summer of 1930 – a month after Yeats stayed here – he brought John Betjeman, who had been at Oxford with him. Betjeman arrived a day earlier than Frank and was welcomed by Edward's two younger sisters, Lady Violet and Lady Julia, Edward and Christine having had to go to Dublin. The two girls did not know his name, which had been illegible in Frank's letter announcing his arrival; they were too polite to ask. They took their anonymous guest on to the roof and up the iron ladder to the flag tower. They then took him round the garden and they picked up fruit that had fallen off the trees in the hothouses. Betjeman began to quote Marvell:

'The nectarine and curious peach
Into my hands themselves do reach.'[20]

Next day Frank arrived, and Betjeman's name was revealed. The Longfords returned and Edward and Betjeman struck up what was to be a lifelong friendship. Then Evelyn Waugh, who had already achieved fame as a novelist with *Decline and*

Evelyn Waugh (left) fooling about with his host Edward, Earl of Longford.

*Fall* and *Vile Bodies*, arrived with his friend Alastair Graham. The house party also included Elizabeth Harman, a girl with whom Frank was in love.

At breakfast, Waugh would ask, 'Who's got any funny letters this morning?'[21] The others, realizing that, as a professional writer, he was looking for copy, would duly hand over any promising letters for him to read. They spent the day walking in the demesne and boating on Lough Derravaragh, which Betjeman was to invoke in 'The Attempt', one of a cycle of poems about County Westmeath in which various obscure Irish peers also feature. Betjeman became fascinated by obscure Irish peers on this first visit to Pakenham, just as he found inspiration in the lakes. 'John B. became a bore rather with Irish peers and revivalist hymns,' Waugh complained in his diary.[22]

The revivalist hymns were sung by the house party in the hall, with Edward, fat and rumbustious, at the piano or the 'wheezy organ',[23] thumping out a hit-or-miss accompaniment. They also sang rebel songs like 'Bold Fenian Men' and 'The Boys of Wexford'; but while Edward was an Irish Nationalist, he would join no less heartily in 'Protestant Boys' and 'The Old Orange Flute'. The evening's entertainment would also include charades and Betjeman would tell ghost stories and do parodies of Shakespeare. Edward would show his appreciation by uncontrollable laughter. 'I have seen at Pakenham what I have seen nowhere else,' Waugh afterwards wrote, 'an entirely sober host rolling about the carpet with merriment . . . His butler and attendant footmen would gravely bestride the spherical form in its velvet smoking-suit as they carried their trays.'[24]

Betjeman's first visit to Pakenham was Waugh's second; for both of them there were many more to come. Betjeman and Waugh were here at the same time in 1931, together with two popular young Oxford dons, Lord David Cecil and Maurice Bowra. Frank Pakenham was also here with Elizabeth Harman, to whom he was now engaged, and his and Edward's sister Pansy, with her husband, the painter Henry Lamb. 'Good painter and funny chap who smokes Irish cigars,' was how Betjeman described Henry Lamb in a letter in which he also spoke of 'Evelyn Waugh with his eyes blazing with religious fanaticism'.[25]

In 1932 Betjeman brought his fiancée Penelope Chetwode to Pakenham. Penelope went riding with Waugh, who was once again a fellow-guest; Waugh got caught in a tree and Penelope sportingly did not tell the others. Meanwhile Betjeman was in the library – which was everything a library should be, spacious and comfortable, with oak bookcases going up the ceiling, and windows facing south over idyllic parkland – reading in leather-bound Grand Jury reports about the wicked Sir John Piers whom he was to make the central figure in his cycle of poems about County Westmeath.

When Betjeman was here on a later occasion, there was a tea party for the village school and he and Lady Pansy Lamb and other people staying in the house helped to pass things round. The local parson, Mr Mouritz, was present; he had an orange-coloured beard and Betjeman put him into his own version of 'Protestant Boys':

> The Protestant Boys are loyal and true,
> And Father Mouritz is coming to tea.

Cathleen Delaney, an attractive dark-haired young actress from the Gate Theatre, was also staying; Betjeman, who admired her, took her out in the boat on Lough Derravaragh and she sang Moore's *Irish Melodies* to him.

In the summer of 1934, Elizabeth Pakenham – as Elizabeth Harman now was – brought the young novelist Anthony Powell to stay for two weeks. As he afterwards recalled, 'London literary patter would be playfully dismissed as much too grand to be valid currency in these wilds.' Edward Longford 'did from time to time display bursts of curiosity about sides of London life, social or intellectual . . . though making such enquiries with a kind of implied guilt, as if a betrayal of principles'.

Powell found his host and hostess 'perfectly friendly, perfectly hospitable, but dep-

The library where John Betjeman read about the wicked Sir John Piers in leather-bound Grand Jury reports.

recatory laughter often suggested that I was rambling on about a society which, even its more bohemian expression, was painfully overcivilised for those with simpler cultural tastes'.[26] He felt a little apprehensive when, in the second week, Elizabeth and her family returned to England, leaving him at Pakenham without a sponsor, so to speak. However, Lady Pansy and Henry Lamb, whom he knew, now arrived, bringing Lady Violet, one of the two unmarried Pakenham sisters, whom he had just met. Henry Lamb felt rather the same as Powell, regarding himself 'equally suspect as purveyor of an alien culture', and escaped whenever he could to the local pub. To keep his hand in, he painted Powell's portrait, setting up his studio in one of the bedrooms into which he moved a large eighteenth-century screen as a background. Lady Violet would attend the sittings, 'to enliven them and keep the model alert'.

For Powell, Lady Violet's presence at Pakenham had momentous consequences. As he himself puts it, 'My personal problem was (to borrow a favoured Jamesian idiom) beautifully solved.' That September, after they had both returned to London, he and Lady Violet became engaged; they were married before the end of the year.

In his autobiography, Anthony Powell touches on the extent to which the Pakenhams are to be identified with the Tollands in *A Dance to the Music of Time*. He admits that there may be 'faint nuances' in Lady Isobel Tolland, whom the narrator marries, just as Powell himself married Lady Violet Pakenham. He also admits that 'a general family orientation is to some extent reproduced'.[27]

Evelyn Waugh felt that the Longfords must have found Frank Pakenham's friends a bit of a strain. 'I had the impression that, when the last of us left, Edward and Christine watched us with something of the relief with which fond parents wave their obstreperous children back to school.'[28] He went further and wrote: 'Edward and Christine used to hate us all but we gave them subjects for conversation for the ensuing year.'[29] The Longfords may have talked about Waugh and the others, but it was certainly untrue to suggest that they hated them; at least one of them, namely Betjeman, became a dear friend. And Waugh contradicts himself by telling of how Edward Longford 'had the gracious habit of tipping his guests on their departure by making bets which he knew he would lose so that he bore the expense of our visits'.[30] However kind and generous a man Edward may have been, it seems unlikely that he would have gone to these lengths with his guests had he not hoped that they would come again.

As they became more taken up with the theatre, Edward and Christine Longford spent less time at Pakenham and preferred having just one or two guests rather than a large house party. During the Second World War, Edward's friend, the Chinese writer and artist Chiang Yee, came to stay. He felt at home in the 'Chinese atmosphere' of the hall and found the meals 'most appetising after the rationed food of England'. They took him in the boat on Lough Derravaragh and fished for pike; he and Edward sat in the bow, the rest of the party in the stern and the oarsman in the middle. When Chiang Yee came down to the hall on the morning after his arrival, he saw four roses for buttonholes laid out on a table near the door.[31]

With the reduction in staff, such flourishes are naturally a thing of the past at Tullynally Castle, as Pakenham Hall is now known, Edward Longford's nephew Mr Thomas Pakenham having restored the original Irish name. In other respects things have not changed all that much since the days when Waugh and Betjeman came to stay. There is the same hospitality. Mr Pakenham follows his uncle and aunt and his parents in being a writer and Mrs Pakenham is a writer also; there are often other writers staying in the house and there is always plenty of good talk. For someone who came to stay in the summer of 1993 there was an unexpected pleasure: also staying was Lady Pansy Lamb, youthful and elegant at the age of eighty-nine and little changed from when he had last seen her more than forty years earlier.

# Source References

*Chapter 1  Adare Manor*

1 Letters of Caroline Countess of Dunraven. Dunraven Papers in P.R.O.N.I.
2 Ibid.
3 Aubrey de Vere, *Recollections*. New York and London 1897.
4 Diaries of Caroline Countess of Dunraven. Dunraven Papers in P.R.O.N.I.
5 Ibid.
6 Letters of second Earl of Dunraven to his wife. Dunraven Papers in P.R.O.N.I.
7 Caroline Countess of Dunraven, *Memorials of Adare Manor*.
8 Diaries of Caroline Countess of Dunraven.
9 Earl of Dunraven, *Past Times and Pastimes*. 2 vols, London n.d.
10. Ibid.
11. Marchioness of Salisbury, in conversation with the author.
12. Pamela Lady Egremont, in conversation with the author.

*Chapter 2  Ardfert Abbey*

1 Letters of Theodosia, Countess of Glandore. Dunraven Papers in P.R.O.N.I.
2 Lady Louisa Stewart, in *Gleanings from an Old Portfolio*, ed. Mrs Godfrey Clark. 3 vols, Edinburgh. Privately printed 1896.
3 Lady Portarlington, in ibid.
4 Letters of Lady Arabella Ward. Dunraven Papers in P.R.O.N.I.

*Chapter 3  Ardfry*

1 Dorothea Herbert, *Retrospections*. London 1929–30.
2 Elizabeth Lady Wallscourt, quoted in Duchess of Sermoneta, *The Locks of Norbury*. London 1940.
3 T. P. O'Connor, *Memoirs of an Old Parliamentarian*. 2 vols, London 1929.

*Chapter 4 Ballyfin*

1  Notes by Thomas Charles Coote, Coote Papers.
2  Ibid.
3  Coote Papers.
4. Notes by Thomas Charles Coote.
5  Ibid.
6  *Leinster Express*, 30 December 1905.


*Chapter 5 Barmeath Castle*

1  Bellew Papers.
2  Ibid.
3  Ibid.
4. M. O'Connor Morris, *Hibernia Venatica*. London 1878.
5  Hon. Bryan Bellew, in conversation with the author.


*Chapter 6 Carton*

1  Quoted in Brian FitzGerald, *Emily Duchess of Leinster*. London n.d. (1949).
2  Ibid.
3  *Gleanings from an Old Portfolio*, ed. Mrs Godfrey Clark. 3 vols, Edinburgh. Privately printed 1896.
4  Quoted in FitzGerald, op. cit.
5  Quoted in ibid.
6  MS in the possession of the Duke of Leinster.
7  *The Creevey Papers*, ed. Sir Herbert Maxwell. London 1905.
8  Quoted in Brian FitzGerald, 'Carton', in *Country Life*, 14 November 1936.
9  M. O'Connor Morris, *Hibernia Venatica*. London 1878.
10 Elizabeth Countess of Fingall, *Seventy Years Young*. London 1937.
11 Ibid.
12 Brigadier Denis FitzGerald, in conversation with the author.


*Chapter 7 Castle Forbes*

1  Granard Papers.
2  Ibid.
3  Ibid.
4  Ibid.
5  Ibid.
6  Ibid.
7  Ibid.

8 Ibid.
9 Pakenham MSS.


*Chapter 8 Castle Leslie (or Glaslough)*

1 Anita Leslie, *The Fabulous Leonard Jerome*. London 1954.
2 Anita Leslie, *The Gilt and the Gingerbread*. London n.d. (1981).
3 Seymour Leslie, *The Jerome Connexion*. London 1964.
4 Shane Leslie, *Long Shadows*. London 1966.
5 Lionel Leslie, *One Man's World*. London 1961.
6 Seymour Leslie, op. cit.
7 Shane Leslie, *The Film of Memory*. London 1938.
8 Seymour Leslie, op. cit.
9 Shane Leslie, *Long Shadows*.
10. Londonderry Papers in P.R.O.N.I.
11. Anita Leslie, *The Gilt and the Gingerbread*.
12. Anita Leslie, *The Fabulous Leonard Jerome*.
13. Anita Leslie, *The Gilt and the Gingerbread*.
14. Sir John Leslie, in conversation with the author.
15. Anita Leslie, *The Gilt and the Gingerbread*.
16. Seymour Leslie, op. cit.


*Chapter 9 Coole Park*

1 Lady Gregory, *Seventy Years, 1852–1922*. Gerrards Cross 1974.
2 Ibid.
3 Mrs Robert Kennedy, in conversation with the author.
4 Anne Gregory, *Me and Nu*. Gerrards Cross 1970.
5 Lady Gregory's Journals, 1916–1930, ed. Lennox Robinson. London 1946.
6 Anne Gregory, op. cit.
7 Ibid.
8 Lady Gregory's Journals.
9 Mrs Robert Kennedy, in conversation with the author.


*Chapter 10 Curragh Chase*

1 *Recollections of Aubrey de Vere*. New York and London 1897.
2 Ibid.
3 Wilfrid Ward, *Aubrey de Vere, a Memoir*. London 1904.
4 Quoted in ibid.
5 Joan Wynne Jones, *The Abiding Enchantment of Curragh Chase*. Cork n.d.
6 James Lees-Milne, letter in *Country Life*, 3 April 1942.

7 Wynne Jones, op. cit.
8 Lees-Milne, loc. cit.


*Chapter 11 Drishane*

1 Somerville and Ross, *Wheel Tracks*. London 1923.
2 Ibid.
3 Ibid.
4 Ibid.
5 Edith Œnone Somerville and Boyle Townshend Somerville, *Somerville Family Records*. Cork 1940.
6 Edith Somerville to Adelaide Somerville, undated (*ca* 1880) in Edith Œnone Somerville Archive.
7 Somerville and Ross, op.cit.
8 Ibid.
9 Moira Somerville, *Edith Œ Somerville, An Intimate Recollection*. Typescript in Edith Œnone Somerville Archive.
10 Ibid.
11 Ibid.
12 Ibid.
13 Edith Somerville to Alice Kinkead, 3 April 1919, in Edith Œnone Somerville Archive.
14 Mr Christopher Somerville, in conversation with the author.
15 Somerville and Ross, *Irish Memories*. London n.d. (1917).
16 Moira Somerville, op. cit.


*Chapter 12 Edgeworthstown*

1 *Memoirs of Richard Lovell Edgeworth*. London 1844.
2 *Life and Letters of Maria Edgeworth*, ed. Augustus Hare. London 1894.
3 Ibid.
4 Quoted in Thomas Pakenham, *The Year of Liberty*. London 1969.
5 *Life and Letters of Maria Edgeworth*.
6 Ibid.
7 Ibid.
8 Ibid.


*Chapter 13 Grey Abbey*

1 Montgomery Papers.
2 *Boswell in search of a Wife 1766–69*, ed. Frank Brady & A. Pottle. Yale 1957.
3 Ibid.

4 Montgomery Papers.
5 Ibid.
6 Mr William Montgomery, in conversation with the author.
7 *Northern Whig*, July 1868.
8 Mr William Montgomery, in conversation with the author.
9 Montgomery Papers.
10 Mrs Hugh Montgomery, in conversation with the author.


*Chapter 14  Gurteen Le Poer*

1 Diary of Edmond, Count de la Poer. De la Poer Papers.
2 Ibid.
3 Ibid.
4 Ibid.
5 Ibid.
6 Ibid.
7 Ibid.
8 Diary of Major John Rivallon de la Poer. De la Poer Papers.
9 Ibid.
10 Ibid.
11 Ibid.
12 Ibid.


*Chapter 15  Kilfane*

1 Anon, *Memoirs of the Kilkenny Hunt*. Dublin 1897.
2 Frances de la Poer MS. De la Poer Papers.
3 Ibid.
4 Ibid.
5 Frances de la Poer, 'Reminiscences of my Married Life'. MS, de la Poer Papers.
6 MS, de la Poer Papers.
7 Earl of Desart and Lady Sybil Lubbock, *A Page from the Past*. London 1936.
8 Ibid.
9 Lord Castletown, *Ego*. London 1923.
10 Mrs Thomas Hal Clarke, in conversation with the author.


*Chapter 16  Lismore Castle*

1 Dorothea Townshend, *Life of Lord Cork*. London 1904.
2 *The Earl of Castlehaven's Review, or his Memoirs of his Engagement and Carriage in the Irish Wars*, Dublin 1815.
3 James Lees-Milne, *The Bachelor Duke*. London 1991.

4 *The Diary of Lady Frederick Cavendish*, ed. John Bailey. 2 vols, London 1927.
5 Lady Clodagh Anson, *Victorian Days*. London 1957.
6 Letters of Humphrey Eley, in the possession of his daughter.
7 The late Molly Keane, in conversation with the author.
8 Letters of Humphrey Eley.
9 *The Letters of Nancy Mitford*, ed. Charlotte Mosley. London 1993.
10 Duchess of Devonshire, in a letter to the author.
11 Ibid.


*Chapter 17  Lissadell*


1 Thomas Goold to The Earl of Dunraven. Dunraven Papers in P.R.O.N.I.
2 Reminiscences of Thomas Kilgallon. Typescript in Gore-Booth Papers.
3 Ibid.
4 Reminiscences of S. A. W. Waters. Typescript in P.R.O.N.I.
5 Ibid.
6 Reminiscences of Thomas Kilgallon.
7 Reminiscences of S. A. W. Waters.
8 Reminiscences of Thomas Kilgallon.
9 Quoted in Anne Marreco, *The Rebel Countess*. London 1967.
10 Marreco, op. cit.
11 Ibid.
12 Quoted in Marreco, op. cit.
13 Marreco, op. cit.
14 The late Sir Cecil Stafford-King-Harman, in conversation with the author.
15 Marreco, op. cit.


*Chapter 18  Mitchelstown Castle*


1 Edward C. McAleer, *The Sensitive Plant*. Chapel Hill, University of North Carolina Press 1958.
2 *Recollections of Aubrey de Vere*. New York and London 1897.
3 Percival-Maxwell Papers in P.R.O.N.I.
4 Elizabeth Bowen, *Bowen's Court*. London 1942.
5 Nora Robertson, *Crowned Harp*. Dublin 1960.
6 Information given to the author by Mr William Power.
7 Bowen, op. cit.
8 Ibid.


*Chapter 19  Mount Stewart*


1 Quoted in H. Montgomery Hyde, *The Londonderrys*. London 1979.

2 Quoted in ibid.
3 De Latocnaye, *A Frenchman's Walk through Ireland, 1796–7*, trans. by John Stevenson. Belfast and Dublin n.d.
4 Castlereagh Papers in P.R.O.N.I.
5 Knight of Kerry Papers in P.R.O.N.I.
6 Quoted in Montgomery Hyde, op. cit.
7 Castlereagh Papers in P.R.O.N.I.
8 Londonderry Papers in P.R.O.N.I.
9 Quoted in Montgomery Hyde, op. cit.
10 Typescript by Theresa Marchioness of Londonderry. Londonderry Papers in P.R.O.N.I.
11 Elizabeth Countess of Fingall, *Seventy Years Young*. London 1937.
12 Montgomery Hyde, op. cit.
13 Oliver St John Gogarty, *In the Steps of St Patrick*. London 1938.
14 Sir John Leslie, in conversation with the author.

## Chapter 20 Newtown Anner

1 *Memorials of Lady Osborne*, ed. Mrs Osborne (her daughter). Dublin 1870.
2 Ibid.
3 Ibid.
4 Mrs Richard Bagwell, *My Recollections*. Unpublished typescript.
5 Diary of Edmond, Count de la Poer. De la Poer Papers.
6 Ibid.
7 Ibid.

## Chapter 21 Rockingham

1 Diary of Lady Eleanor King, in the possession of Col. A. L. King-Harman.
2 Robert Douglas King-Harman, *The Kings, Earls of Kingston*. Privately printed 1959.
3 Reminiscences of Thomas Kilgallon. Typescript in Gore-Booth Papers.
4 Londonderry Papers in P.R.O.N.I.
5 The late Sir Cecil Stafford-King-Harman, in conversation with the author.
6 Mrs George Dennehy, in conversation with the author.
7 Ibid.
8 Ibid.

## Chapter 22 Springhill

1 Mina Lenox-Conyngham, *An Old Ulster House*. Dundalk 1946.
2 Ibid.
3 Ibid.

4 Ibid.

5 Ibid.

6 Told to the author by Mr Henry Clark.

7 Lenox-Conyngham, op. cit.

8 Ibid.


Chapter 23 *Tullynally Castle (formerly Pakenham Hall)*

1 *Memoirs of Richard Lovell Edgeworth*. London 1844.

2 Ibid.

3 Mark Girouard, 'Modernising an Irish County House' and 'Comforts for a Victorian Household'. Articles in *Country Life*, 23 and 30 December 1971.

4 *Life and Letters of Maria Edgeworth*, ed. Augustus Hare. London 1894.

5 Ibid.

6 Ibid.

7 Ibid.

8 Pakenham MSS.

9 Ibid.

10 Ibid.

11 Ibid.

12 Ibid.

13 Ibid.

14 Quoted in Girouard, op. cit.

15 Pakenham MSS.

16 Ibid.

17 Girouard, op. cit.

18 Pakenham MSS.

19 Girouard, op. cit.

20 Bevis Hillier, *Young Betjeman*. London 1988.

21 Ibid.

22 *The Diaries of Evelyn Waugh*, ed. Michael Davie. London 1976.

23 Hillier, op. cit.

24 Evelyn Waugh, obituary of Edward, Earl of Longford in the *Observer*, 2 December 1961.

25 *John Betjeman Letters,* vol. I, ed. Candida Lycett Green. London 1994.

26 Anthony Powell, *Faces in my Time*. London 1980.

27 Ibid.

28 Evelyn Waugh, obituary of Edward, Earl of Longford in the *Observer*, 2 December 1961.

29 Evelyn Waugh to Anne Fleming, in *The Letters of Evelyn Waugh*. London 1980.

30 Evelyn Waugh, obituary of Edward, Earl of Longford in the *Observer*, 2 December 1961.

31 Chiang Yee, *The Silent Traveller in Dublin*. London 1953.

# Select Bibliography

MANUSCRIPT AND OTHER UNPUBLISHED SOURCES

Bellew papers, in the possession of Hon. Bryan Bellew.
Castlereagh papers, in the Public Record Office of Northern Ireland.
Coote papers, in the possession of Sir Christopher Coote, Bt.
de la Poer papers, in the possession of Mr Nigel de la Poer.
Dunraven papers, in the Public Record Office of Northern Ireland.
Letters of Humphrey Eley, in the possession of his daughter Mrs Martin Moyes.
Gore-Booth papers, in the possession of Sir Josslyn Gore-Booth, Bt.
Granard papers, in the possession of Lady Georgina Forbes.
Diary of Lady Eleanor King, in the possession of Col. A.L. King-Harman.
Knight of Kerry papers, in the Public Record Office of Northern Ireland.
Londonderry papers, in the Public Record Office of Northern Ireland.
Montgomery papers, in the possession of Mr William Montgomery.
Pakenham MSS, in the possession of Mr Thomas Pakenham.
Perceval-Maxwell papers, in the Public Record Office of Northern Ireland.
Edith Œnone Somerville Archive at Drishane, County Cork.


PRINTED SOURCES

*Ancestral Voices, The Big House in Anglo-Irish Literature*, A Collection of Interpretations
    edited by Otto Rauchbauer, Dublin and Hildesheim 1992.
ANON: *Memoirs of the Kilkenny Hunt*, Dublin 1897.
ANSON, LADY CLODAGH: *Victorian Days*, London 1957.
BENCE-JONES, MARK: *A Guide to Irish Country Houses*, London 1988.
BENCE-JONES, MARK: *Twilight of the Ascendancy*, London 1987.
*Boswell in Search of a Wife 1766–69* (ed Frank Brady and A. Pottle), Yale 1957.
BOWEN, ELIZABETH: *Bowen's Court*, London 1942.
CASTLETOWN, LORD: *Ego*, London 1923.

*The Diary of Lady Frederick Cavendish* (ed John Bailey), 2 vols, London 1927.

*The Creevey Papers* (ed Sir Herbert Maxwell), London 1905.

DE LATOCNAYE: *A Frenchman's Walk through Ireland, 1796–7* (trans John Stevenson), Belfast and Dublin ND.

DESART, EARL OF AND LADY SYBIL LUBBOCK: *A Page from the Past*, London 1936.

*Recollections of Aubrey de Vere*, New York and London 1897.

DUNRAVEN, CAROLINE COUNTESS OF: *Memorials of Adare Manor*, with Historical Notices of Adare by her son the Earl of Dunraven, Oxford, privately printed 1865.

DUNRAVEN, EARL OF: *Past Times and Pastimes*, 2 vols, London ND.

DUNSANY, LORD: *Patches of Sunlight*, London 1938.

*Life and Letters of Maria Edgeworth* (ed. Augustus Hare), London 1894.

*Memoirs of Richard Lovell Edgeworth*, London 1844.

EVERETT, KATHERINE: *Bricks and Flowers*, London 1950.

FINGALL, ELIZABETH COUNTESS OF: *Seventy Years Young*, London 1937.

FITZGERALD, BRIAN: *Emily Duchess of Leinster*, London ND (1949).

FLEMING, LIONEL: *Head or Harp*, London 1965.

*Gleanings from an Old Portfolio* (ed Mrs Godfrey Clark), 3 vols, Edinburgh, privately printed 1895.

GOGARTY, OLIVER ST JOHN: *In the Steps of St Patrick*, London 1938.

GREGORY, ANNE: *Me and Nu*, Gerrards Cross 1970.

GREGORY, LADY: *Seventy Years, 1852–1922*, Gerrards Cross 1974.

*Lady Gregory's Journals, 1916–1930* (ed Lennox Robinson), London 1946.

HAVERTY, ANNE: *Constance Markievicz*, London 1988.

HERBERT, DOROTHEA: *Retrospections*, London 1929–30.

HILLIER, BEVIS: *Young Betjeman*, London 1988.

HYDE, H. MONTGOMERY: *The Londonderrys*, London 1979.

KING-HARMAN, ANTHONY LAWRENCE: *The Kings of King House*, Bedford 1996.

KING-HARMAN, ROBERT DOUGLAS: *The Kings, Earls of Kingston*, privately printed 1959.

LEES-MILNE, JAMES: *The Bachelor Duke*, London 1991.

LENOX-CONYNGHAM, MINA: *An Old Ulster House*, Dundalk 1946.

LESLIE, ANITA: *The Fabulous Leonard Jerome*, London 1954.

LESLIE, ANITA: *The Gilt and the Gingerbread*, London ND (1981).

LESLIE, LIONEL: *One Man's World*, London 1961.

LESLIE, SEYMOUR: *The Jerome Connexion*, London 1964.

LESLIE, SHANE: *The Film of Memory*, London 1938.

LESLIE, SHANE: *Long Shadows*, London 1966.

MCALEER, EDWARD C., *The Sensitive Plant*, Chapel Hill, University of North Carolina Press 1958.

MARRECO, ANNE: *The Rebel Countess*, London 1967.

O'BRIEN, JACQUELINE AND DESMOND GUINNESS: *Great Irish Houses and Castles*, London 1992.

ORIGO, IRIS: *Images and Shadows*, London 1970.

*Memorials of Lady Osborne* (ed Mrs Osborne), Dublin 1870.

ROBERTSON, NORA: *Crowned Harp*, Dublin 1960.

SERMONETA, DUCHESS OF: *The Locks of Norbury*, London 1940.

SMYTHE, COLIN: *A Guide to Coole Park*, Gerrards Cross 1973.

SOMERVILLE, EDITH Œ and BOYLE TOWNSHEND SOMERVILLE: *Somerville Family Records*, Cork 1940.

*The Edith Œnone Somerville Archive*, A Catalogue and an Evaluative Essay by Otto Rauchbauer, Irish Manuscripts Commission 1994, 1995.

SOMERVILLE, E. Œ and MARTIN ROSS: *Irish Memories*, London 1917.

SOMERVILLE, E. Œ and MARTIN ROSS: *Some Irish Yesterdays*, London 1906.

SOMERVILLE, E. Œ and MARTIN ROSS: *Wheel Tracks*, London 1923.

SOMERVILLE-LARGE, PETER: *The Irish Country House, a Social History*, London 1995.

TILLYARD, STELLA: *Aristocrats*, London 1994.

TOWNSHEND, DOROTHEA: *Life of Lord Cork*, London 1904.

WARD, WILFRID: *Aubrey de Vere, a Memoir*, London 1904.

WYNNE JONES, JOAN: *The Abiding Enchantment of Curragh Chase*, Cork ND.

# Index